Tourism and Sustainable Economic Development

THE FONDAZIONE ENI ENRICO MATTEI (FEEM) SERIES ON ECONOMICS,
THE ENVIRONMENT AND SUSTAINABLE DEVELOPMENT

Series Editor: Carlo Carraro, *University of Venice, Venice*
and Research Director, Fondazione Eni Enrico Mattei
(FEEM), Milan, Italy

Editorial Board

The Fondazione Eni Enrico Mattei (FEEM) was established in 1989 as a non-profit, non-partisan research institution. It carries out high-profile research in the fields of economic development, energy and the environment, thanks to an international network of researchers who contribute to disseminate knowledge through seminars, congresses and publications. The main objective of the Fondazione is to foster interactions among academic, industrial and public policy spheres in an effort to find solutions to environmental problems. Over the years it has thus become a major European institution for research on sustainable development and the privileged interlocutor of a number of leading national and international policy institutions.

The Fondazione Eni Enrico Mattei (FEEM) Series on Economics, the Environment and Sustainable Development publishes leading-edge research findings providing an authoritative and up-to-date source of information in all aspects of sustainable development. FEEM research outputs are the results of a sound and acknowledged co-operation between its internal staff and a worldwide network of outstanding researchers and practitioners. A Scientific Advisory Board of distinguished academics ensures the quality of the publications.

This series serves as an outlet for the main results of FEEM's research programmes in the areas of economics, energy and the environment.

Titles in the series include:

Sustainable Management of Water Resources
An Integrated Approach
Edited by Carlo Giupponi, Anthony J. Jakeman, Derek Karssenberg and Matt P. Hare

Valuing Complex Natural Resource Systems
The Case of the Lagoon of Venice
Edited by Anna Alberini, Paolo Rosato and Margherita Turvani

Tourism and Sustainable Economic Development
Macroeconomic Models and Empirical Methods
Edited by Rinaldo Brau, Alessandro Lanza and Stefano Usai

Tourism and Sustainable Economic Development

Macroeconomic Models and Empirical Methods

Edited by

Rinaldo Brau

University of Cagliari and CRENoS, Italy

Alessandro Lanza

Eni Corporate University, Italy

Stefano Usai

University of Cagliari and CRENoS, Italy

THE FONDAZIONE ENI ENRICO MATTEI (FEEM) SERIES ON
ECONOMICS, THE ENVIRONMENT AND SUSTAINABLE
DEVELOPMENT

Edward Elgar

Cheltenham, UK • Northampton, MA, USA

Published by
Edward Elgar Publishing Limited
Glensanda House
Montpellier Parade
Cheltenham
Glos GL50 1UA
UK

Edward Elgar Publishing, Inc.
William Pratt House
9 Dewey Court
Northampton
Massachusetts 01060
USA

A catalogue record for this book
is available from the British Library

Library of Congress Control Number: 2007941681

.

ISBN 978 1 84720 650 3

Printed and bound in Great Britain by MPG Books Ltd, Bodmin, Cornwall

Contents

Contributors

Sophie Avila-Foucat, University of York, UK

Rinaldo Brau, CRENoS, University of Cagliari, Italy

Guido Candela, University of Bologna, Italy

Davide Cao, CRENoS, University of Cagliari, Italy

Fabio Cerina, CRENoS, University of Cagliari, Italy

Chi-Chur Chao, University of Hong Kong, China

Juan L. Eugenio-Martin, University of Nottingham, UK

Paolo Figini, University of Bologna, Italy

Sauveur Giannoni, IDIM, University of Corsica, France

Bharat R. Hazari, Victoria University, Australia

Jean-Pierre Laffargue, CEPREMAP, France

Alessandro Lanza, Eni Corporate University, Italy

Anil Markandya, FEEM, Italy, Bath University, UK and World Bank, USA

Silva Marzetti Dall'Aste Brandolini, University of Bologna, Italy

Marie-Antoinette Maupertuis, University of Corsica, France

Michael McAleer, University of Western Australia

Renzo Mosetti, University of Trieste, Italy

Jean-Jacques Nowak, University of Lille, France

Suzette Pedroso-Galinato, World Bank, USA

Mondher Sahli, Victoria University of Wellington, New Zealand

Antonello E. Scorcu, University of Bologna, Italy

Pasquale M. Sgrò, Deakin University, Australia

Riaz Shareef, University of Western Australia

Stefano Usai, CRENoS, University of Cagliari, Italy

Simone Valente, ETH Zurich, Switzerland

Bernardo da Veiga, University of Canterbury, New Zealand

Eden S.H. Yu, University of Hong Kong, China

Introduction

Rinaldo Brau, Alessandro Lanza and Stefano Usai

International tourist arrivals have grown from a mere 25 million in 1950 to an estimated 842 million in 2006 and tourism now accounts for approximately 10 per cent of world economic activity. In particular, in many countries it is one of the main industries in terms of income generation, employment creation and provision of foreign exchange.

Moreover, substantial growth is predicted in the future due to the addition to the market of tourists from some highly populated countries such as Russia and China, in the first instance, and, hopefully, soon after India and Brazil. This will provide excellent opportunities for economic growth in both the developed and the developing world.

However, this prospect is also a potential source of major challenges and considerable threats. Tourism has proven to imply important externalities affecting the natural and built environments and having controversial effects on the wellbeing and culture of host populations. This is why the concept of sustainable tourism development has become the focus of the debate on this subject. According to UNEP (2005), 'sustainable tourism is not a discrete or special form of tourism. Rather, all forms of tourism should strive to be more sustainable'.

This book has originated from the 'Second International Conference on Tourism and Sustainable Economic Development: Macro and Micro Economic Issues', held in Sardinia, Italy, on 15–16 September 2005, jointly organized by the Centre for North–South Economic Research (CRENoS) and the Fondazione Eni Enrico Mattei (FEEM). Through a selection of some of the contributions presented therein, this volume aims to provide a few useful analytical and empirical tools in support of the idea that sustainability is not just about regulating and controlling the negative impacts of tourism, but also about policies and actions which aim to reinforce the benefits and reduce the costs of tourism, in order to make it more profitable now and in the future.

The potential of tourism specialization has been widely studied, both from a theoretical and an empirical perspective. However, the positive impact of tourism cannot be taken for granted given that, from a long-term economic perspective, a number of negative effects appear evident. The list of now well-established drawbacks includes dependence on foreign capital and volatile demand (Sinclair, 1998), disturbances in the labour market (Nowak et al., 2005), 'Dutch disease' effects (Nowak and Sahli, 1999; Nowak et al., 2005) and will be expanded by some of the more theoretically-oriented contributions in this book. An increased awareness of the potential problems is a necessary first step in fostering the sustainable management of natural resources and other non-replicable tourist attractions, which may increase tourists' willingness to pay and, ultimately, tourism receipts (e.g. Lanza and Pigliaru, 1994; Rey-Maquieira et al., 2005), thereby ensuring a positive overall balance from the development of tourism.

Rigorous analytical framework and adequate empirical measures are self-evidently fundamental. Consequently, the empirical contributions in this book focus on these critical aspects, in particular the volatility of tourism receipts, the effective impact of environmental preservation on tourists' preference and the identification of social sustainability in tourism development policies.

THEORY

A stylized fact which has recently attracted the attention of applied researchers is that small tourism economies appear to grow faster than big industrialized countries specialized in 'conventional' consumer goods (Brau et al., 2005). This poses some interesting theoretical questions regarding whether economic growth in small open economies specialized in tourism, based on environmental resources, can be sustainable in the long run and under what conditions. The six theoretical chapters which follow all focus on this question from different perspectives.

The perspective offered by Cerina is a very broad one that presents a general dynamic framework suited to an analysis of the role of externalities in models of economic growth with tourism specialization based on environmental resources. In particular, the chapter studies the steady-state and transitional dynamics properties of the economy while considering the possibility of pollution abatement technologies aimed at limiting the negative environmental effects caused by tourist arrivals. In this framework, a small open economy specialized in tourism activities based on environmental resources maximizes the long-term welfare of its residents by 'choosing' not only the level of consumption, but also the number of tourists to be hosted and the fraction of income to be devoted to pollution abatement.

It is shown that the number of tourists has an ambiguous effect on welfare. On the one hand, visitors increase tourism revenues and consumption possibilities. On the other hand, by drawing on the stock of environmental resources, the number of tourists has a negative impact on welfare both directly (environmental resources enter the residents' utility function) and indirectly by shifting tourist demand (tourists also give a positive value to environmental quality).

Two types of abatement technology are studied: the first considers an increase of the rate of regeneration capacity of the environment, while the second allows for a reduction in the marginal impact of tourists on the environment. While both kinds of abatement allow for a higher number of tourists, tourism revenues and consumption (in spite of the presence of an abatement tax), only the first abatement form ensures higher environmental quality. As for the tax required for financing pollution prevention policies, this proves to be positively related to the effectiveness of the abatement technology and negatively related to the degree of tourists' aversion to crowding. Consequently, countries that welcome, or can attract, tourists who are highly averse to crowding are able to ensure a higher welfare equilibrium and lower abatement taxes on residents.

Most importantly, Cerina shows that growth cannot be sustained in the long run by endogenous factors unless some exogenous aspects, such as the terms of trade dynamics, is given prominence. Such an exogenous factor becomes endogenous in the second chapter by Valente, who provides an analysis of the relationship between tourism specialization and economic growth in a two-country setting. Accordingly, he can focus on relative demand effects, which explain terms-of-trade evolution as the result of dynamic increases or decreases in the growth gap between consumption expenditures among countries. Movements in relative prices are therefore closely related to individual inter-temporal saving choices. Relative demand effects take place independently of whether trading economies converge or diverge over the long run.

Two models of specialized trade, where at least one country displays transitional dynamics, are considered. A first model considers technological gaps and convergence by imitation. In this set-up, no structural gaps arise in the long run, and signs of transitional growth differentials depend on whether the technological follower catches up with, or falls behind, the innovation leader. It is shown that, during transition, terms-of-trade effects always dominate, implying a positive growth differential for the innovation follower when the technological gap with the leader increases over time. The second model classifies the two countries as tourism-based and manufacturing-based economies, and assumes that production possibilities in the former economy depend on available environmental goods.

Both models show how, during transition to the steady state, terms-of-trade effects always dominate, leading to a positive growth differential in favour of tourism specialized economies, in spite of a persisting technological gap with respect to industrialized countries. In particular, when the availability of environmental goods is considered, structural gaps and relative demand effects arise and, in the long run, the growth rate of the tourism-based economy is exclusively determined by natural regeneration and time-preference rates.

The first two chapters are, therefore, able to provide a solid analytical rationale for economic growth in a tourism-based economy when environmental quality and externalities are at stake. However, the perspective is mainly within a macro framework, which provides few hints about the cyclical evolution of many tourism economies. The chapter by Giannoni and Maupertuis is, by contrast, able to offer some clues. The contribution starts by assessing if and how a balanced path between resource exploitation and resource preservation can be achieved. The analysis is based on recent economic literature which has provided new keys for the analysis of the inter-temporal trade off between investments in tourism infrastructures and pollution. This framework is able to imitate a cyclical evolution of investments, number of tourists, pollution stock and infrastructures which originates in different phases of tourism development, thus providing an analytical basis to Butler's lifecycle hypothesis.

In this model, tourism development may be sustainable if alternative phases of high and low tourism pressure permits ecosystems to regenerate. The authors actually show that deterioration is an equilibrium result in a model where tourist attractions are managed monopolistically and price is used as a control variable. This creates the conditions for government intervention in the form of a tax on tourism income. The authors show that such a tax makes it possible to preserve both the environment and the profitability of tourism in the long run, with a differential effect depending on tourists' preferences. If tourists are sufficiently sensitive to environmental quality, the implementation of a corrective tax may even lead to a higher private profit level than when no corrective action is taken.

The chapter by Candela, Figini and Scorcu adopts a different framework, while still providing a microeconomic setting to explain some specific features of tourism specialization. Given that the tourist product is comprised of a set of heterogeneous complementary goods and services supplied by firms which are mainly located in the destination area, they argue that there is scope for the introduction of the analytical notion of Local Tourist System (LTS). As an economic concept, the LTS shares some characteristics of both the Industrial District (ID), that shows that firms have a tendency to cluster geographically, and the Cultural District (CD), based on the integration in the same region of artistic and cultural activities that acquire their own idiosyncratic characteristics.

The main potential of an LTS includes production externalities and complementarities in the composition of the tourist product enjoyed by tourist firms. The risks are represented by the possible emergence of coordination failures, since the tourist good is exposed to a so-called anti-common problem. In other words, when private firms supply different goods and services comprising the tourist product, the fact that a single firm denies its own service to a tourist (e.g., with high prices or limiting the kind of services provided), may imply a loss for all the other firms. Technically, we are in a situation where there is excess of property rights among firms supplying single parts of the final good. In view of this, coordination policies by policy makers are likely to be welfare improving, since they may lead to both an increase in profits for all firms, and an increase in overnight stays demanded by tourists.

Finally, the last two chapters of the theoretical section provide valuable theoretical contributions to the understanding of the sectoral effects induced by tourism-related economic activities. The focus is on the mechanisms by which tourism can affect the host economy, in particular sectoral outputs, factor incomes, prices, other exports and, most importantly, domestic welfare. Unlike standard partial equilibrium approaches with fixed prices and unlimited endowments of inputs, a general equilibrium approach is used. This allows for an analysis of indirect and feedback mechanisms, such as those generated by competition among sectors for scarce resources (e.g., labour, land and capital).

The chapter by Nowak and Sahli focuses on feedback mechanisms which are more likely to occur in developing countries specializing in tourism. The framework adopted considers the dualistic structure of the labour market, sectoral unemployment, inter-regional migrations and competition between agriculture and tourism for labour and land. In other words, the authors consider a small open economy that is made up of two regions: an urban region and a coastal area. The former is specialized in a manufacturing sector which is partially non-tradable, while the latter is made up of two sectors: agriculture and tourism. Readers familiar with this kind of literature, may recognize that this economic structure is based on the Harris–Todaro model, which accounts for the coexistence in developing countries of massive urban unemployment and rural-urban labour migrations.

The chapter shows that, with substantially realistic assumptions, indirect and feedback effects may prove so strong that a tourism boom may have a negative impact on incomes and welfare. In addition to negative environmental and socio-cultural impacts traditionally recognized in the literature, tourism could be the origin of economic costs in such countries. Thanks to the focus on land use, the authors point out that ad hoc tourism policies which encourage land-intensive tourism may be as unsustainable (from an economic, and not just an environmental, perspective) since they draw an important and scarce input to the rest of the economy.

The chapter by Chao, Hazari, Laffargue, Sgrò and Yu examines unemployment, capital accumulation and resident welfare effects in a dynamic model of tourism specialization. The relationship between tourism, employment and welfare has been poorly explored in the literature. In the short term, one expects that an expansion in tourism, because of the nature of labour intensity in the tourism industry, influences demand for labour and leads to an increase in employment. However, in the long run, capital adjustments must be considered too: in this case, a tourism boom lowers capital accumulation, especially in other traded sectors.

Therefore, in evaluating the effect of tourism on the economy, a trade-off exists between the gains in employment and the losses in capital decumulation. This may have very different implications for national welfare, depending on the degree of capital intensity of traded sectors. When the tourist country trades on low capital-intensive goods, the expansion of tourism improves overall welfare. The opposite happens when traded sectors are highly capital intensive.

The model considers perfectly mobile labour and capital between sectors, but there are also factors that are specific to each sector. So, the model considered is a hybrid of the Heckscher–Ohlin and the specific-factors model. By calibrating the model with Cobb–Douglas production functions, the 'dynamic immiserizing' possibility of tourism on resident welfare is confirmed by conducting simulations using German data.

EMPIRICS

The second part of the book comprises five chapters. The first chapter focuses on the volatility of international receipts, among which those from tourism, and its determining impact. The second examines such aspects more closely by considering the impact of idiosyncratic events on growth. The last three chapters take a more micro-economic approach and look at the underlying bases for the sustainable development of tourism from an economic and social point of perspective, respectively.

The chapter by Markandya and Pedroso-Galinato focuses on the determinants of GDP volatility by extending the discussion on this topic to export earnings from different sources, including tourism. The originality of the chapter rests not only on this interesting extension but also on the treatment of volatility as a factor of interest in its own right, and not only because of its effects on economic growth, given that large fluctuations in earnings result in instability in employment, changes in government budgets and uncertainties which may all have important welfare consequences.

In order to identify what kind of action is necessary to reduce volatility, it is essential to understand its main causes. The empirical analysis shows that a number of factors cause volatility and, as a result, affect growth; these include financial, structural and institutional variables. Overall, results suggest that measures which reduce fluctuations of capital flows and encourage a shift to a more service sector-oriented economy will reduce growth variability.

From this viewpoint, tourism can contribute to expanding the service sector, which helps reduce volatility. Moreover, earnings from tourism prove relatively less volatile than a number of other sources of foreign exchange, such as remittances, aid or the export of energy.

Risks and volatility are also the focus of the chapter by McAleer, Shareef and da Veiga, even though from the perspective of individual countries. Cross-section data are substituted by time series observations, which make it possible to use advanced econometric methods.

The authors argue that tourism volatility is particularly critical in those countries where tourism tax revenue is one of the principal determinants of public expenditure. In other words, volatility in tourist arrivals and their growth rate may be associated conceptually with volatility in financial returns, which is interpreted as a financial risk. The focus of the chapter is on international tourism in Small Island Tourism Economies (SITEs) where economic development, employment, and foreign exchange depend greatly on tourist arrivals. The case study is on one important SITE, the Maldives, whose government needs constant and detailed information on potential shocks that may adversely affect international tourist arrivals and, as a result, have a direct impact on earnings from tourism and indirectly on related sectors across the entire economy.

This chapter, consequently, provides a template for an analysis of earnings from international tourism and discusses the direct and indirect monetary benefits from international tourism, as if it were a financial phenomenon. It also provides a framework for the design and implementation of tourism taxes.

One novelty of the exercise undertaken by the authors for tourism research literature is the use of daily tourism data with a view to analysing volatility by modelling and forecasting the Value-at-Risk (VaR) thresholds for the number of tourist arrivals and their growth rates. This implies the application of the typical VaR portfolio management approach to manage the risks associated with tourism revenues. The empirical results, based on two widely-used conditional volatility models, show that volatility is affected asymmetrically by positive and negative shocks, with negative shocks to the growth in tourist arrivals having a greater impact on volatility than previous positive shocks of a similar magnitude.

The analysis therefore may have an important impact on the public and private ability to interact successfully with a volatile market such as international tourism. In fact, the exercise makes it possible to quantify, on a daily basis, the potential fall in tax receipts, which in turn hinders the ability of the Maldivian Government to service its debt obligations. This analysis may therefore enable potential creditors to decide what should be the appropriate interest rate on loans to the Maldivian Government. Financial institutions that provide loans to the governments of tourist countries could incorporate VaR thresholds for tourism tax receipts into loan covenants to provide a greater level of protection for their investments. The authors also suggest that the VaR analysis presented in their contribution could also be used by private firms, such as resort operators, in a 'Real Options' framework, with a view to achieving optimal risk management strategies.

International and domestic tourism may have a considerable impact on both macroeconomic phenomena and public policy-making. On the one hand, visitors may also influence the social, cultural and economic activities of a site, and its residents' lifestyle. On the other hand, tourists appear to be rather sensitive to social, cultural and environmental quality, which implies that tourist sites need to be managed according to sustainable criteria otherwise they risk losing their ability to generate welfare. The three concluding chapters of the book aim to provide direct measures to ensure an appropriate evaluation of tourist and resident preferences concerning some relevant characteristics of the composite good that makes up tourism.

The chapter by Brau and Cao examines the application of stated preference techniques (in particular discrete choice modelling) applied in order to understand how to design appropriate policies to achieve 'sustainable tourism development'.

The chapter aims to understand whether frequent transformations of tourist sites are the result of a rational attempt to respond to tourist preferences, or an undesirable consequence of market failures typical in the presence of common natural resources. If the latter is true, many economies are currently on a sub-optimal, and unsustainable, economic path. The chapter therefore attempts to provide substantial empirical evidence of tourist trade-offs from among the several characteristics that comprise tourism, in order to identify the 'pure demand' size of 'green preferences' and 'aversion to overcrowding' found in the theoretical literature, as a necessary condition for long-term sustainable growth.

The empirical research method used in the analysis of the relationship between product characteristics and consumer behaviour is the discrete choice modelling technique. Its use in tourism economics has a certain appeal from a scholarly perspective, as a useful research method applicable to empirically testing some theoretical hypotheses on tourist–consumer behaviour and, from a more policy-oriented viewpoint, as a tool for policy makers and promotion agencies to adapt their 'tourism products' to existing and new target markets.

The study is based on an analysis of a sample of tourists interviewed at airports of the Italian region of Sardinia, and aims to examine how tourist preferences are differentially affected by high or low degrees of accessibility to the tourist attraction, by the existence of protected areas in the vicinity of the accommodation, and by the quality of the natural resources, as well as by the overcrowding of tourist destinations. Results show that tourists are found to appreciate the lack of overcrowding and environmental quality, especially where substantial losses, with respect to original conditions, are prospected. On the contrary, only high levels of accessory recreational services seem to be a relevant determinant of destination choice.

Useful policy indications emerge from such results. For example, tourists seem ready to give up having a room on the beach, if they can get a certain access to the natural resource, or if environmental quality is only slightly affected by tourism activities. Therefore, compensating effects, in the form of granting access to the main attractive areas or ensuring the conservation of high standards of environmental quality, appear to be feasible options.

The subsequent chapter by Avila-Foucat and Eugenio-Martin is also aimed at quantifying the link between changes in environmental quality and their effects on tourism demand. In particular, they propose a methodology which integrates ecological and socio-economic perspectives and evaluates how changes in environmental quality affects the willingness to repeat a visit in a tourist site.

The main assumption is that only a few environmental impacts have a real effect on the way tourists perceive the environmental quality. In this sense, from the tourist's perspective, it is necessary to identify those ecological attributes which specifically define environmental quality. The methodological suggestion is that willingness to repeat the visit should be differently affected by different kinds of environmental impacts, depending on the importance which tourists assign to these effects.

The model is applied to a case study of Ventanilla, in the region of Oaxaca, Mexico, which is one of the few successful examples of community-based ecotourism management, located alongside a coastal lagoon exposed to the polluting effects by fertilizers run-off from upland activities. Preferences for environmental attributes are examined in relation to four attributes: presence of crocodiles, birds, mangroves and the fact that Ventanilla is a community based on ecotourism. In turn, the 'biomass' of the first three attributes of the site are related to polluting releases by means of an ecological model of the site.

The econometric analysis of tourists' answers shows that crocodiles (and to a lower extent mangroves) are the only aspects that become relevant when assessing the willingness to repeat a visit. On the contrary, the presence of birds and the existence of a community-based ecotourism system are not seen as relevant by current tourists. On the basis of econometric estimates, a few simulations of the ecological model and of the related tourist attractiveness are presented.

In a similar vein, Marzetti Dall'Aste Brandolini and Mosetti introduce the concept of tourism carrying capacity (TCC) of a site, where such a TCC refers not only to preservation and improvement of the local natural environment, but also to attention for the local society and its cultural values, as well as for traditional local economic activities. Again trade-offs may appear, implying that policy-makers have to mediate between different aspects of the carrying capacity concept applied to tourism.

In this chapter the focus is on the social aspect of the carrying capacity related to overcrowding. Tourism is generally a seasonal economic activity and, on the most crowded days of the year, traffic, criminality, waiting time, and noise, during the day and at night, are major causes of residents' discomfort (and the quality of visitors' recreational experience may also deteriorate). A joint analysis is performed on these two aspects of the TCC: residents' and visitors' perceptions of crowding. Two methods are used: i) the cost–benefit analysis (CBA), based on the maximization of individual cardinal preferences; and ii) the majority voting rule (MR), when sufficient data for applying the CBA are not available.

The idea underlying this chapter is that the site TCC is the result of a compromise between residents' and visitors' interests. Depending on the information available to policy-makers, different procedures can be adopted to measure TCC and establish a tax level that would constitute a good compromise for both visitors and residents. With complete information the policy-maker may resort to the maximization procedure; while with incomplete information, the best procedure depends on the nature of the missing data. More generally, it is clear that this methodology is extremely effective for policy-makers, specialized agencies and operators who need to be better informed about the determinants of tourists' behaviour, given the growing level of competition from new tourist destinations, and the necessity to limit the market failures usually associated with a laissez faire management of natural resources.

The many facets of the growing debate on the relationship between tourism and sustainability concepts can only be touched on within a single book. Nonetheless, we are confident that the focus on the economic potential of this industry, as well as on some crucial drawbacks usually disregarded, may offer several interesting suggestions regarding those strategies that would aid the optimal exploitation of the potential of nature-based tourism for economic development. Moreover, the chapters which illustrate the use of a number of empirical instruments may provide an useful reference for academicians and policy-makers interested in how to put theory into practice.

REFERENCES

Brau, R., A. Lanza and F. Pigliaru (2005), 'An investigation on the growth performance of small tourism countries', in A. Lanza, A. Markandya and F. Pigliaru (eds), *The Economics of Tourism and Sustainable Development*, Cheltenham, UK and Northampton, MA, USA: Edward Elgar, pp. 8–29.

Lanza A. and F. Pigliaru (1994), 'The tourism sector in the open economy', *Rivista Internazionale di Scienze Economiche e Commerciali*, **41**, 15–28.

Nowak J.J. and M. Sahli (1999), 'L'analyse d'un boom touristique dans une petite économie ouverte', *Revue d'Economie Politique*, **109**(5), 729–49.

Nowak, J.J., M. Sahli and P.M. Sgrò (2005), 'Tourism, increasing returns and Welfare', in A. Lanza, A. Markandya and F. Pigliaru (eds), *The Economics of Tourism and Sustainable Development*, Cheltenham, UK and Northampton, MA, USA: Edward Elgar, pp. 87–103.

Rey-Maquieira, J., J. Lozano and G.M. Gomez (2005), 'Land, environmental externalities and tourism development', in A. Lanza, A. Markandya and F. Pigliaru (eds), *The Economics of Tourism and Sustainable Development*, Cheltenham, UK and Northampton, MA, USA: Edward Elgar, pp. 56–86.

Sinclair, M.T. (1998), 'Tourism and economic development: a survey', *Journal of Development Studies*, **34**, 1–51

UNEP (2005), 'Making tourism more sustainable. A guide for policy makers', UNEP and WTO.

PART I

Modelling Tourism Development

1. Tourism, Growth and Pollution Abatement

Fabio Cerina

1.1 INTRODUCTION

Recent empirical studies, such as Brau et al. (2005), have documented that, in recent years, small 'tourism economies' have grown significantly faster than non-tourism ones and their income level is above the average for small economies. Moreover, during the last 20 years, the growth performance of tourism economies has been better than the average of the OECD countries. Several papers (Lanza and Pigliaru, 1994, 2000; Hazari and Sgrò, 1995; Smeral, 2003; and Nowak et al., 2007 among others) have tried to provide an explanation for such stylized facts. A common result of these works is that the positive growth performance can be considered a long-run equilibrium phenomenon once we allow tourism countries to 'import' growth from abroad by means of continual gains in the terms of trade. Notably, none of these papers considers the role of the environmental amenities and natural resources in the process of tourism development where the positive growth performance has involved in particular countries whose tourism sector is based on natural and environmental resources. On the other hand, many authors (Davies and Cahill, 2000 and Tisdell, 2001, among others) pointed out that environmental resources interact with the process of tourism development in at least two different ways: they positively affect tourists' preferences towards the destination but, at the same time, they are negatively affected by inflows of tourists.

Once environmental resources are taken into account, some interesting questions arise: can growth be sustained in the long run for a small open economy specializing in tourism based on environmental resources? What are the dynamic interactions between tourism development, residents' welfare and environmental resources? Under which conditions might a small country specializing in tourism decide to invest in the abatement industry? And what are the effects of such investment?

The main aim of this chapter is to build a simple analytical framework where such issues can be analyzed in a proper way. We develop a dynamic general equilibrium model where the main task of a small open economy specializing in tourism based on environmental resources is to choose the number of tourists to be hosted, the level of consumption and the fraction of income to be devoted to abatement efforts in order to maximize the long-run welfare of its residents, which is assumed to depend on consumption level and environmental quality. This choice has to take into account two dynamic trade-offs. First, the number of tourists has an ambiguous effect on welfare: on the one hand, visitors increase tourism revenues and consumption possibilities; on the other, since tourists are assumed to negatively affect the environmental stock of resources, they also have a negative impact on welfare both directly (the environmental resources enter the residents' utility function) and indirectly (tourists are assumed to give a positive value to the environmental quality and to be crowding-averse). Second, financing public abatement expenditures might lead to distortions in consumption decisions but they might guarantee a higher welfare level.

We analyze the dynamic properties of the model with and without public abatement expenditures. We focus on two different kinds of abatement technology: the first allows increasing the regeneration rate of the environment while the second is able to reduce the negative impact of tourists on the environment. In each set-up of the model, the unique steady state is found to be saddle-point stable and the characteristics of the transitional dynamics allows us to interpret as temporary and transitional some stylized facts such as the positive growth performance of small open tourism economies and the worldwide increasing inflow of tourists (WTO, 2006). In the steady state, both kinds of abatement allow for a higher number of tourists and higher tourism revenues. Despite the need to finance abatement expenditure through taxation, both kinds of abatement technology allow for higher steady state consumption, but only the technology acting on the rate of regeneration allows for a higher equilibrium level of environmental quality. As for the abatement tax rate, we find that in both cases it increases with the productivity of the abatement technology and decreases with the degree of tourists' aversion to crowding, so that a country which addresses primarily tourists who are highly averse to crowding is able to impose a lower abatement tax on residents. In both cases, when the productivity of the abatement industry is low enough and/or the degree of crowding aversion is high enough, the country has no incentive to invest in the abatement industry so that the respective tax is zero.

There are two main strands of literature to which the chapter primarily refers. The first one, which deals explicitly with tourism economics issues from a dynamic point of view, includes the already cited group of works by Lanza and Pigliaru (1994 and 2000), Hazari and Sgrò (1995), Smeral (2003),

Nowak et al. (2007). This chapter investigates the environmental consequences of their main results and offers an alternative (and out-of-equilibrium) explanation for such a positive performance. Among this strand we also include Gomez Gomez et al. (2004), Giannoni and Maupertuis (2005), Lozano et al. (2005), Rey-Maquieira et al. (2005), Cerina (2006, 2007) and Candela and Cellini (2006). Explicitly dealing with environmental issues, the aims of this group of works are similar to ours though crucial differences in the modelling strategies and in the level of investigation exist. Moreover, none of these papers allows for an explicit investigation of the transitional dynamics so that numeric simulations are necessary. Finally, none of these paper addresses the issue of pollution abatement.

The other important branch of literature to which this chapter refers is the massive 'environmental and growth' literature (Tahvonen and Kuuluvainen, 1991; Gradus and Smulders, 1993; Smulders and Gradus, 1996; Stokey, 1998; etc., see Beltratti, 1996 and Smulders, 2000 for a comprehensive survey of the literature). What distinguishes this chapter from this group of works is that, as suggested by Papatheodoru (2003), the peculiarities of the tourism sector are explicitly taken into account. In particular, our framework focuses on the interplay between the number of tourists and environmental sustainability and highlights a distinctive feature of the tourism industry where the excessive demand for tourism services provided by a given destination may lead to an impoverishment of the quality of the same and, ultimately, to a worsening of the economic performance.

The rest of the chapter is organized as follows: section 1.2 presents the general analytical framework, section 1.3 studies the social optimum in the model without abatement while section 1.4 analyses and compares the consequences of the introduction of two different kinds of abatement technologies. Section 1.5 concludes.

1.2 THE ANALYTICAL FRAMEWORK

Tourists' Preferences and the International Tourism Market

According to the existing literature (Crouch and Louvière, 2001; Brau and Cao, 2005), a foreign visitor might obtain satisfaction from several sources such as:

1. the quality and the quantity of services supplied by private tourist operators (accommodation, restaurants, leisure facilities);
2. the quality and the quantity of public goods provided by local authorities (public transport, information, safety);

3. the quality and the quantity of the environmental (amenities, landscapes, beaches, mountains, parks, climate), cultural (traditional customs and events, typical food, historic buildings, museums) and social (people's behavior, general atmosphere, fascinating attitudes) resources;
4. the degree of availability and enjoyability of public goods and cultural and environmental amenities, which is highly correlated and negatively influenced by the aggregate number of visitors.

Since this chapter principally focuses on the interplay between the number of tourists and the stock of environmental, social and cultural resources, we restrict our attention on the last two factors. Accordingly, we assume that, at any time t tourists' satisfaction is negatively influenced by the current aggregate number of tourists N_t and positively influenced by the current stock of environmental, social and cultural resources which we gather in a general index of 'environmental quality' denoted by E_t.[1]

In formalizing tourists' preferences we follow the approach used by Gomez Gomez et al. (2004) which relies on the hedonic price theory (Rosen, 1974). The willingness to pay for tourism services is then given by

$$p_t = \gamma_t p(E_t, N_t). \qquad (1.1)$$

Where $p_E > 0$, $p_N < 0$ and $\gamma_t = \gamma_0 e^{gt}$ is a parameter whose constant growth rate $g \geq 0$ reflects upward pressure on the relative price of tourism for any perceived quality of tourism services depending on the interplay between growth in foreign income and the luxury nature of the tourism good (Crouch, 1995 and Smeral, 2003) or its small elasticity of substitution with other kinds of goods (Lanza and Pigliaru, 1994, 2000; Lanza et al., 2003). Our economy supplies tourism services in an international tourism market where a large number of small tourism economies participate. It is important to highlight that although international competition fixes the price for a given quality of the services, a country could charge a higher price provided that its services are considered of a higher quality (i.e. characterized by a higher stock of environmental, cultural and social resources) than other countries'. In other words, the international market consists in a continuum of tourism markets differentiated by their quality and the (equilibrium) price paid for the tourism services. In each of them the suppliers are price-takers but they can move along the quality ladder due to changes in their environmental quality.

Tourism Revenues and Residents' Behavior

We assume that each tourist, at any time t, buys one unit of tourism services so that output at time t is measured in terms of tourist entries N_t. The supply side of the economy is made up of a large number of identical 'households–firms' which we normalize to 1. We assume that the international demand for tourism is infinite for the price level which corresponds to tourists' WTP and is nil for any other price level.[2] So the market clears all the time and the quantity of N_t exchanged is totally determined by the supply side. For the sake of simplicity, we assume that the country provides tourism services without any labor or capital costs. In other words, we are assuming that tourists are satisfied by simply enjoying the environmental, social and cultural resources of which the country is naturally endowed. As we will see in the next section, the only cost associated with tourists, the one which prevents the number of tourists from being infinite, is an environmental one.

Given the absence of labor and capital costs, aggregate tourism revenues correspond to aggregate profits obtained by the households–firms and is represented by the value of the economy's output

$$TR = N_t \gamma_t p(E_t, N_t). \tag{1.2}$$

Conceptually, this is not different from a 'production function' of tourism services where N_t and E_t enter as input factors.

The demand side is represented by the same continuum of infinitely-lived 'households–firms'. Their aggregate utility at time t is positively influenced by the aggregate level of consumption at time t of an homogenous good purchased from abroad at a unitary price C_t and by the stock of environmental, cultural and social resources at time t (E_t). Their lifetime utility is given by an infinite discounted sum of logarithmic instantaneous utility[3]

$$U = \int_0^\infty u(C_t, E_t) e^{-\rho t} dt = \int_0^\infty (\ln C_t + \beta \ln E_t) e^{-\rho t} dt. \tag{1.3}$$

Notice that the stock of environmental, social and cultural resources has not only an (indirect) economic value (by positively affecting the tourists' willingness to pay) but also a value *per se* (by entering the residents' utility function).

The Evolution of the Environmental Quality

We model environmental quality as an accumulable stock of renewable resources. The motion equation of the stock of environmental quality is then given by

$$\dot{E}_t = f\left(E_t, N_t, z_t\right)$$
$$f_E < 0; f_N < 0; f_z > 0, \tag{1.4}$$

where $\dot{E}_t$ is the derivative of E_t with respect to time, N_t is the number of tourists at time t and z_t is the fraction of national income devoted to public abatement expenditures. We assume $f_E < 0$ so that the natural absorption capacity of the environment always decreases as the current stock of environment grows. Apart from some works (like Van Marrewijk et al., 1993; Brock and Taylor, 2003; Ramirez et al., 2006), the literature tends to accept the view according to which there is an upper bound to environmental quality. The motivation for this view (extensively described in Smulders, 2000) is highly related to the merely 'physical' interpretation that the literature generally gives to the environmental quality index and relies on the fact that the higher the quality of the environment, the more eco-services are needed to sustain this level, whereas the supply of these services is ultimately limited by solar energy because of the entropy law. It is questionable whether the assumption of an upper bounded environmental quality is appropriate even when the latter is intended in our broader sense (which fits better with tourism-related issues). Nonetheless, leaving the investigation of the issue for future research, we conform to the standard approach and we then assume that there is an upper bound $\bar{E}$ above which environmental quality is not able to grow.

We also assume $f_N < 0$ as already said we abstract from physical capital in this model so that all the potential negative impacts of the tourism industry, extensively discussed by Davies and Cahill (2000),[4] are embodied in the variable N.

As for $f_z > 0$, we assume that the country may undertake some actions in order to positively affect the evolution of the environmental quality. Reasonably enough, the abatement effort is costly so that a country willing to undertake an abatement policy should extract resources from the output of the economy.

1.3   A MODEL WITHOUT PUBLIC ABATEMENT

In this section we analyze and discuss a particular case of the general model presented above in which abatement efforts are totally ineffective in reducing the negative impact of tourists. Hence, we assume $f_z = 0$. Since abatement is useless, the country need not devote any resources to it and the whole national income is used to purchase the consumption good. In order to obtain a closed-form solution we introduce explicit functional forms for the relation introduced before. In particular, we assume a Cobb–Douglas form for tourists' preferences

$$\gamma_t p\left(E_t, N_t\right) = \gamma_t E_t^{\phi} N^{-\theta}, \tag{1.5}$$

where ϕ can be interpreted as a measure of preference for the environmental quality, while θ is a measure of crowding aversion. We assume that both ϕ and θ belong to the interval $[0,1) \subset \mathbb{R}^2$ so that $p_E > 0, p_{EE} < 0$ and $p_N < 0, p_{NN} > 0$.[5]

The accumulation equation of the environmental quality takes the following form which can be also found in Becker (1982), Cazzavillan and Musu (2001), Gomez Gomez et al. (2004), Lozano et al. (2005)

$$\dot{E} = f\left(E_t, N_t\right) = m\left(\overline{E} - E_t\right) - \alpha N_t. \tag{1.6}$$

As already anticipated, $\overline{E}$ represents the upper bound to the environmental quality and $\left(\overline{E} - E_t\right)$, the difference between the maximum and the current level of the environmental quality, can be interpreted as the current stock of pollution. $m \in (0,1)$ is the constant proportion of the stock of pollution which is assimilated at each date t by the natural factors that govern the economy. α is a positive scaling parameter measuring the (negative) impact of tourists on environmental quality. When no resources can be devoted to abatement expenditures, residents can influence the dynamics of the pollution stock only by controlling tourist entries N_t.

The problem of the country is to maximize (1.3) under (1.6) and the resource constraint

$$C_t = \gamma_t N_t^{1-\theta} E_t^{\phi}. \tag{1.7}$$

This is an optimal control problem with one state variable E_t and two control variables (C and N). However, one control variable can be eliminated by means of the previous budget constraint. The resulting optimal dynamic system is

$$\begin{aligned} \frac{\dot{N}_t}{N_t} &= \frac{(\phi + \beta)\alpha N_t}{(1-\theta)E_t} - \rho + m, \\ \dot{E}_t &= m\left(\overline{E} - E_t\right) - \alpha N_t. \end{aligned} \tag{1.8}$$

Transitional Dynamics and Steady State Analysis

We are interested in an equilibrium which implies sustainability for the stock of cultural, environmental and natural resources, i.e., $\dot{E} = 0$. As we can easily see from (1.6), $\dot{E} = 0$ implies $\dot{N} = 0$. The two equilibrium manifolds

$\dot{N} = 0$ and $\dot{E} = 0$ are given by

$$\dot{N} = 0 \ : \ N_1(E) = \frac{(\rho + m)(1 - \theta)E}{(\phi + \beta)\alpha},$$

$$\dot{E} = 0 \ : \ N_2(E) = \frac{m}{\alpha}\overline{E} - \frac{m}{\alpha}E. \tag{1.9}$$

Existence and uniqueness are easily proved by a quick inspection of the geometrical properties of the two loci. They are two straight lines with positive and negative inclination, respectively. Since $N_2(E)$ has a positive vertical intercept, they intersect only once in the positive orthant of the (E, N) plane and the unique steady state is given by

$$E_{ss} = \frac{m(\phi + \beta)}{(\rho + m)(1 - \theta) + m(\phi + \beta)}\overline{E},$$

$$N_{ss} = \frac{m}{\alpha}\frac{(\rho + m)(1 - \theta)}{(\rho + m)(1 - \theta) + m(\phi + \beta)}\overline{E}. \tag{1.10}$$

As for stability, we can state the following

Proposition 1.1. *The equilibrium* (E_{ss}, N_{ss}) *is locally a saddle point for the system (1.9).*
Proof *See the appendix.*

The phase diagram is shown in Figure 1.1.
The characteristics of the transitional path towards the steady state deserve some comments.

First, notice that along the lower stable arm, both N and E increase over time and eventually reach the stable equilibrium for $t = \infty$. Since consumption is a positive function of both the number of visitors ($\theta < 1$) and of the environmental quality, consumption grows over time as well along the lower stable arm. Finally, as a consequence, instantaneous welfare is also increasing along the same manifold. On the other hand, along the upper stable arm, both N and E decrease over time before reaching the steady state asymptotically and the same happens to consumption and welfare. If we take this model seriously and if we accept the idea that real world situations might be better interpreted in terms of transitional dynamics than with steady states configurations, some interesting remarks can be made. A country starting from an initial level belonging to the lower stable arm might be interpreted as a country whose optimal size of the tourist sector has not

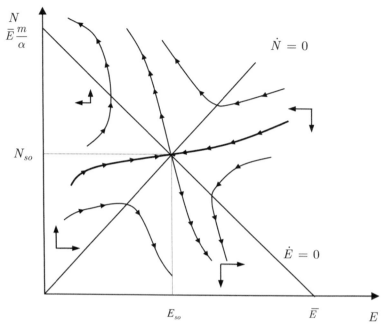

Figure 1.1   Phase diagram in the case without abatement

yet been reached. Think of a country that has only recently discovered how to 'employ' its environmental amenities for tourism purposes. For such a country, the model predicts a relatively fast increase in the number of visitors per unit of time, jointly with an increase in the environmental quality.[6] This positive and sustainable growth performance will last forever because the steady state is reached only for $t = \infty$, but its relative speed will decrease as the economy get closer to the steady state. According to this view, the well-known high-growth performance of many small open tourism economies need not be interpreted as exogenous and equilibrium phenomena as part of the literature on tourism tends to do (Lanza and Pigliaru, 1994 and 2000; Nowak et al., 2007), but rather as a temporary and transitional phenomenon with no need to invoke exogenous growth in the terms of trade.[7] Tourism development will eventually stop in the steady state, but such economies will reach this situation only asymptotically. This not-too-optimistic way to interpret this result might be counterbalanced by a less pessimistic one: a country specializing in tourism, granted that it places itself along the saddle path, need not deplete its environmental resources completely which, on the contrary, tends to a constant value. Hence, tourism specialization appears to be compatible with a sustainable use of the environmental resources. These observations lead us to a second important issue related to the transitional dynamics.

What the phase diagram is telling us is that, for any initial value of the environmental quality, there is only one initial value of the number of tourists such that the country is able to place itself along one of the two stable arms. This is a typical feature of dynamic systems characterized by saddle point stability, where the dynamic path which tends to the unique steady state is represented by a manifold having measure zero with respect to the whole state space. Nonetheless, investigating the economic implications of this somewhat obvious observation can be highly instructive. It is clear from Figure 1.1 that if the country starts from an initial value of N which is too high with respect to the initial value of E then it will not be able to move along the stable arm and, sooner or later, it will experience a fast growth in the number of visitors associated with a fast decrease in the environmental quality. This progressive reduction will lead, within a finite time, to a zero value of the environmental quality and therefore to a situation where both consumption and utility are null. In other words, this path is not sustainable. Then our model envisages the eventuality of a country experiencing a too fast and unbalanced tourism development which eventually leads to the death of the tourist destination. For such a country, both visitors and environmental quality will initially increase jointly, providing a growing welfare. But there comes a time when the number of visitors will be so high that the regenerative capacity of the environment is not sufficient to restore the pollution flow provoked by tourist inflows. Hence, within a finite interval of time environmental quality will start to decrease while the number of visitors continues to grow. Initially, this situation has ambiguous effects on welfare but these effects are progressively less ambiguous the more environmental quality approaches a zero value, which is associated with the death of the country. On the other hand, the model also takes into account the case of an economy which fails to employ its environmental amenities for tourism purposes and then its dynamic evolution ends up (within a finite time) with a perfectly virgin environment ($E = \bar{E}$) but with no tourists at all and, therefore, with no consumption.

Finally, it is worth reflecting on the effect that (exogenous) growth might have on the variables C, N and E. As already said, exogenous growth is introduced in this model by assuming that $\gamma_t = \gamma_0 e^{gt}$ (where $g \geq 0$ is the rate of growth of the WTP) and can be thought as the result of continual gains in the terms of trade.[8] By (1.10) we note that both tourist inflows N and the environmental quality E are not affected by γ so that they remain constant in steady state even if exogenous growth is introduced. It is worth noticing that this result still holds when a more general CES instantaneous utility is used in place of a logarithmic one[9] but, on the other hand, it is a direct consequence of the fact that the parameter γ enters the WTP in a multiplicative way. However, since steady state consumption is equal to $C_{so} = \gamma_t N_{so}^{1-\theta} E_{so}^{\phi}$ it grows at rate g, and growing instantaneous utility in the long run is obtained preserving both sustainability of the environment and a constant number of visitors. In other words, an ever-increasing equilibrium price of the tourist services does not affect individuals' decision over the number of tourists to be hosted in the destination and the additional monetary resources are employed, day by day, in additional consumption. This result might have important policy implications since if we accept the conclusion according to which tourism specialization is associated with ever-increasing terms of trade, as suggested by both empirical and theoretical works, then specializing in tourism might allow for an ever-increasing welfare level in the long run (which is an obvious consequence of the exogenous growth in the price of tourism) without compromising environmental sustainability and keeping the tourist inflows at a constant level.

Comparative Statics

The steady state level of the environmental quality E_{ss}: (1) increases with residents' environmental care β; (2) increases (proportionally) with the maximum level of environmental quality $\bar{E}$; (3) increases with the natural rate of regeneration capacity m; (4) decreases with impatience ρ; (5) increases with tourists' crowding aversion θ and (6) increases with tourists' care for the environment ϕ.

As for tourist inflows N_{ss} they: (1) decrease with care of the environment β; (2) increase with the maximum level of environmental quality $\bar{E}$; (3) increase with the regeneration capacity m; (4) decrease with the impact of tourists α; (5) increase with impatience ρ; (6) decrease with tourists' aversion to crowding θ; (7) decrease with tourists' care for the environment ϕ.

As for consumption, it is interesting to analyze its behavior with respect to environmental care β. A low level of β means a low level of E but a high level of N. As β grows, the effect on the tourist revenues (and therefore on consumption) is ambiguous: on the one hand, it allows for a higher steady state level of the environmental quality and therefore increases tourist revenues through a higher tourists' WTP. On the other, a higher β means a lower steady state level of N which reduces consumption. By calculations we find that there is a level of $\beta^* = \frac{\rho\phi}{m}$ such that steady state consumption is maximized.[10] If β is low ($\beta < \beta^*$) an increase in the love for the environment (e.g. as a result of campaigns to sensitize individuals) gives rise to an increase in consumption too. This is because, when E is very low, the marginal value that tourists will assign to the environment is very high so that their WTP grows significantly when E increases. This is what happens when

β grows starting from very low values. As long as this positive effect of an increase in β is larger (in absolute term) than the negative effect of β on N_{ss}, there will be an increase in tourist expenditures and therefore in consumption too. The relationship reverses when a further increase in β leads to a value of E such that the increase in tourists' WTP is not able to compensate any longer for the reduction in the number of tourists. In other words, our model suggests that too much love for the environment means low consumption levels but, on the other hand, an increase in the environmental care might lead to an increase in consumption. Hence, we obtain a sort of golden rule level of β with respect to consumption.

1.4   A MODEL WITH PUBLIC ABATEMENT

In the following sections we analyze, discuss and compare the model's results in the most general case when the country can affect the dynamics of the environmental quality even by employing resources in the abatement industry ($f_z < 0$). There are several ways in which a pollution abatement technology can be introduced in this model. In this section we focus on the effects of the two different kinds of abatement technologies: (1) an increase in the natural rate of regeneration capacity m; (2) a reduction in the impact α that tourist inflows produce on the environmental quality. Assuming that the country can devote part of its national income on either the first or the second abatement technology, we find the respective optimal abatement tax rate and finally we analyze how these abatement technologies affect the dynamics of the relevant variables.

Abatement 1: Increasing the Rate of Regeneration Capacity

We introduce a continuous function $m\left(z_t^m \right)$ such that the dynamics of the environmental asset is given by

$$\dot{E}_t = m\left(z_t^m \right)\left(\bar{E} - E_t \right) - \alpha N_t, \tag{1.11}$$

where z_t^m represents the fraction of national income devoted to abatement technology. We exclude the possibility that the country can borrow resources from abroad, so that abatement expenditures must be drawn from national income and reduce consumption possibilities. We assume that the function $m(\cdot)$ has the following characteristics

$$m\left(z^m\right)|_{z^m=0} = m > 0,$$
$$m\left(z^m\right)|_{z^m=1} = 1,$$
$$m'(\cdot) > 0.$$

(1.12)

The first assumption tells us that there is a positive natural rate of regeneration capacity: when no resources are devoted to abating pollution, the proportion of the pollution stock assimilated by natural factors is given by m, as in the previous section. The second assumption tells us that when all the resources of the economy are devoted to abatement expenditures, the whole current stock of pollution is assimilated. The third assumption tells us that the regeneration rate is monotonically increasing in z^m.

In order to find explicit solutions for the state and control variables, we assign the following explicit form to $m(\cdot)$ which satisfies the previous three properties

$$m\left(z^m\right) = m + (1-m)z^m.$$

(1.13)

The motion equation for E then becomes

$$\dot{E}_t = \left[m + (1-m)z_t^m\right]\left(\bar{E} - E_t\right) - \alpha N_t.$$

(1.14)

The problem for the country is now to choose the optimal level of consumption C_t, the optimal level of tourists to be hosted N_t and the optimal abatement tax rate z_t^m in order to maximize residents' welfare:

$$\max_{\left(C_t, N_t, z_t^m\right)} U = \int_0^\infty \left(\ln C_t + \beta \ln E_t\right)e^{-\rho t}dt$$
$$s.t.: \dot{E} = \left[m + (1-m)z_t^m\right]\left(\bar{E} - E_t\right) - \alpha N_t,$$
$$C_t = \left(1 - z_t^m\right)\gamma_t E_t^\phi N_t^{1-\theta}$$

(1.15)

where $z_t^m \in [0,1)$.

By equating the first-order conditions we get

$$z_t^m\left(N_t, E_t\right) = \frac{(1-\theta)(1-m)\left(\bar{E} - E_t\right) - \alpha N_t}{(1-\theta)(1-m)\left(\bar{E} - E_t\right)},$$

(1.16)

which gives us the expression of the optimal abatement tax rate as a (negative) function of the aggregate number of tourists N and of the environmental quality E. Differentiating the first-order condition on N and substituting into the Euler equation we find optimal dynamics for N which is given by

$$\frac{\dot{N}}{N} = \frac{\alpha(\phi+\beta)N_t}{(1-\theta)E} - \rho + \left[m + (1-m)z_t^m \right]. \tag{1.17}$$

By using (1.16) we can eliminate one control variable and completely characterize the optimal dynamic system as

$$\frac{\dot{N}}{N} = \frac{\alpha N_t}{1-\theta}\left(\frac{\phi+\beta}{E} + \frac{1}{\overline{E}-E_t} \right) - \rho + 1,$$

$$\dot{E} = \overline{E} - E_t - \alpha N_t\left(\frac{2-\theta}{1-\theta} \right). \tag{1.18}$$

Transitional dynamics and steady state analysis
The two equilibrium manifolds $\dot{N} = 0$ and $\dot{E} = 0$ are given by

$$\dot{N} = 0 \ : \ N_1^m(E) = \frac{1}{\alpha}\frac{(\rho+1)(1-\theta)E(\overline{E}-E)}{E+(\overline{E}-E)(\phi+\beta)},$$

$$\dot{E} = 0 \ : \ N_2^m(E) = \frac{(1-\theta)}{\alpha(2-\theta)}(\overline{E}-E). \tag{1.19}$$

Unlike in the model without abatement expenditures, the $\dot{N} = 0$ locus is now a bell-shaped curve. The $\dot{E} = 0$ locus, by contrast, remains a decreasing curve but with different inclination and vertical intercept. The steady state with non-negative z, N and E is unique and is given by

$$E_{ss}^m = \frac{(\phi+\beta)}{(\rho+1)(1-\theta)+\rho+(\phi+\beta)}\overline{E}$$

$$N_{ss}^m = \frac{(\rho+1)(1-\theta)+\rho}{(\rho+1)(1-\theta)+\rho+(\phi+\beta)}\frac{(1-\theta)\overline{E}}{(2-\theta)\alpha} \tag{1.20}$$

Substituting in (1.16) we obtain the steady state value for z^m

$$\overline{z}_{ss}^m = \begin{cases} \dfrac{(1-m)(2-\theta)-1}{(1-m)(2-\theta)} & \text{when } m < \dfrac{1-\theta}{2-\theta} \\ 0 \text{ when } m \geq \dfrac{1-\theta}{2-\theta} \end{cases}. \tag{1.21}$$

Hence, the government chooses to devote resources to abatement only when m, the natural regeneration rate, is not too high. Roughly speaking, if the environment is in a good shape, there is no need to spend money to safeguard it. It is worth stressing that an increase in m leads to a reduction in the marginal productivity of the abatement technology, which is measured by $(1 - m)$, so that the abatement tax can be viewed as a positive function of the productivity of the abatement. Note that the value of the threshold m such that the country decides to employ resources to increase significantly the regeneration rate depends on the degree of tourists' aversion to crowding: the higher θ, the lower the threshold value of m such that the abatement tax z^m is positive. But aversion to crowding reduces the abatement tax also in a direct way since, ceteris paribus, the more our small open tourist economy encourages crowding-adverse tourists, the lower the need to tax residents in order to safeguard the environment.

As for stability, we can state the following

Proposition 1.2. *The equilibrium* $\left(E_{ss}^m, N_{ss}^m \right)$ *is locally a saddle point for the system (1.18).*
Proof: *See the appendix.*

Except for the bell-shaped equilibrium locus of N, the phase diagram (Figure 1.2) does not look so different with respect to the no-abatement case, so that the previous arguments apply here also.

As already anticipated, when $m \geq (1-\theta)/(2-\theta)$ the country finds it optimal not to employ any resources in the abatement technology, so that $z_{ss}^m = 0$ and the solution collapses to the no-abatement case. By contrast, whenever $m < (1-\theta)/(2-\theta)$ it can be easily shown that

$$E_{ss}^m > E_{ss},$$
$$N_{ss}^m > N_{ss}.$$

Hence, when this kind of abatement technology is available and the country has incentives to invest in it, the country achieves a higher environmental quality and a higher number of tourists in the steady state and therefore tourism revenues (which are a positive function of both E and N) are higher than in the no-abatement case. And despite the presence of the

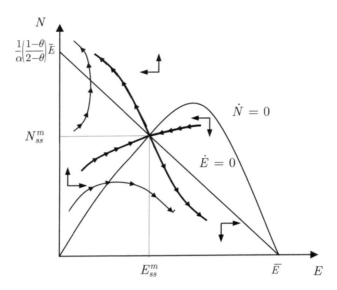

Figure 1.2   The phase diagram in the case with abatement

abatement tax, it can be shown also that consumption is always higher with respect to the no-abatement case.

$$C_{ss}^m = \frac{\gamma_t \left(E_{ss}^m \right)^{\phi} \left(N_{ss}^m \right)^{1-\theta}}{(1-m)(2-\theta)} > C_{ss}$$

Abatement 2: Reducing the Impact of Tourist Inflows

In the following section we analyze the consequences of a different kind of abatement technology. We assume that our small open economy is able to use a fraction of the national income in order to reduce the tourists' impact on the environmental quality, represented by the parameter α. In doing so, having defined by z^α the fraction of national income employed in this abatement technology, we introduce a function $\alpha \left(z^\alpha \right)$ satisfying the following properties

$$\alpha \left(z^\alpha \right)\big|_{z^\alpha = 0} = \alpha$$
$$\alpha'(\bullet) = 0$$

The first property assures that when no resources are dedicated to abatement, the impact of tourists on the environment is the same as the case without abatement, that is α. The second property assures that an increase in the fraction of income devoted to abatement leads to a reduction of the negative impact of tourists. In order to find explicit solutions for the state and control variables, we assign an explicit form to $\alpha(\cdot)$ satisfying the previous two properties

$$\alpha\left(z^{\alpha}\right) = \alpha e^{-(1+\mu)z^{\alpha}}, \tag{1.22}$$

where μ is a positive parameter measuring the productivity of this abatement technology.

The problem for the country now is to choose the optimal level of consumption C_t, the optimal level of tourists to be hosted N_t and the optimal abatement tax rate z_t^{α} in order to maximize residents' welfare:

$$\max_{\left(C_t, N_t, z_t^{\alpha}\right)} U = \int_0^{\infty} \left(\ln C_t + \beta \ln E_t\right) e^{-\rho t} dt$$

$$s.t.: \dot{E} = m\left(\bar{E} - E_t\right) - \alpha e^{-(1+\mu)z_t^{\alpha}} N_t, \tag{1.23}$$

$$C_t = \left(1 - z_t^{\alpha}\right) \gamma_t E_t^{\phi} N_t^{1-\theta}$$

where $z_t^{\alpha} \in [0,1)$.

By equating the first-order conditions on z_t^{α} and N we get

$$z_t^{\alpha} = \bar{z}^{\alpha} = \begin{cases} \dfrac{(1-\mu)(1-\theta)-1}{(1-\mu)(1-\theta)} & \text{when } \mu > \dfrac{\theta}{1-\theta} \\ 0 \text{ when } \mu \le \dfrac{\theta}{1-\theta} \end{cases}. \tag{1.24}$$

Hence, the optimal tax rate z_t^{α} is constant along the transitional dynamics. Moreover, it increases with the productivity of the abatement technology μ and, similarly to z^m, it decreases with the tourists' aversion to crowding θ. Finally, when the productivity of the abatement technology is too low, or the degree of crowding aversion is too high, the optimal abatement tax rate is 0 and the solution collapses to the case without abatement.

The dynamics of the economy are completely characterized by the following system

$$\frac{\dot{N}_t}{N_t} = \frac{\alpha\left(\overline{z}^\alpha\right)(\phi+\beta)N_t}{(1-\theta)E_t} - \rho + m,$$

$$\dot{E}_t = m\left(\overline{E} - E_t\right) - \alpha\left(\overline{z}^\alpha\right)N_t.$$

(1.25)

Transitional dynamics and steady state analysis
The transitional dynamics to the steady state looks very similar to the case without abatement. The two equilibrium loci are the following

$$\dot{N} = 0 : N_1^\alpha\left(E\right) = \frac{(\rho+m)(1-\theta)}{\alpha\left(\overline{z}^\alpha\right)(\phi+\beta)}E,$$

$$\dot{E} = 0 : N_2^\alpha\left(E\right) = \frac{m\left(\overline{E} - E\right)}{\alpha\left(\overline{z}^\alpha\right)}.$$

(1.26)

As in the case without abatement, the equilibrium loci are two straight lines with positive ($\dot{N} = 0$) and negative ($\dot{E} = 0$) inclination. The only difference is represented by the presence of $\alpha\left(\overline{z}^\alpha\right)$ in place of α which makes the two loci steeper than in the no-abatement case. As a consequence, the qualitative behavior of the system (uniqueness and saddle point stability of the equilibrium) looks very similar to the no-abatement case, so we can simply refer to the latter (see Figure 1.1).[11]

Despite the investment in the abatement technology, the steady-state value of the environmental quality does not change with respect to the no-abatement case, so that the only effect of this kind of abatement technology is to increase the optimal number of tourists in the steady state:

$$E_{ss}^\alpha = \frac{m(\phi+\beta)}{(\rho+m)(1-\theta)+m(\phi+\beta)}\overline{E} = E_{ss},$$

$$N_{ss}^\alpha = \frac{(\rho+m)(1-\theta)}{(\rho+m)(1-\theta)+m(\phi+\beta)}\frac{m\overline{E}}{\overline{\alpha}\left(z^\alpha\right)} > N_{ss}.$$

(1.27)

Since tourists are crowding-averse, their willingness to pay is surely reduced with respect to the no-abatement case, so that the tax burden can not be transferred to tourists. However, since tourism revenues always increase with the number of tourists,[12] national income is surely larger than in the no-abatement case. As for consumption, we should take into account the fact that in the case with abatement residents cannot use their whole income to buy the consumption good because the country needs to finance the abatement technology. However, it is easy to conclude that when the abatement tax rate is positive ($\mu > \theta/(1-\theta)$) consumption should be higher than in the no-abatement case: utility, which depends on consumption and environmental quality, should increase by definition but environmental quality remains constant. Hence we have

$$C_{ss}^{\alpha} > C_{ss}.$$

1.5 CONCLUSIONS

The positive growth performance of small open economies specializing in tourism poses interesting questions regarding the role that environmental resources play in the long-term prospects of such countries and in the sustainability and efficiency of their process of development. Our chapter presents a simple analytical framework where some of these questions can start to be answered properly. We have built a dynamic general equilibrium model where a small open economy specializing in tourism based on environmental resources has to choose the number of tourists to be hosted, the level of consumption and the fraction of income to be devoted to abatement efforts in order to maximize the long-run welfare of its residents by taking into account the several dynamic trade-offs associated with this choice. We have first analyzed the dynamic properties of the model in the case without abatement and the unique steady state is found to be a saddle point. The analysis of the transitional dynamics allows us to provide an alternative and 'out-of-equilibrium' interpretation for some stylized facts that the literature tends to explain as equilibrium phenomenon. As a consequence of our particular set-up, growth cannot be sustained in the long run by any endogenous factor, but the presence of exogenous growth in the terms of trade allows for an increasing consumption in the long run without compromising environmental sustainability. Then we have studied the effect of two different kinds of abatement technology, the first allowing for an increase in the rate of regeneration capacity of the environment and the second allowing for a reduction in the marginal impact of tourists on the environment. We have analyzed the dynamic properties of the solutions and in both cases the qualitative dynamics look very similar to the no-abatement case (uniquess and saddle point stability of the equilibrium). In the steady state, both kinds of abatement allow for a higher number of tourists, higher tourism revenues and higher consumption (despite the presence of an abatement tax), but only the first kind of abatement allows for a higher level of environmental quality. The latter is the main difference between these two kinds of abatement so that a country willing to increase environmental quality should adopt the an abatement technology which increases the rate of regeneration capacity. As for the abatement tax rate, we find that in both cases it increases with the productivity of the abatement technology and decreases with the degree of tourists' aversion to crowding, so that a country which addresses primarily tourists who are highly averse to crowding is able to impose a lower abatement tax on residents. In both cases, when the productivity of the abatement industry is low enough and/or the degree of crowding aversion is high enough, the country has no incentive to invest in the abatement technology so that the abatement tax is zero.

Although the model presented is very stylized, we believe it raises interesting policy implications and provides information about the role of the environment in the development of the tourist sector. This information can be useful for policymakers who are facing the choice between investing their resources in tourism or in more high-intensive technology sectors.

NOTES

1. Taking into account the implications of the difference between purely physical aspects of the environment and its less tangible aspects, related to the social and cultural sphere, can raise interesting issues but the economic implications of this distinction go beyond the purposes of this chapter and we leave it to future works.
2. This assumption might look quite restrictive but it helps in capturing the volatility of some kinds of tourism demand.
3. As discussed in the appendix, using a more general instantaneous CES function would not add much.
4. Davies and Cahill give an account of the environmental impacts of tourism such as energy consumption, water consumption, wasters, impact on water and air quality, ecosystems alteration and fragmentation, impacts on wildlife and on aesthetic and cultural environment.
5. Notice that (1.5) can be also written as $p_t = \gamma_t \left(E_t / N_t \right)^\phi N_t^{\phi - \theta}$ so that the willingness to pay can be viewed as an increasing and concave function of 'per-capita environment' (E / N) and an increasing or decreasing concave function of the number of tourist entries depending on whether $\phi - \theta$ is positive or negative. Alternatively, we can interpret the inverse of per-capita environment (N / E) as a measure of the crowding of the destination so that we are basically assuming that tourists are crowding-averse. The term $N_t^{\phi - \theta}$ can be considered as an additional preference (if $\phi > \theta$) or aversion (if $\phi < \theta$) over the number of tourists in the destination. In particular, we can associate $\phi > \theta$ with a preference for mass tourism and $\phi < \theta$ with a preference for 'elite' or snobbish tourism.
6. It is not difficult to associate this situation with the case of many developing (mostly Mediterranean) regions (such as Morocco, Tunisia, Egypt, Malta, Corsica, etc) that have experienced a quite relevant increase in the number of visitors per year associated with a sharp increase in the gross national product. This increase in visitors does not seem to have compromised, so far, the beauty of their natural resources. On the contrary, it seems that the discovery of the 'economic value' of the environment (ϕ in our model) has resulted in more attention towards the environmental issues.
7. It is easy to see that previous observations hold even if $g = 0$.
8. This approach is used, for example, by Rey-Maquieira et al. (2005).
9. As shown in the appendix, with CES utility the rate of growth g affects the level of N and E, but not their constancy in the steady state.
10. The same level of β represents instead a maximum when steady state consumption is considered as a function of impatience ρ, so that an increase in impatience ρ may give rise to a higher consumption in the steady state if the love for the environment is sufficiently high.

11. Proof is available on request.
12. National income is $\gamma_t E_t^{\phi} N_t^{1-\theta}$ and by assumption $\theta < 1$.

REFERENCES

Becker, R. (1982), 'Intergenerational equity: The capital–environment trade-off', *Journal of Environmental Economics and Management*, **9**, 165–85.
Beltratti, A. (1996), *Models on Economic Growth with Environmental Assets*, Dordrecht: Kluwer Academic Publishers.
Brau, R. and D. Cao (2005), 'Uncovering the macrostructure of tourists' preferences. A choice experiment analysis of tourism demand to Sardinia', CRENoS Working Paper 2005/14.
Brau, R., A. Lanza and F. Pigliaru (2005), 'How fast are tourism countries growing? The cross country evidence', in A. Lanza, A. Markandya and F. Pigliaru (eds), *The Economics of Tourism and Sustainable Development*, Cheltenham, UK and Northampton, MA, USA: Edward Elgar, pp. 8–29.
Brock, W.A. and M.S. Taylor (2003), 'Economic growth and the environment: matching the stylized facts', University Wisconsin Madison, Social Systems Working Papers, 2003/16.
Candela, G. and R. Cellini (2006), 'Investment in the tourism market: a dynamic model of differentiated oligopoly', *Environmental and Resource Economics*, **35**, 41–58.
Cazzavillan, G. and I. Musu (2001), 'Transitional dynamics and uniqueness of the balanced-growth path in a simple model of endogenous growth with an environmental asset', FEEM Working Paper 65.2001.
Cerina, F. (2006), 'Tourism specialization and environmental sustainability: a long-run policy analysis', FEEM Working Paper 11.2006.
Cerina, F. (2007), 'Tourism specialization and environmental sustainability in a dynamic economy', *Tourism Economics*, **13**, 553–582.
Crouch, G.I. (1995), 'A meta-analysis of tourism demand', *Annals of Tourism Research*, **22**, 103–18.
Crouch, G.I. and J.J. Louvière (2001), 'A review of choice modelling research in tourism, hospitality and leisure', in J.A. Mazanec, G.I. Crouch, J.R.B. Ritchie and A.G. Woodside (eds), *Consumer Psychology of Tourism, Hospitality and Leisure*, Vol. 2, Wallingford: CABI Publishing.
Davies, T. and S. Cahill (2000), 'Environmental implications of the tourism industry, resources for the future', Discussion paper 00–14.
Giannoni, S. and M.A. Maupertuis (2005), 'Environmental quality and long run tourism development: a cyclical perspective for small island tourist economies', paper presented at the Second CRENoS–FEEM International Conference on 'Tourism and Sustainable Economic Development', held in Chia, Italy, 16–17 September 2005.
Gomez Gomez, C., J. Lozano and J. Rey-Maquieira (2004), 'A dynamic analysis of environmental and tourism policies', in Economìa del Turismo, proceedings of the first 'Jornadas de Economìa del Turismo', held in Palma de Mallorca, 28–29 May 2004, pp. 435–56.
Gradus, R. and S. Smulders (1993), 'The trade-off between environmental care and long-term growth: pollution in three prototype growth models', *Journal of Economics*, **58**, 25–51.

Hazari, B. and P.M. Sgrò (1995), 'Tourism and growth in a dynamic model of trade', *Journal of International Trade and Economic Development*, **4**, 243–52.

Lanza, A. and F. Pigliaru (1994), 'The tourism sector in the open economy', *Rivista Internazionale di Scienze Economiche e Commerciali*, **41**, 15–28.

Lanza, A. and F. Pigliaru (2000), 'Tourism and economic growth: does country's size matter?', *Rivista Internazionale di Scienze Economiche e Commerciali*, **47**, 77–85.

Lanza, A., G. Urga and P. Temple (2003), 'The Lucas model of economic growth: an empirical application to tourism specialisation using multivariate cointegration', *Tourism Management*, **24**, 315–21.

Lozano, J., C. Gòmez Gòmez and J. Rey-Maquieira, (2005), 'An analysis of the evolution of tourism destinations from the point of view of the economic growth theory', FEEM Working Paper No. 146.2005.

Nowak, J.J., M. Sahli and I. Cortés-Jiménez (2007), 'Tourism, capital good imports and economic growth: theory and evidence for Spain', *Tourism Economics*, **13**, 515–536.

Papatheodoru, A. (2003), 'Modelling tourism development: a synthetic approach', *Tourism Economics*, **9**, 407–30.

Ramirez, D.T.J., M. Khanna and D. Zilbermann (2005), 'Conservation capital and sustainable economic growth', *Oxford Economic Papers*, **57**, 336–59.

Rey-Maquieira, J., J. Lozano and C. Gòmez Gòmez (2005), 'Land, environmental externalities and tourism development', in A. Lanza, A. Markandya and F. Pigliaru (eds), *The Economics of Tourism and Sustainable Development*, Cheltenham, UK and Northampton, MA, USA: Edward Elgar, pp. 56–86.

Rosen, S. (1974), 'Hedonic prices and implicit markets: product differentiation in pure competition', *Journal of Political Economy*, **82**, 34–55.

Smeral, E. (2003), 'A structural view of tourism growth', *Tourism Economics*, **9**, 77–93.

Smulders, S. (2000), 'Economic growth and environmental quality', in H. Folmer and L. Gabel (eds), *Principles of Environmental and Resource Economics*, Cheltenham, UK and Northampton, MA, USA: Edward Elgar.

Smulders, S. and R. Gradus (1996), 'Pollution abatement and long-term growth', *European Journal of Political Economy*, **12**, 505–32.

Stokey, N. (1998), 'Are there limits to growth?', *International Economic Review*, **39**, 1–31.

Tahvonen, O. and J. Kuuluvainen (1991), 'Optimal growth with renewable resources and pollution', *European Economic Review*, **35**, 650–61.

Tisdell, C.A. (2001), *Tourism Economics, the Environment and Development*, Cheltenham, UK and Northampton, MA, USA: Edward Elgar.

Van Marrewijk, C., F. Van der Ploeg and J. Verbeek (1993), 'Pollution, abatement and endogenous growth', World Bank Working Paper Series, 1151.

WTO (2006), *Yearbook of Tourism Statistics, data 2000–2004*.

1.A. APPENDIX

A.1 Proof of proposition 1.1

Linearizing the system (1.8) around the unique steady state we yield

$$\begin{bmatrix} \dot{N} \\ \dot{E} \end{bmatrix} = J \begin{bmatrix} N - N_{ss} \\ E - E_{ss} \end{bmatrix},$$

where

$$J = \begin{bmatrix} \rho + m & -\dfrac{(\rho + m)^2 (1 - \theta)}{\alpha (\phi + \beta)} \\ -\alpha & -m \end{bmatrix}.$$

So that

$$\det J = -m(\rho + m) - \frac{(\rho + m)^2 (1 - \theta)}{(\phi + \beta)} < 0,$$

Hence the unique steady state is locally a saddle.

A.2 Proof of Proposition 1.2

Linearizing (1.18) around $\left(E_{ss}^m, N_{ss}^m \right)$ we yield

$$\begin{bmatrix} \dot{N} \\ \dot{E} \end{bmatrix} = J_m \begin{bmatrix} N - N_{ss}^m \\ E - E_{ss}^m \end{bmatrix},$$

where

$$J_m = \begin{bmatrix} \rho + 1 & \dfrac{1}{\alpha} \dfrac{1 - \theta}{(2 - \theta)^2} \left(1 + \dfrac{[1 + 2\rho - \theta(1 + \rho)]^2}{\phi + \beta} \right) \\ -\dfrac{2 - \theta}{1 - \theta} \alpha & -1 \end{bmatrix},$$

the Jacobian is always negative since

$$\det J_m = \frac{1 - \theta}{2 - \theta} - \rho - \frac{1}{2 - \theta} \frac{[1 + 2\rho - \theta(1 + \rho)]^2}{\phi + \beta} < 0,$$

so the equilibrium $\left(E_{ss}^m, N_{ss}^m \right)$ is locally a saddle point.

A.3   CES instantaneous utility

Our results do not change significantly when a CES utility function is used in place of a more restrictive logarithmic utility. The steady-state analysis still displays uniqueness and saddle-point stability and the only relevant difference is related to the equilibrium level of the state and control variables. For simplicity we limit our analysis to the no-abatement case. The central planner now solve the following problem:

$$\max_{(C_t, N_t)} U = \int_0^\infty \frac{\left(C_t E_t^\beta\right)^{1-\sigma}}{1-\sigma} e^{-\rho t} dt$$

$$s.t.: \dot{E} = m\left(\overline{E} - E_t\right) - \alpha N_t,$$

$$C_t = \gamma_t E_t^\phi N_t^{1-\theta}$$

First-order and Euler conditions are:

$$H = \frac{\gamma_t^{(1-\sigma)} N_t^{(1-\theta)(1-\sigma)} E_t^{(\phi+\beta)(1-\sigma)} - 1}{1-\sigma} + \lambda_t \left[m\left(\overline{E} - E_t\right) - \alpha N_t \right],$$

$$H_N = 0 : (1-\theta)\gamma_t^{(1-\sigma)} N_t^{(1-\theta)(1-\sigma)-1} E_t^{(\phi+\beta)(1-\sigma)} - \alpha \lambda_t = 0,$$

$$\dot{\lambda}_t = \rho \lambda_t - (\phi + \beta)\gamma_t^{(1-\sigma)} N_t^{(1-\theta)(1-\sigma)-1} E_t^{(\phi+\beta)(1-\sigma)-1},$$

by differentiating the FOC with respect to time we get

$$(1-\sigma)g - [(1-\theta)(1-\sigma)-1]\frac{\dot{N}_t}{N_t} + (\phi+\beta)(1-\sigma)\frac{\dot{E}_t}{E_t},$$

which shows that, unlike in the logarithmic case, the rate of growth of the shadow price is affected (negatively or positively according to whether σ is greater or smaller than unity) by the exogenous rate of growth of tourists' WTP. As we can see from the first-order condition, this is due to the fact that, when σ is different from 1, the marginal utility of N is also affected by tourists' WTP which incorporates the growing term γ_t. In particular the marginal utility of N is increasing or decreasing in tourists' WTP according to whether σ is smaller or greater than 1, that is, according to whether the substitution or the income effect prevails. This feature, however, has no influence on the equilibrium dynamics of N and E which remain constant in steady state, but only on their level. In fact, with CES utility,

$$E_{ss} = \frac{m(\phi + \beta)}{(\rho + m)(1 - \theta) + (1 - \sigma)g + m(\phi + \beta)} \bar{E},$$

$$N_{ss^*} = \frac{m}{\alpha} \frac{(\rho + m)(1 - \theta) + (1 - \sigma)g}{(\rho + m)(1 - \theta) + (1 - \sigma)g + m(\phi + \beta)} \bar{E}.$$

In other words, if the substitution effect prevails ($\sigma < 1$), an exogenous rise in the equilibrium price of tourists services leads to an increase in the marginal utility of N and so individuals are induced to choose a higher steady-state level of N which, in turn, determines a lower steady-state level of the environmental stock. The opposite happens if $\sigma > 1$ and the income effect prevails. In any case, the constancy of the steady-state level of the tourism flows and of the environmental quality is preserved even under CES utility.

2. Specialised Trade, Growth Differentials and the Performance of Tourism Economies

Simone Valente

2.1 INTRODUCTION

The link between trade specialisation and economic development has recently been subject to extensive research at both the theoretical and the empirical level. A major reason for the renewed interest in trade and growth issues is the vast empirical evidence on cross-country differences in income levels: observed gaps exhibit persistence, and terms-of-trade effects between countries trading heterogeneous goods have likely played an active role in this regard. One of the stylised facts that recently grabbed the attention of applied research is that small, resource-intensive economies specialising in tourism appear to grow faster than big industrialised countries specialising in 'conventional' consumption goods. In particular, international data show that, despite their small size and relative scarcity of human capital, tourism-dependent economies have exhibited a better economic performance over the last two decades (Brau et al., 2007), suggesting a systematic link between tourism development, product specialisation, and international trade with manufacturing-based economies.[1] A possible explanation of the economic performance of countries specialising in tourism is that of a favorable trend in terms of trade with conventional consumption goods (Lanza and Pigliaru, 1994). In general, the direction of terms-of-trade dynamics in a developing world can be given two interpretations, which may be labelled as the 'structural gaps view' and the 'relative demand view'. Under the former perspective, movements in relative prices directly result from the existence of persistent gaps in physical output growth, implying ever-changing market shares for trading countries. The second view, instead, emphasizes the role of individual expenditures: movements in relative prices are determined by the differential in the consumption growth rates of trading countries, and are thus intimately linked with intertemporal saving choices. The structural gap view underlies the analysis of Lanza and Pigliaru (1994), who argue that the typical features of tourism-based economies – small relative size, extensive use of environmental resources, lower labour skills – may result in persistent productivity growth gaps with respect to larger economies specialising in manufactured goods. In this setting, the sign of the long-run growth differential is exclusively determined by the preference-elasticity of substitution between traded goods: if consumers perceive such goods as complements, terms-of-trade effects dominate growth in physical output.

This chapter tackles the issue from the perspective of 'relative demand effects' and considers two models of specialised trade where at least one country displays transitional dynamics. A first model considers technological gaps and convergence by imitation, following Barro and Sala-i-Martin (1997). In this set-up, no structural gaps arise in the long run, and the sign of transitional growth differentials depends on whether the technological follower catches up with, or falls behind, the innovation leader. It is shown that, during transition, terms-of-trade effects always dominate, implying a positive growth differential for the innovation follower when the technological gap with the leader increases over time. In a second model we identify the two countries as tourism-based and manufacturing-based economies, and assume that production possibilities in the former economy depend on available environmental goods. In this framework, both structural gaps and relative demand effects arise, and transitional growth differentials are crucially determined by the dynamics of the propensity to consume in the tourism-based economy. It is shown that propensity effects push the growth differential in favor of the tourism-based economy along any dynamically efficient path. The above conclusions provide support to the view that the observed performance in tourism countries can also be explained by dynamic increases in the relative foreign demand for tourism services.

2.2   RELATIVE DEMAND EFFECTS

As noted in the Introduction, the direction of terms-of-trade effects can be either interpreted from the perspective of 'structural gaps' or explained as the result of 'relative demand' dynamics. These views differ in both means and ends as long as the economies involved in trade exhibit balanced growth (at least) in the long run. Structural gaps explain persistent divergence with ever-changing market shares: in this case, winners and losers are crucially determined by the degree of substitution between exchanged goods, which is all that matters in the long run (Feenstra, 1996). The relative demand approach, instead, describes terms-of-trade effects as the result of dynamic increases or decreases in the growth gap between consumption expenditures in the two countries. On the one hand, this interpretation yields additional insights about growth differentials in situations where at least one of the trading countries is not (yet) along the balanced-growth path – which is the case in most growth models where the economy displays transitional adjustment before reaching the long-run equilibrium. On the other hand, relative demand effects take place independently of whether trading economies converge or diverge in the long run. This implies that the explanation of terms-of-trade effects provided by relative demand dynamics is different, but not necessarily conflicting with the interpretation given in models with structural gaps, such as Feenstra (1996) and Lanza and Pigliaru (1994). A formal treatment of this reasoning is presented below.

Growth Differentials and Terms of Trade

Time is continuous and indexed by t. The instantaneous variation of the generic variable $x(t)$ is denoted by $\dot{x} = dx/dt$ and its growth rate by $\hat{x} = \dot{x}/x$. Assume a world consisting of two countries indexed by $i = M, T$ with full specialization: goods M and T are perceived as heterogeneous, and international trade allows all consumers to enjoy both goods. Population in country i equals L_i and is assumed constant for simplicity. Denoting by Y_i aggregate output of country i, and by p_i its relative price on the world market, the growth differential Δ between country T and country M is defined as

$$\Delta = \hat{Y}_T - \hat{Y}_M + \hat{p}_T - \hat{p}_M = \Delta^Y + \hat{p}, \tag{2.1}$$

where $\Delta^Y \equiv \hat{Y}_T - \hat{Y}_M$ represents the physical output effect, and the growth rate of the price index, $p \equiv p_T/p_M$, is the terms-of-trade effect. The dynamics of the market shares of the two countries are exclusively determined by the sign of the growth differential, since $\Delta > 0$ ($\Delta < 0$) implies that the value of output of country T is increasing (decreasing) relative to world output.

Consumer preferences are identical between the two economies, and instantaneous utility of country i's residents is

$$u\left(c_i^M, c_i^T\right) = \log\left[\beta\left(c_i^M\right)^{\frac{\sigma-1}{\sigma}} + (1-\beta)\left(c_i^T\right)^{\frac{\sigma-1}{\sigma}}\right]^{\frac{\sigma}{\sigma-1}}, \tag{2.2}$$

where c^M and c^T are individually consumed quantities of good M and good T, respectively, $\beta \in (0,1)$ is a weighting parameter, and $\sigma > 0$ is the elasticity of substitution between the two types of goods. Since c_i^j is the quantity of good j consumed in country i, c_i^j with $j \neq i$ indicates per capita imports in country i. Individual spending for consumption goods in country i can be expressed in terms of the home-produced good as

$$c_i = p_i^{-1} \left(p_M c_i^M + p_T c_i^T \right). \tag{2.3}$$

When choosing how to allocate consumption between c^M and c^T, agents maximise instantaneous utility taking expenditure c_i as given: first-order conditions for utility maximisation imply

$$c_M^M / c_M^T = c_T^M / c_T^T = \left[p\beta(1-\beta)^{-1} \right]^{\sigma}. \tag{2.4}$$

Ruling out international lending and borrowing, trade balance requires

$$p_T c_M^T L_M = p_M c_T^M L_T \tag{2.5}$$

in each point in time. From (2.3), (2.4), and (2.5), terms-of-trade dynamics are governed by the differential in aggregate consumption growth rates, and by the elasticity of substitution between traded goods:

$$\hat{p} = -\sigma^{-1} \left(\hat{C}_T - \hat{C}_M \right) = -\sigma^{-1} \Delta^C, \tag{2.6}$$

where $C_i = L_i c_i$ is aggregate consumption expenditure and the consumption growth differential Δ^C is defined as the term in brackets. Substituting (2.6) in (2.1) we obtain

$$\Delta = \Delta^Y - \sigma^{-1} \Delta^C. \tag{2.7}$$

The two interpretations of terms-of-trade effects can be easily described on the basis of (2.7). The structural gap interpretation is as follows: assume that each country exhibits balanced growth ($\hat{Y}_i = \hat{C}_i$) and that the two economies display persistent differences in physical productivity growth ($\hat{Y}_T \neq \hat{Y}_M$). In this case we have $\Delta^Y = \Delta^C \neq 0$ and the growth differential reads

$$\Delta = (\sigma - 1)\sigma^{-1} \Delta^Y \neq 0, \tag{2.8}$$

which implies that the structural gap effect dominates if traded goods are perceived as substitutes ($\sigma > 1$), whereas terms-of-trade effects dominate when traded goods are perceived as complements ($\sigma < 1$). That is, the economy with higher (lower) physical productivity growth progressively increases its market share when the elasticity of substitution is greater (less) than unity. Lanza and Pigliaru (1994) implement this approach in a learning-by-doing model *à la* Lucas (1988) where a first economy, say *T*, trades tourism services against manufactured goods produced by a second economy, M, which displays persistently higher growth rates in physical productivity ($\Delta^Y < 0$). In this setting, Lanza and Pigliaru (1994) show that tourism specialisation guarantees a positive growth differential – and hence increasing market shares for country T – when tourism and conventional commodities are perceived as complements. Indeed, in the Lucas (1988) setting, balanced growth and persistent gaps occur at each point in time, so that (2.8) is always valid and yields $\Delta > 0$ for $\sigma < 1$. This result is quite general, and even seems robust to the inclusion of international financial markets as long as the two economies do not converge in productivity growth rates: as shown by Feenstra (1996), the preference elasticity determines the sign of long-run growth differentials in specialised multisector economies, where growth is based on R&D activity and international borrowing and lending is also allowed.

The relative demand approach emphasizes the different nature of the endogenous terms, Δ^Y and Δ^C, appearing in (2.7). The departure from the previous interpretation is maximal when we relax both the assumptions made above – that is, considering situations in which (i) at least one economy does not exhibit balanced growth, $\hat{Y}_i \neq \hat{C}_i$, and (ii) economies converge in physical productivity growth rates in the long run, $\hat{Y}_T \rightarrow \hat{Y}_M$. This is the case in most growth models where the economies display transitional dynamics before achieving the balanced growth path, and exhibit the same long-run growth rate due to technology diffusion (Grossman and Helpman, 1990) or knowledge spillovers (Rivera-Batiz and Romer, 1991): see e.g. Barro and Sala-i-Martin (1997), Rogers (2003), Smulders (2004). In this setting, the analysis of growth differentials is modified in two respects: first, the preference elasticity does not matter in the long run, since convergence implies $\Delta = \Delta^Y = \Delta^C = 0$ as time goes to infinity; second, growth differentials along the transition are determined by (2.7) with Δ^Y differing from Δ^C, the latter being determined by intertemporal choices regarding consumption and saving decisions. Since terms-of-trade dynamics reflect the accumulation processes of the two countries, transitional growth differentials become dependent on technological parameters and on each country's distance to the frontier (the gap between current input endowments and long-run equilibrium quantities), with a possible but not exclusive role played by the preference elasticity.

The aim of this chapter is twofold. First, we study whether and under what circumstances an economy displaying slow physical productivity growth enjoys positive growth differentials induced by terms-of-trade effects, with the favorable trend in prices being generated by dynamic increases in the relative foreign demand for the traded good. By extension, the general principle of relative demand can be reasonably applied to tourism-based economies, where slow physical productivity growth can be induced by small relative size, extensive use of environmental resources, and lower labour skills. In order to describe the general principle, however, we initially rule out environmental resources and other tourism-specific technological features: in section 2.3 we formalise transitional growth differentials assuming that one country (*M*) is the innovation leader, whereas the second country (*T*) is a follower, improving its technological base by imitation. Second, it should be clear from the above discussion that relative demand effects and structural gaps provide different, but not necessarily conflicting explanations for the good economic performance of tourism-based economies. Section 2.4 builds a hybrid model where both structural gaps and differentiated transitional dynamics arise between tourism-based and manufacturing-based economies along the equilibrium path, as a consequence of the peculiar role played by environmental goods in the 'production' of tourism services. In both models presented, the intertemporal behavior of consumers is represented by the necessary optimality conditions for present-value utility maximisation, as shown below.

Optimal Consumption Dynamics

Following a standard procedure (Frenkel and Razin, 1985; Gardner and Kimbrough, 1990), the consumer problem is solved in two steps. First, as shown above, each agent chooses how to allocate consumption expenditure between the two goods in order to maximise instantaneous utility (2.2) subject to the expenditure constraint (2.3). Plugging the resulting first-order conditions (2.4) in (2.2), we obtain the indirect utility functions

$$U_M = U\left(c_M; p\right) = \log c_M + \Phi_M\left(p\right), \qquad (2.9)$$

$$U_T = U\left(c_T; p\right) = \log c_T + \Phi_T\left(p\right), \qquad (2.10)$$

where Φ_M and Φ_T are functions of p and exogenous parameters σ, β. In the second step, each agent maximises the standard objective function

$$\int_0^\infty U_i\left(c_i\left(t\right); p\left(t\right)\right) e^{-\delta t} dt, \qquad (2.11)$$

where $\delta > 0$ is the utility discount rate. Agents choose $\{c_i(t)\}$ taking $\{p(t)\}$ as given, and maximise (2.11) subject to the dynamic wealth constraint

$$\dot{a}_i\left(t\right) = \mu_i\left(t\right) a_i\left(t\right) + w_i\left(t\right) h_i\left(t\right) - c_i\left(t\right), \qquad (2.12)$$

where all variables are expressed in terms of output (per capita) produced in country i. Private wealth per capita a_i is held in the form of assets yielding a rate of return equal to μ_i, and labour income equals the wage rate w_i times units of labour efficiency supplied, h_i. Agents supply labour inelastically, so that h_i represents per worker productivity in country i. By definition, w_i and μ_i are domestic-price deflated rates. Optimality conditions of the second-step problem yield the standard Keynes–Ramsey rule

$$\hat{c}_i = \mu_i - \delta \,, \tag{2.13}$$

according to which the growth rate of consumption expenditure is proportional to the observed gap between real interest rates and utility discount rates. As a consequence, the dynamics of terms of trade in the present analysis are exclusively determined by the interest rate differential: from (2.6) and (2.13),

$$\hat{p} = \mu_T - \mu_M \,. \tag{2.14}$$

In section 2.3 we complete the model by specifying the supply side of the two economies following Barro and Sala-i-Martin (1997), obtaining a two-country–two-goods variant of the expanding-varieties model with technology diffusion. In section 2.4, instead, we build a hybrid model featuring both persistent gaps and relative demand effects induced by tourism-specific inputs.

2.3   TECHNOLOGY DIFFUSION

The purpose of this section is to describe relative demand effects in a general setting featuring endogenous growth and long-run convergence. Hence, some specific features of tourism-based economies, like natural resource dependence, are ruled out here, and countries T and M can be interpreted as two generic economic areas trading heterogeneous commodities. However, two crucial assumptions of the model – i.e. that country T is smaller, and exhibits lower labour skills and lower ability to generate innovations – are consistent with the typical features of most economies specialised in tourism. Besides the sake of clarity, this is the reason why in this section we will refer to countries M and T as manufacturing-based and tourism-based countries.

In this section we employ the two-country model of Barro and Sala-i-Martin (1997): the only difference is that, in the original model, a single homogeneous good is traded, whereas countries are fully specialising in the present setting. Each economy produces final output by means of labour and a set of intermediate goods. In aggregate, labour efficiency units in country i equal $H_i = h_i L_i$, and we assume that efficient labour is relatively more abundant in country M than in the tourism-based economy,

$$H_M > H_T. \tag{2.15}$$

Note that, since human capital accumulation plays no role in this section, it is also possible to obtain (2.15) by normalising per-worker efficiency $h_i = 1$ while assuming $L_M > L_T$ instead. The only difference would be to shift the focus from aggregate labour productivity to population size – an interpretation which remains consistent with empirical evidence about tourism countries. The demand side is that described in the previous section, where individual wealth a_i is represented by assets of firms operating in the home country.

Final output Y is obtained by means of labour H and a number of intermediate inputs x_n (where the type of intermediate good is indexed by $n = 1, ..., N$), according to the aggregate production function

$$Y_i = H_i^{1-\alpha} \sum_{n=1}^{N_i} x_{ni}^{\alpha}, \tag{2.16}$$

where $\alpha \in (0,1)$. Since (2.16) exhibits constant returns to scale, the whole final sector behaves as a single competitive firm. Denoting by w^x_n the price of the n-th intermediate good, profit maximisation in the final sector implies

$$w_{ni}^x x_{ni} = \alpha H_i^{1-\alpha} x_{ni}^{\alpha}. \tag{2.17}$$

Each intermediate variety is produced with unit marginal cost by monopolists. Instantaneous profits for the n-th type of intermediate thus equal $\pi_{ni} = x_{ni} (w^x_{ni} - 1)$. Maximisation of π_{ni} subject to the demand schedule (2.17) gives the standard solution of a constant mark-up over marginal costs, $w^x_{ni} = 1/\alpha$, for each n. Since w^x_{ni} is invariant across varieties, each monopolist produces the optimal quantity

$$x_{ni} = \bar{x}_i = H_i \alpha^{\frac{2}{1-\alpha}}, \tag{2.18}$$

and equilibrium instantaneous profits read

$$\pi_{ni} = \bar{\pi}_i = (1-\alpha)\alpha^{\frac{1+\alpha}{1-\alpha}} H_i. \tag{2.19}$$

From (2.18) and (2.16), equilibrium output equals

$$Y_i = H_i N_i \alpha^{\frac{2\alpha}{1-\alpha}} . \tag{2.20}$$

Expression (2.20) shows that output per worker is proportional to the number of intermediates, N_i. In line with the basic idea of the 'expanding-varieties' model pioneered by Spence (1976) and Dixit and Stiglitz (1977), the source of endogenous growth is represented by increases in N_i obtained through innovations. An 'innovation' is the development of a new variety of intermediates, and the innovator becomes its sole supplier by virtue of a patent which is perfectly enforced within the country. As in Barro and Sala-i-Martin (1997), we assume that countries are able to expand N_i not only by 'original' innovation, but also 'by imitation': new types of intermediates developed e.g. in country M can be readapted as intermediates for producing tourism goods in country T, thereby raising N_T.[2] Hence, countries may in principle obtain new varieties by means of two alternative strategies. On the one hand, country i may act as the innovation leader by inventing new intermediates: the associated marginal cost (which will be called 'R&D cost') is assumed constant and denoted λ_i. On the other hand, if innovators in country $j \neq i$ are actually developing new blueprints on their own, country i may choose to be a follower: technology monopolists readapt intermediates invented abroad as inputs for the different good produced in country i. This second strategy implies a marginal 'readaptation cost' denoted by $fi > 0$. Obviously, innovators would find it profitable to invest resources in discovering new types 'by themselves' as long as $\lambda i < fi$, and if this inequality holds in both countries, none of the two will act as a follower. We assume that country M exhibits a higher ability to generate innovations with respect to country T. Formally, the technological gap is characterised by three assumptions: (i) at time $t = 0$ the set of intermediates existing in the tourism-based economy is a subset of that employed in country M, with NM (0) > NT (0); (ii) inventing new intermediates is relatively more expensive in the tourism-based economy, $\lambda_M < \lambda_T$; (iii) readaptation costs are specified according to the 'cost of imitation' function,

$$f_T = \lambda_T \left(N_T / N_M \right)^v . \tag{2.21}$$

The cost function (2.21) exhibits two important properties. First, $N_M > N_T$ implies $f_T < \lambda_T$, which means that if there is a 'technological gap' in favor of country M, readapting is more convenient than innovating for the tourism-based economy: this property implies that it is profitable for country T to act as a follower at time zero, because $N_M(0) > N_T(0)$ yields $f_T(0) < \lambda_T$. Second, since f_T is increasing in (N_T/N_M), so that the wider is the technological gap the lower is the cost of readaptation, followers imitate foreign intermediates beginning with the variety which is the easiest to readapt, so that marginal costs rise with the number of varieties already readapted.[3]

Free-entry conditions for firms in R&D sectors can be derived as follows: the present value of profits from inventing a new type of intermediate at instant t equals

$$V_i(t) = \int_t^\infty \pi_{ni}(s) e^{-\int_t^s \mu_i(b)db} \, ds. \tag{2.22}$$

If there is free entry in innovation in country M, and free entry in 'readaptation' in country T as well, we have

$$V_M = \lambda_M \text{ and } V_T = f_T, \tag{2.23}$$

because an equilibrium with positive amounts of resources devoted to obtaining new intermediates requires that R&D costs be equal to the market value of R&D firms, represented by V_M and V_T. Notice that (2.23) implies that V_M is constant over time, whereas V_T is generally time-varying since readaptation costs depend, through (2.21), on the technological gap between the two countries. This has important consequences for economic dynamics and growth differentials between the two countries, as shown below.

Equilibrium Dynamics

As shown in the Appendix, the intertemporal equilibrium is characterised by

$$\hat{N}_i = \mu_i + (1-\alpha) Y_i (V_i N_i)^{-1} - C_i (V_i N_i)^{-1} - \hat{V}_i, \tag{2.24}$$

and equilibrium interest rates in the two economies equal

$$\mu_M = \bar{\pi}_M / \lambda_M, \tag{2.25}$$

$$\mu_T = \hat{f}_T + (\bar{\pi}_T / f_T). \tag{2.26}$$

Equation (2.24) represents the growth rate of the number of intermediate varieties in country i, while equations (2.25)–(2.26) result from the equilibrium between the value of total household assets and the market value of R&D firms. Equilibrium interest rates, μ_M and μ_T, are endogenously determined within the respective countries, and variations in terms of trade occur as a consequence of interest rate differentials according to the equilibrium condition (2.14). The peculiar feature of this model is that the equilibrium interest rate in the leading country is constant over time along the entire path, whereas μ_T is generally time-varying: in (2.25), marginal costs of innovation λ_M and instantaneous profits are constant, whereas readaptation costs imply non-trivial dynamics in (2.26), because f_T depends on the technological gap observed in each point in time. Assumption (2.21) thus implies that the tourism-based economy generally exhibits non-constant growth rates in C_T. The asymmetric behavior of output growth and interest rates between the two economies generates the following result.

Lemma 2.1 *(Barro and Sala-i-Martin, 1997) Country* M *immediately achieves balanced growth at time zero and exhibits a* constant *growth rate* g_M *in each instant. Country* T *displays transitional dynamics, and growth rates converge to* g_M *in the long run.*

The proof of Lemma 2.1 is identical to that in Barro and Sala-i-Martin (1997), and is explained as follows. From (2.13) and (2.25), a constant interest rate in country M implies a constant growth rate of C_M. From (2.20), output and the number of intermediates grow at the same rate $g_M = \hat{Y}_M$, implying that the only possible equilibrium path is

$$\hat{C}_M = \hat{Y}_M = \hat{N}_M = g_M \text{ for each } t \in [0, \infty). \tag{2.27}$$

In the tourism-based country, a non-constant interest rate implies that $\hat{C}_T$ be time-varying. Defining control-like and state-like variables $\chi_T \equiv C_T/N_T$ and $N_x \equiv N_T/N_M$, respectively, the following dynamic equations can be derived (see Appendix):

$$\hat{N}_x = \frac{1}{\lambda_T N_x^v}\left[\left(\frac{1+\alpha}{\alpha}\right)\bar{\pi}_T - \chi_T\right] - g_M, \tag{2.28}$$

$$\hat{\chi}_T = \frac{1}{\lambda_T N_x^v}\left[(1-v)\chi_T - \bar{\pi}_T\frac{(1-v)(1+\alpha)-\alpha}{\alpha}\right] - v g_M - \delta. \tag{2.29}$$

Equations (2.28)–(2.29) describe economic dynamics in country T for each t, provided that the tourism-based economy is always acting as a follower. A little algebra shows that equation (2.28) is dynamically stable regardless of different combinations of parameters: N_x approaches a steady state value as time goes to infinity, and the numbers of intermediate varieties in the two countries, N_T and N_M, will consequently grow at the same rate in the long run. Since Y_i is proportional to N_i from (2.20), it follows that

$$\lim_{t\to\infty} \hat{N}_T = \lim_{t\to\infty} \hat{Y}_T = \lim_{t\to\infty} \hat{C}_T = g_M \,. \tag{2.30}$$

Convergence of the growth rate $\hat{C}_T$ towards g_M is ensured by saddle-point stability, as shown in the phase diagram depicted in Figure 2.1. Only one stable arm exists, and all diverging paths would violate either optimality conditions or the aggregate resource constraint in the long run.[4] The economy jumps onto the stable arm of the saddle at time zero, which brings χ_T and N_x towards equilibrium values χ_T^{ss} and N_x^{ss}. In the long run, C_T and N_T (and hence, also Y_T) grow asymptotically at the same rate, implying balanced growth in country T. From (2.30), convergence in growth rates of C_T and C_M requires that interest rates be equalised in the long run, by virtue of the Keynes–Ramsey rule (2.13). This in turn implies

$$\lim_{t\to\infty} \mu_T = \mu_M \Rightarrow \lim_{t\to\infty} \hat{p} = 0 \,. \tag{2.31}$$

Asymptotic convergence with balanced growth implies that no type of specialisation – tourism or manufacturing – may be labelled as growth maximising in the long run, since $\Delta^Y = \Delta^C = 0$ as $t \to \infty$. However, output and terms-of-trade effects do not compensate each other along the transitional path, where growth rates of Y_T and C_T clearly differ. It derives from (2.28)–(2.29) that the long-run equilibrium is characterised by $N_x^{ss} < 1$, which means that the technological gap between the two economies is never filled: countries will grow at the same rate, but the innovation leader will always exhibit a higher number of intermediate varieties (see Valente, 2005b). The fact that $N_x^{ss} < 1$, implies that two types of transitional dynamics are possible, which we label as convergence from below and convergence from above.[5] This classification reflects the positive slope of the stable arm in the phase plane: if $N_x(0) < N_x^{ss} < 1$, the economy converges from below, starting e.g. in point B of Figure 2.1. If $N_x^{ss} < N_x(0) < 1$, instead, the economy converges from above, starting e.g. in point A.[6] The direction of convergence is of crucial importance for the present analysis, since it ultimately determines the sign of the growth differential during the transition. The following propositions characterise the two cases:

Proposition 2.2 *Convergence from below: if $N_x(0) < N_x^{ss}$, the technological gap is reduced over time*

$$\dot{N}_x > 0 \,, \tag{2.32}$$

and

$$\hat{C}_T > \hat{Y}_T > \hat{Y}_M = \hat{C}_M \qquad (2.33)$$

along the transitional path.

Proposition 3.3 *Convergence from above: if* $N_x(0) > N_x^{ss}$ *the technological gap increases over time,*

$$\dot{N}_x < 0, \qquad (2.34)$$

and

$$\hat{C}_T < \hat{Y}_T < \hat{Y}_M = \hat{C}_M \qquad (2.35)$$

along the transitional path.

Propositions 2.2 and 2.3 provide all the information needed to determine the sign of growth differentials along the transitional path. For the sake of clarity, we begin by discussing the case in which tourism and manufactured goods are neither substitutes nor complements ($\sigma = 1$).

Growth differentials with $\sigma = 1$. When the elasticity of substitution between the two types of goods is $\sigma = 1$, the growth differential (2.1) reduces to

$$\Delta = \Delta^Y - \Delta^C. \qquad (2.36)$$

That is, the terms-of-trade effect coincides with (minus) the difference between the growth rates of C_T and C_M. In this case, it follows from (2.33) and (2.35) that

Proposition 2.4 *If country* T *converges from above (below), tourism specialisation implies higher (lower) growth rates during the transition.*

The economic reason for this result is as follows. When country *T* converges from below, the technological gap is gradually reduced, implying that both the physical output and the internal consumption indices, Y_T and C_T, are growing at higher rates than in country *M*; however, Δ^C exceeds Δ^Y, so that the terms-of-trade effect dominates and the resulting growth differential is negative. In the opposite case, country *T* converges from above, the technological gap increases during the transition, implying that physical output and consumption grow at lower rates than in country *M*. However, Δ^C

dominates in absolute value Δ^Y, and the terms-of-trade effect is favorable to tourism specialisation, yielding $\Delta > 0$. The conclusion is that, since terms-of-trade effects always dominate output effects, tourism specialisation guarantees higher growth when tourism-based countries fall behind the innovation leader: as the technological gap increases over time (the economy starts in point A), the relative price of tourism rises due to the increase in the relative foreign demand, and country T obtains higher growth rates by virtue of the terms-of-trade effect. Conversely, technological catching-up is bad for growth: if the tourism-based economy reduces the technological gap with the industrialised country (starting from point B), the resulting growth differential is negative because the relative demand for manufactured goods by consumers in country T is increased, implying a transitional reduction in the relative price of the tourism good. It should, however, be stressed that the above results hold provided $\sigma = 1$, i.e. tourism and manufactured goods are neither complements nor substitutes: in this case, the individual demand for one good is not affected by variations in the price of the second, all other things being equal. Conclusions are slightly modified when the elasticity of substitution differs from unity, as shown below.

Growth differentials with $\sigma \neq 1$. When tourism and manufactured goods are either complements ($\sigma < 1$) or substitutes ($\sigma > 1$), the relative strength of the terms-of-trade effect changes: it is intuitive that whether these substitution effects are sufficient to overturn previous conclusions is a matter of parameters. In a structural-gap model, Lanza and Pigliaru (1994) showed that specialisation in tourism guarantees higher growth rates if the preference elasticity of substitution is strictly less than unity. We will refer to this result as the LP condition. The LP condition builds on the assumption that physical productivity in the tourism-based economy grows at a lower rate with respect to the manufacturing-based economy. In our model, this situation corresponds to the case 'convergence from above', where the growth rate of physical output is lower in country T during the transition. The growth differential is now redefined as $\Delta = \Delta^Y - \sigma^{-1}\Delta^C$. Following the same steps as in Proposition 2.4, it can be easily shown that

Proposition 2.5 *If country* T *converges from above, tourism specialisation implies higher growth rates along the* transition *path as long as*

$$\sigma < \Delta^C/\Delta^Y, \tag{2.37}$$

where $\Delta^C/\Delta^Y > 1$ during the transition.

Proposition 2.5 implies that a modified LP condition holds in the present model, though inequality (2.37) must be re-interpreted in a dynamic context.

More precisely, the growth differential exhibits different dynamics depending on whether (2.37) is satisfied at time zero. In particular, Δ is time-varying during transition, and its sign is crucially determined by the adjustment speeds of Δ^C and Δ^Y. Since $\Delta^C/\Delta^Y > 1$ along the entire transitional path, the speed at which Δ^C approaches zero will not exceed the adjustment speed of Δ^Y, implying that Δ^C/Δ^Y is non-declining over time and bounded below by unity. As a consequence, if inequality (2.37) holds at time zero, it will also be satisfied along the entire transitional path: when $\sigma < \Delta^C/\Delta^Y$ at $t = 0$, the tourism-based economy (converging from above) exhibits higher growth during the whole transition to the long-run equilibrium. When $\sigma > \Delta^C/\Delta^Y > 1$ at $t = 0$, instead, the growth differential Δ may approach zero following a non-monotonic transition path: since the adjustment speed of Δ^C is strictly less than that of Δ^Y, if (2.37) is initially violated, the ratio Δ^C/Δ^Y will grow over time so as to achieve $\Delta^C/\Delta^Y = \sigma$ at some instant, with inequality (2.37) being satisfied from that time onwards. The associated path of Δ is therefore non-monotonic: in this case, tourism specialisation is growth reducing in the short run, and growth improving in the medium run. At the beginning the increase in the relative demand for tourism is more than offset by the negative impact of increasing the technological gap with the leader; subsequently, terms-of-trade effects dominate, implying higher growth in the tourism-based economy before achieving balanced growth.

Clearly, the non-monotonic case does not occur when the preference-elasticity is below unity: $\sigma < 1$ implies $\sigma < \Delta^C/\Delta^Y$ at any point in time. This is indeed the link between Proposition 2.5 and the LP condition: in the present

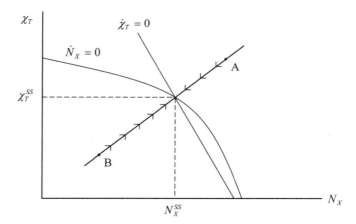

Figure 2.1   Phase diagram of system (2.28)–(2.29). If country T starts at point A (B), the technological gap with the leader increases (decreases) over time

model, $\sigma < 1$ is not strictly necessary to have positive growth differentials for tourism countries, but is sufficient to ensure that tourism specialisation is growth improving along the entire transition path.[7]

Remarks

The previous analysis suggests two main remarks. First, the sign of transitional growth differentials is opposite to that predicted by the original expanding-varieties model. The reason is that we have extended the single-good version developed by Barro and Sala-i-Martin (1997) to include full specialisation in non-homogeneous final goods, and terms-of-trade effects. When both countries produce the same final good, relative prices disappear and the growth rate of physical output is all that matters. As a consequence, conclusions about growth differentials are radically overturned: in a one-good set-up, technological catching up (i.e. converging from point B) guarantees higher growth rates along the transition for the follower; conversely, converging from point A, the technological gap increases over time and transitional growth rates are lower with respect to the innovation leader.

The second remark is that, in the model presented, tourism-based economies exhibit higher growth when the technological gap with industrialised countries increases over time. It should be stressed, however, that technological falling-behind need not be thought of as the requirement for obtaining higher growth, since the above results can be interpreted more generally as follows. In a two-country–two-good set-up, the growth effects of increasing physical output are more than offset by price movements. Consequently, tourism specialisation is growth improving when the increase in the foreign relative demand is sufficient to drive terms of trade in the favorable direction. With standard specifications for preferences and technology, this process occurs when growth rates of physical output are lower than those experienced by trading partners: in general, any specialisation is growth improving as long as the relative scarcity of the home-produced good is increased over time. From this broad perspective, it is clear that other sources of 'relative scarcity' may play the same role as the technological gap in our model. Considering tourism-dependent economies, a standard index of 'physical output' is likely to be subject to finite upper bounds, by virtue e.g. of land availability, accommodation capacity, depletable environmental resources, etc.; in this case, good economic performance is necessarily driven by either quality improvements or increasing relative prices for tourism. Similarly, product-differentiation strategies pursued by tourism-dependent economies may be interpreted as a way of implementing an equivalent 'scarcity principle' when facing industrialised countries, where the levels of conventional production steadily increase. On the one hand, whether and to what extent relative scarcity and differentiation strategies actually explain the observed economic performance of tourism-based economies is an empirical question. On the other hand, it is possible to address the problem of environmental constraints at the theoretical level by means of a simple model of specialised trade with asymmetric technologies. The next section analyses a two-country model where both relative demand effects and structural gaps are induced by the essential role played by environmental goods in tourism-based economies.

2.4 TOURISM-SPECIFIC INPUTS

In the previous section, the structural differences between the manufacturing-based and the tourism-based economy were represented by 'technological inferiority', modeled in terms of R&D capacity and relative endowments. However, real-world tourism countries (i) exploit tourism-specific inputs, e.g. environmental resources, that do not have homologues in the set of factors used to produce manufactured goods, and (ii) may exhibit persistent gaps in physical productivity growth, as in Lanza and Pigliaru (1994). Building on this point, this section tackles issues (i) and (ii) by considering a hybrid model where both persistent gaps and transitional dynamics arise, due to the presence of asymmetric technologies and tourism-specific inputs.

Industrialised country. The reference model for country M is the Frenkel–Romer model of endogenous growth. There exist J firms indexed by $j = 1, ..., J$ that produce y_M units of final output employing k_M units of capital and $h_M l_M$ labour-efficiency units. Each firm's technology is represented by

$$y_M^{(j)} = \left(k_M^{(j)}\right)^\rho \left(h_M l_M^{(j)}\right)^{1-\rho}, \tag{2.38}$$

where per-worker productivity h_M is now time-varying. The standard assumption in this regard is that the level of h_M is subject to aggregate externalities. Each firm chooses input quantities k_M and $h_M l_M$ taking per-worker productivity as given. This guarantees that (2.38) exhibits constant returns to scale at the firm's level. Profit-maximising conditions thus imply

$$\mu_M = \rho\left(y_M^{(j)}/k_M^{(j)}\right), \tag{2.39}$$

$$w_M = (1-\rho)\left(h_M l_M^{(j)}\right)^{-1} y_M^{(j)}. \tag{2.40}$$

Assuming that all firms are of identical size, each firm employs the same amount of each input, and total output $Y_M = Jy_M$ thus equals

$$Y_M = K_M^\rho \left(h_M L_M \right)^{1-\rho},$$ (2.41)

where $K_M = Jk_M$ is aggregate capital and $L_M = Jl_M$ is total employment in country M. Following Romer (1989), we assume that h_M is positively related to the aggregate capital stock K_M, in line with the idea that human knowledge develops together with the economy through a process of learning-by-doing (Arrow, 1962; Frankel, 1962). Formally,

$$h_M(t) = b_M K_M(t),$$ (2.42)

where $b_M > 0$ is the intensity of learning-by-doing. Substituting (2.42) in (2.43), we obtain

$$Y_M(t) = B_M K_M(t),$$ (2.43)

where $B_M \equiv (b_M L_M)^{1-\rho}$. Expression (2.43) implies that, looking at the economy as a whole, the aggregate technology displays increasing returns to scale, with aggregate output being linear in aggregate capital. As a consequence, the equilibrium interest rate is constant and equal to

$$\mu_M = \rho B_M = \rho \left(b_M L_M \right)^{1-\rho},$$ (2.44)

and consumption grows at the constant rate ($\mu_M - \delta$). The aggregate constraint $\dot{K}_M = B_M K_M - C_M$, in turn, implies that the industrialised economy displays balanced growth from time zero onwards:

$$\hat{K}_M = \hat{C}_M = \hat{Y}_M = \rho B_M - \delta \text{ at any } t \in [0, \infty),$$ (2.45)

where we assume $\rho B_M > \delta$ in order to have a well-defined equilibrium with a positive growth rate.

Tourism country. A typical feature of tourism-based economies is the strong dependence on environmental goods and natural resources. Accordingly, we model the production process in country T by including environmental goods as a third input in the aggregate technology. The stock of environmental goods is denoted by E, and obeys the transition law

$$\dot{E}(t) = -X(t) + \Omega(E(t)),$$ (2.46)

where Ω represents environmental regeneration and $X(t)$ is the amount of environmental goods subtracted to the stock at time t in order to produce an intermediate good, Q_T, which is essential for the tourism industry. In this specification, E can be either interpreted as livestock or quantity of environmental resources/amenities, so that Ω can be accordingly interpreted as a biological regeneration function or resources renewal function. In order to obtain neat results, we assume $\Omega(E) = \varphi E$, where $\varphi \geq 0$ is the constant marginal rate of regeneration. Environmental 'extraction' occurs at zero cost, and there is a linear technology for the intermediate good $Q_T = \upsilon X$, where $\upsilon > 0$ is the (constant) marginal productivity of environmental goods. The present-discounted value at time $t = 0$ of the stream of profits from intermediate inputs is

$$\upsilon \int_0^\infty w^q(t) X(t) e^{-\int_0^t \mu_M(j)dj} dt, \tag{2.47}$$

where w^q is the price of the intermediate good. The optimal extraction plan consists of choosing the sequence of the rates of environmental use $\{X(t)\}$ that maximises (2.47) subject to the environmental constraint (2.46), taking prices $\{w^q(t)\}$ as given. The resulting first-order conditions imply the modified Hotelling rule

$$\hat{w}^q = \mu_M - \varphi. \tag{2.48}$$

Final output is produced by S firms indexed by $s = 1, ..., S$ that produce y_T units of final output employing k_T units of capital, $h_T l_T$ labour-efficiency units, and q_T units of the intermediate good. Each firm's technology is represented by

$$y_T^{(s)} = \left(k_T^{(s)}\right)^{\varepsilon_1} \left(h_T^{(s)} l_T^{(s)}\right)^{\varepsilon_2} \left(q_T^{(s)}\right)^{\varepsilon_3},$$

which displays constant returns to scale. Assuming that all firms are of identical size, employed quantities are symmetric across firms and total output $Y_T = S y_T$ reads

$$Y_T = K_T^{\varepsilon_1} \left(h_T L_T\right)^{\varepsilon_2} Q_T^{\varepsilon_3}, \tag{2.49}$$

where $K_T = S k_T$ is aggregate capital, $L_T = S l_T$ is total employment, and $Q_T = S q_T$ is the amount of environment-intensive intermediate inputs. As before, knowledge h_T depends on the aggregate capital stock through the learning-by-doing process $h_T(t) = b_T K_T(t)$, where b_T is the intensity of learning-by-doing. Hence, aggregate output can be rewritten as

$$Y_T = B_T K_T^{1-\varepsilon_3} Q_T^{\varepsilon_3}.$$ (2.50)

Expression (2.50) implies that environmental endowments constrain the tourism-based economy both in the short and in the long run. On the one hand, (2.50) rules out the stable linear relation between output and capital observed in (2.43), so that country T displays transitional dynamics. On the other hand, the presence of Q_T in (2.50) implies that the interest rate will depend on the capital–environmental goods ratio, so that the long-run interest rate will also be affected by the resource constraint. In fact, the role of environmental scarcity is prominent: contrary to economy M, the long-run growth rate in economy T is actually independent of learning-by-doing, as shown below.

Long-run Growth Differentials

As shown in the Appendix, equilibrium dynamics in country T imply asymptotic balanced growth, the long-run growth rate being exclusively determined by natural regeneration:

$$\hat{K}_T = \hat{C}_T = \hat{Y}_T = \varphi - \delta \text{ as } t \to \infty.$$ (2.51)

Two well-known results underlie this outcome. First, if we interpret E as a non-renewable resource ($\varphi = 0$), we obtain the unsustainability result of Dasgupta and Heal (1974): if the resource stock is essential and exhaustible, consumption is bound to decrease in the long run. Second, technical progress improves the long-run growth rate only if it is, directly or indirectly, resource-augmenting (Stiglitz, 1974): in fact, learning-by-doing is here equivalent to capital-embodied technical progress, and it does not enhance the long-run growth rate in our model.[8] The fact that natural regeneration relieves the environmental constraint is intuitive, and is emphasised in general equilibrium models by Mourmouras (1993), Krautkraemer and Batina (1999) and Valente (2005a).

From (2.7), (2.43) and (2.51), the long-run growth differential can be expressed as

$$\lim_{t \to \infty} \Delta = \left(\frac{\sigma - 1}{\sigma} \right) (\varphi - \rho B_M),$$ (2.52)

which recalls the discussion on persistent gaps in section 2.2. If $\sigma > 1$ ($\sigma < 1$), the growth differential is in favor of the economy displaying a positive (negative) structural gap in physical output growth. In the present setting, this means that if the rate of natural regeneration in country T falls short of the (weighted) intensity of learning-by-doing in country M, tourism specialisation is growth maximising if traded goods are perceived as complements, as in Lanza and Pigliaru (1994). The opposite is true when $\varphi > \rho B_M$: in this case, the structural gap is positive for the tourism-based economy, and terms-of-trade effects push in the unfavorable direction for country T. However, due to the presence of relative demand effects during the transition, these results are not necessarily valid at each point in time, as shown below.

Relative Demand Effects

In the tourism-based economy, the growth rates of consumption and output differ along the transition. To address this point, define the marginal propensity to consume in country T as $\tau \equiv C_T/Y_T$ and rewrite the growth differential (2.7) as

$$\Delta = \sigma^{-1}\left[(\sigma-1)\Delta^Y - \hat{\tau}\right]. \tag{2.53}$$

Comparing (2.53) with (2.52), the differences between transitional and long-run results may be substantial. In particular, in the polar case $\sigma = 1$, the two economies exhibit convergence towards constant market shares and, during transition, the growth differential is exclusively determined by the dynamics of the marginal propensity to consume in the tourism economy. Also in the more general case, $\sigma \neq 1$, the last term in (2.53), which may be called the 'propensity effect', has the potential to overturn the sign of growth differentials with respect to the predictions of the structural gap approach. This effect is particularly relevant when economy T at time zero is far distant from the long-run equilibrium, since propensity effects become stronger and influence the sign of Δ over an arbitrarily large interval.

The sign of propensity effects can be characterised as follows. Figure 2.2 shows that the marginal propensity to consume is stationary in the long run, and it may approach the long-run equilibrium either from above or from below. In particular, the trajectory is determined by whether the initial output–capital ratio, $z \equiv Y_T/K_T$, is below or above the long-run equilibrium level. In this regard, the main conclusion is

Proposition 2.6 *During the transition, propensity effects* increase *(reduce)* Δ *if the economy follows a path along which the interest rate* μ_T *decreases (increases).*

It follows immediately from Proposition 2.6 that when $\sigma = 1$, the growth differential is totally independent of the sign of long-run productivity gaps, and Δ is strictly positive (negative) if the economy follows a path along which the interest rate declines (decreases). When $\sigma \neq 1$, various subcases are possible, depending on the combination of the parameters that determine whether output effects dominate propensity effects, and vice versa. In any case, it should be stressed that propensity effects push growth differentials in the favourable direction for country T along any dynamically efficient path. By dynamically efficient path we mean the typical development path of an economy that is initially scarce of capital (relative to other inputs), and increases its capital intensity during the transition to the long-run equilibrium. This is the classical transitional path considered in the Ramsey–Cass–Koopmans model, where the capital–labour ratio increases over time until the modified golden rule is reached, and the interest rate therefore exhibits a decreasing time-path. In the present model, the dynamically efficient path exhibits decreasing interest rates and therefore propensity effects that tend to increase Δ. Propensity effects thus represent a possible additional explanation for the positive growth differentials experienced by tourism-based economies.

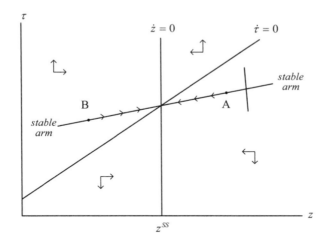

Figure 2.2 Dynamics of the marginal propensity to consume (τ) and the output–capital ratio (z) in the model with tourism-specific inputs

2.5 CONCLUSION

Empirical evidence suggests that terms-of-trade effects between countries trading heterogeneous goods likely play an active role in determining cross-country income gaps. In general, the direction of terms-of-trade dynamics can be interpreted in terms of 'structural gaps' or 'relative demand effects'. Taking the perspective of modern growth theory, the two approaches yield independent results when considering growth differentials in models that display transitional dynamics: the behaviour of market shares is determined by (i) structural gaps and the preference-elasticity of substitution in the long run, whereas growth differentials along the transition are crucially influenced by (ii) the dynamics of consumption expenditures. In the literature on tourism and growth, Lanza and Pigliaru (1994) implement the structural gap approach in a learning-by-doing model *à la* Lucas (1988), and show that tourism specialisation is growth maximising when traded goods are perceived as complements.

   This chapter implemented relative demand effects in two models of specialised trade featuring transitional dynamics. A first model considered technological gaps and convergence by imitation, as in Barro and Sala-i-Martin (1997). In this set-up, no structural gaps arise in the long run, and the sign of transitional growth differentials depends on whether the technological follower catches up with, or falls behind the innovation leader. If the lagging economy reduces the technological gap over time, it experiences higher growth rates in physical output with respect to the innovation leader; however, terms-of-trade effects are stronger and the growth differential is in favor of the technological leader. Conversely, if the technological gap increases over time, growth rates in physical output are below those experienced by the innovation leader, and terms-of-trade effects imply that the growth differential is positive for the innovation follower. The above conclusions are also interesting in that they contradict the results of the standard one-good model, where technological falling-behind is bad for growth.

   The second model identified trading countries as tourism-based and manufacturing-based economies, and assumed that production possibilities in the tourism country are constrained by available environmental goods. In this framework, both structural gaps and relative demand effects arise. In the long run, although there is a symmetric learning-by-doing process, the growth rate of the tourism-based economy is exclusively determined by natural regeneration and time-preference rates. During the transition, the industrialised country displays endogenous balanced growth, whereas the tourism-based economy exhibits monotonic convergence of the interest rate towards the long-run equilibrium value. Transitional growth differentials are determined by the dynamics of the marginal propensity to consume in the tourism country, and these propensity effects push the growth differential in favour of the tourism-based economy along any dynamically efficient path. All the above results emphasise the possibility that positive growth differentials in tourism-based economies are driven by internal consumption dynamics, suggesting that the observed performance can also be explained by dynamic increases in the relative foreign demand for tourism services.

ACKNOWLEDGEMENTS

I thank Anna Maria Pinna for insightful discussion, Barbara Annicchiarico, Rinaldo Brau, and Christa Brunnschweiler for comments, and seminar participants at the CRENoS–FEEM Conference on Tourism and Sustainable Economic Development (Cagliari, 2005) for useful suggestions. The working paper version of this chapter was circulated under the title 'Growth, Conventional Production and Tourism Specialisation: Technological Catching-Up versus Terms-of-Trade Effects'. This is a substantially revised and expanded version of Valente (2005b).

NOTES

1. While tourism specialisation is positively associated with growth as such, the effects on residents' welfare may be ambiguous. Possible channels through which tourism specialisation may impoverish residents are analysed by Chao et al. (in this book) and Nowak et al. (2004).
2. For the readaptation process to be possible in the present context, it is not strictly necessary to assume that laws for copyright protection are ineffective at the international level: countries are producing different goods, and the readaptation process may generate intermediates x_{kT} featuring specific differences (and hence not violating international laws) with respect to their 'original versions' x_{kM} developed in country M. The lack of effective copyright protection at the international level is instead an implicit assumption in Barro and Sala-i-Martin (1997), as they assume that countries produce exactly the same final good.
3. An alternative interpretation is that readaptation proceeds chronologically: countries bearing a relatively wide technological gap first readapt intermediates that are relatively 'old' with respect to those being pioneered by the leader in that moment; if the technological gap is reduced thereafter, imitating becomes more expensive because intermediates available for readaptation are 'technologically closer' to the frontier currently determined by the leader.
4. The conclusion that the growth rate $\hat{C}_T$ also converges to g_M can be reached heuristically by applying the same reasoning used to rule out non-balanced growth paths in country M.
5. The characterisation of economic dynamics in the two countries developed above, and Lemma 1 in particular, postulates that readaptation costs always remain below innovation costs in country T. As shown in Valente (2005b), the relative scarcity of labour (skills) in country T and the assumption $N_T(0) < N_M(0)$ imply that the tourism-based country is always a follower, because readapting is cheaper than innovating in every instant.
6. Our use of the terms 'above' and 'below' relates to the phase diagram in Figure 2.1, and does *not* refer to initial output levels as often done in the growth literature. The analysis will clarify that 'above' and 'below' are then associated with the growth differential between the

follower and the leader, but this is peculiar to the present model since the opposite result holds in the original Barro and Sala-i-Martin (1997) model – see subsection 'Remarks'.

7. Also note that, due to an exactly symmetric reasoning, when country T converges from below, tourism specialisation is growth reducing as long as $\sigma < \Delta^C/\Delta^Y$: if this inequality holds at time zero, country T exhibits lower growth rates along the entire transition path; if σ initially exceeds Δ^C/Δ^Y and adjustment speeds differ between Δ^C and Δ^Y, the non-monotonic case is also reversed, and tourism specialisation is growth improving in the short run but growth reducing in the medium run.

8. For simplicity, the present discussion ignores resource-augmenting technical progress, which is likely an outcome of competitive R&D sectors when the direction of technical change is endogenous, as shown in Di Maria and Valente (2006).

REFERENCES

Arrow, K. (1962), 'The economic implications of learning by doing', *Review of Economic Studies*, **80**, 155–73.

Barro, R. and X. Sala-i-Martin (1997), 'Technological diffusion, convergence, and growth', *Journal of Economic Growth*, **2**, 1–26.

Brau, R., A. Lanza and F. Pigliaru (2007), 'Tourism specialisation, cross country growth evidence, in African Analyst Quarterly, **2**(2), 61–68.

Dasgupta, P.S. and G.M. Heal (1974), 'The optimal depletion of exhaustible resources', *Review of Economic Studies, Symposium on the Economics of Exhaustible Resources*, 3–28.

Di Maria, C. and S. Valente (2006), 'The direction of technical change in capital-resource economies', Economics Working Paper Series 06/50, March 2006. ETH Zurich.

Dixit, A. and J. Stiglitz (1977), 'Monopolistic competition and optimum product diversity', *American Economic Review*, **67**, 297–308.

Feenstra, R. (1996), 'Trade and uneven growth', *Journal of Development Economics*, **49**, 229–56.

Frankel, M. (1962), 'The production function in allocation and growth: a synthesis', *American Economic Review*, **52**, 995–1022.

Frenkel, J. and A. Razin (1985), 'Government spending, debt, and international economic interdependence', *Economic Journal*, **95**, 619–36.

Gardner, G. and K. Kimbrough (1990), 'The effects of trade-balance-triggered tariffs', *International Economic Review*, **31**, 117–29.

Grossman, G. and H. Helpman (1990), 'Comparative advantage and long-run growth', *American Economic Review*, **80**, 796–815.

Krautkraemer, J.A. and R.G. Batina (1999), 'On sustainability and intergenerational transfers with a renewable resource', *Land Economics*, **75**(2), 167–84.

Lanza, A. and F. Pigliaru (1994), 'The tourism sector in the open economy', *Rivista Internazionale di Scienze Economiche e Commerciali*, **41**(1), 15–28.

Lucas, R. (1988), 'On the mechanics of economic development', *Journal of Monetary Economics*, **22**, 3–42.

Mourmouras, A. (1993), 'Conservationist government policies and intergenerational equity in an overlapping generations model with renewable resources', *Journal of Public Economics*, **51**, 249–68.

Nowak, J.-J., M. Sahli and P. Sgrò (2004), 'Tourism, trade and domestic welfare', FEEM Note di Lavoro, No. 24.04.

Rivera-Batiz, L. and P. Romer (1991), 'Economic integration and endogenous growth', *Quarterly Journal of Economics*, **106**, 531–56.

Rogers, M. (2003), *Knowledge, Technological Catch-Up and Economic Growth*. Cheltenham, UK and Northampton, MA, USA: Edward Elgar.

Romer, P.M. (1989), 'Capital accumulation in the theory of long-run growth', in R. Barro (ed.), *Modern Business Cycle Theory*, Oxford: Basil Blackwell.

Smulders, S. (2004), 'International capital market integration: Implications for convergence, growth, and welfare', *International Economics and Economic Policy*, **1**, 173–94.

Spence, M. (1976), 'Product selection, fixed costs, and monopolistic competition', *Review of Economic Studies*, **43**, 217–35.

Stiglitz, J. (1974), 'Growth with exhaustible natural resources, efficient and optimal growth paths', *Review of Economic Studies, Symposium on the Economics of Exhaustible Resources*, 123–37.

Valente, S. (2005a), 'Sustainable development, renewable resources and technological progress', *Environmental and Resource Economics*, **30**, 115–25.

Valente, S. (2005b), 'Growth, conventional production and tourism specialisation', FEEM Working Paper, No. 140.05.

2.A   APPENDIX

Model with Technology Diffusion

Derivation of (2.24)

Setting $A_i = a_i L_i$ in (2.12), and recalling that aggregate wealth equals the value of firms, $A_i = N_i V_i$, the aggregate wealth constraint can be rewritten as

$$\dot{N}_i V_i + N_i \dot{V}_i = \mu_i N_i V_i + w_i^h H_i - C_i. \tag{2.A1}$$

Substituting the profit-maximising condition $w^h H = (1 - \alpha) Y$ together with (2.20) yields

$$\dot{N}_i V_i + N_i \dot{V}_i = \mu_i N_i V_i + (1 - \alpha) H_i N_i \alpha^{\frac{2\alpha}{1-\alpha}} - C_i \tag{2.A2}$$

Dividing by $N_i V_i$ yields equation (2.24) in the text.

Proof of Lemma 2.1

See Barro and Sala-i-Martin (1997).

Derivation of equations (2.25)–(2.26)

Time-differentiating V_i yields

$$\dot{V}_i = \mu_i V_i - \bar{\pi}_i, \tag{2.A3}$$

where we have used (2.19). Substituting equilibrium free-entry conditions (2.23) in (2.A3), we obtain (2.25)–(2.26).

Derivation of equations (2.28)–(2.29)

Equation (2.28) is derived as follows. Equations (2.18) and (2.20) imply $Y_T = \alpha^{-2} \bar{x}_T N_T$, which can be substituted in (2.19) to obtain

$$(1 - \alpha)(Y_T / N_T) = (\bar{\pi}_T / \alpha). \tag{2.A4}$$

Now rewrite (2.24) as

$$\hat{N}_T = \mu_T + \left[(1 - \alpha)(Y_T / N_T) - \chi_T - \dot{V}_T \right] V_T^{-1}, \tag{2.A5}$$

where $\chi_T \equiv C_T / N_T$. Substituting (2.23), (2.26) and (2.A4) in (2.A5) gives

$$\hat{N}_T = \left[\alpha^{-1}(1+\alpha)\bar{\pi}_T - \chi_T\right]f_T^{-1}, \tag{2.A6}$$

Setting $N_x \equiv N_T/N_M$, we obtain, from (2.27) and (2.A6),

$$\hat{N}_x = \left[\alpha^{-1}(1+\alpha)\bar{\pi}_T - \chi_T\right]f_T^{-1} - g_M.$$

Substituting (2.21) in the above expression yields equation (2.28) in the text. Equation (2.29) is derived as follows. Substituting (2.26) in (2.13) gives

$$\hat{C}_T = v\hat{N}_x + (\bar{\pi}_T - \delta)(\lambda_T N_x^v)^{-1}, \tag{2.A7}$$

where we have used (2.21) and its time-derivative. Using (2.A6) and (2.A7),

$$\hat{\chi}_T = v\hat{N}_x + (\lambda_T N_x^v)^{-1}\left[(\bar{\pi}_T - \delta) - \alpha^{-1}(1+\alpha)\bar{\pi}_T + \chi_T\right]. \tag{2.A8}$$

Substituting (2.25) and rearranging terms gives equation (2.29) in the text.

Proof of Propositions 2.2 and 2.3
Both propositions hinge on the fact that the stable path towards the steady-state equilibrium is upward-sloping in the phase plane (χ_T, N_x), as shown in Figure 2.1. First, consider Proposition 2.2, which corresponds to a situation where the economy starts at point B. As the economy converges from below we have χ_T increasing during the transition, implying $\hat{C}_T > \hat{N}_T = \hat{Y}_T$, which proves the first inequality in (2.33). On the other hand, starting at point B implies N_x be increasing during the transition, so that $\hat{N}_T > \hat{N}_M$. Since $\hat{N}_i = \hat{Y}_i$, the second inequality in (2.33) is also proved. Second, consider Proposition 2.3, which corresponds to a situation where the economy starts at point A in Figure 2.1. As the economy converges from above we have χ_T decreasing during the transition, so that $\hat{C}_T < \hat{N}_T = \hat{Y}_T$, which proves the first inequality in (2.35). Starting at point A also implies N_x be decreasing during the transition: since $\hat{N}_T < \hat{N}_M$ corresponds to $\hat{Y}_T < \hat{Y}_M$, the second inequality in (2.35) is also proved. The last equality $\hat{Y}_M = \hat{C}_M$ in both (2.33) and (2.35) simply follows from balanced growth in country M, which completes the proof.

Proof of Proposition 2.4
When country T converges from below, the growth differential is positive because expression (2.33) implies

$$\Delta^C > \Delta^Y > 0 \quad \Rightarrow \quad \Delta < 0. \tag{2.A9}$$

Conversely, when country T converges from above, the growth differential is negative because expression (2.35) implies

$$\Delta^C < \Delta^Y < 0 \quad \Rightarrow \quad \Delta > 0. \tag{2.A10}$$

Proof of Proposition 2.5

This result is easily proved following the same steps as above with $\sigma \neq 1$.

Model with Tourism-Specific Inputs

Equilibrium in country T

In country T, each firm chooses input quantities with first order conditions implying

$$\mu_T = \varepsilon_1 \left(y_T^{(s)}/k_T^{(s)} \right), \tag{2.A11}$$

$$w^q = \varepsilon_3 \left(y_T^{(s)}/q_T^{(s)} \right). \tag{2.A12}$$

Assuming that all firms are of identical size, employed quantities are symmetric across firms and total output equals (2.49). From (2.48) and (2.A12) we have

$$\hat{w}^q = \hat{Y}_T - \hat{Q}_T = \mu_M - \varphi. \tag{2.A13}$$

Time-differentiating (2.50), and substituting (2.A11)–(2.A13) in the resulting expression we obtain

$$\hat{z} = \varepsilon_3 \left(1 - \varepsilon_3 \right)^{-1} \left(\varphi - \varepsilon_1 z \right), \tag{2.A14}$$

where we have defined $z \equiv Y_T/K_T$. Equation (2.A14) displays a unique steady-state equilibrium

$$z_{ss} = \varphi/\varepsilon_1 > 0, \tag{2.A15}$$

which is globally stable from (2.A14). As a consequence, $z(t) \to z_{ss}$ in the long run, which implies, from (2.A11), that the interest rate converges to the marginal rate of regeneration:

$$\lim_{t \to \infty} \mu_T = \lim_{t \to \infty} \varepsilon_1 z(t) = \varphi . \qquad (2.A16)$$

It follows from the aggregate constraint of the economy,

$$\dot{K}_T = Y_T - C_T , \qquad (2.A17)$$

that $z(t) \to z_{ss}$ implies consumption, capital and output be growing at the same balanced rate $(\varphi - \delta)$ suggested by the Keynes–Ramsey rule (2.13). This proves expression (2.51) in the text. As regards the marginal propensity to consume, $\tau \equiv C_T/Y_T$, we have by definition

$$\hat{\tau} = \hat{C}_T - \hat{Y}_T = \hat{C}_T - \hat{K}_T - \hat{z} . \qquad (2.A18)$$

Substituting (2.A14) and, from the aggregate constraint, the growth rate of capital with $z - \tau$, we obtain

$$\hat{\tau} = \tau - \frac{\varepsilon_2}{1-\varepsilon_3} z - \left(\delta + \frac{\varepsilon_3}{1-\varepsilon_3} \varphi \right). \qquad (2.A19)$$

The simultaneous steady state in (2.A14) and (2.A19) features

$$\hat{z} = 0 \quad \to \quad z = \varphi/\varepsilon_1,$$

$$\hat{\tau} = 0 \quad \to \quad \tau = \frac{\varepsilon_2}{1-\varepsilon_3} z + \left(\delta + \frac{\varepsilon_3}{1-\varepsilon_3} \varphi \right),$$

and is represented in Figure 2.2. Since $\partial(\hat{\tau})/\partial \tau > 0$ and $\partial(\hat{z})/\partial z < 0$, the direction of the arrows in the phase diagram is such that the stable arm is upward-sloping in the (z, τ) plane. As a consequence, the sign of $\hat{\tau}$ is unambiguously determined by whether country T converges from above (e.g. starting from point A in Figure 2.2) or converges from below (e.g. starting from point B in Figure 2.2).

Proof of Proposition 2.6

Since the equilibrium interest rate in country T is given by $\mu_T = \varepsilon_1 z$, the main conclusion is easily proved by means of Figure 2.2. When $z(0) < z_{ss}$, the interest rate increases over time (z increases) and, since the stable arm is upward-sloping, τ increases during the whole transition: from (2.53), this implies that Δ tends to be reduced by propensity effects. Instead, when $z(0) > z_{ss}$ interest rates are declining (z decreases) and τ decreases during the whole transition, so that Δ tends to be increased by propensity effects.

3. Tourism Development and Environmental Quality: Long-Run Effects of Monopoly Power

Sauveur Giannoni and Marie-Antoinette Maupertuis

3.1 INTRODUCTION

In a context of intense tourism expansion all over the world, lots of developing countries and regions of developed ones specialize in tourism in order to exploit natural comparative advantages. From a growth perspective, this specialization seems to be successful for most of them (Brau et al., 2007).

Nonetheless little attention has been devoted to what is at stake when speaking of tourism development: the preservation or the deterioration of natural and heritage resources.

Indeed tourism development is based on some kind of paradox. On the one hand the attractiveness of a destination relies on natural capital (water and land endowment, landscapes, biodiversity, climate, etc.) and heritage. On the other hand tourism frequentation induces pollution, environmental degradation, and more or less irreversible damage of natural and heritage assets, the intensity of which may threaten tourism development in the long run.

Following the World Tourism Organisation (1995), tourism development will be sustainable if it enhances the way of living of the population without damaging the environmental and cultural capital of the destination. But there are no clear criteria in order to measure the sustainability of a given tourism strategy. Then the key question is to find an equilibrium point between resource exploitation and resource preservation because it is the only way to maintain attractiveness over time. Mainstream economics generally defines sustainability as a situation in which utility is non-decreasing in the long run. In this chapter, we consider that development is sustainable if a minimal stock of natural and cultural assets is preserved in the long run.

From that point of view, recent economic literature highlights new arguments to understand the inter-temporal trade off between investments in tourism infrastructures and pollution (Casagrandi and Rinaldi, 1999, 2002; Kort et al., 2002; Léon et al., 2003). These authors develop an optimal control model highlighting two kinds of sustainable trajectories when maximizing tourism profits. The first one is a steady state where investments in infrastructures just equal the depreciation of their stock. The number of tourists remains constant over time and the increase in pollution is absorbed by the environment. The second sustainable path is given by a cyclical evolution in investments, in the number of tourists, in the pollution stock and in infrastructures inducing different phases in tourism development and confirming Butler's (1980) life-cycle hypothesis. Tourism development may be sustainable because of alternative phases of high and low frequentation permitting ecosystems to regenerate. It has been shown (Giannoni and Maupertuis, 2005) that introducing an environmental quality variable – instead of a pollution variable – the model broadly confirms Butler's life-cycle hypothesis and Kort et al.'s (2002) conclusion according to which the competitive tourism industry must limit over time the number of visitors to preserve future profits. When the perceived environmental quality is decreasing, the tourism lobby may be incited to disinvest in order to preserve the environment. The question that remains unanswered is how to and to what extent frequentation can be limited. Here we propose to evaluate how the presence of monopoly power limiting the number of tourists may be, from the destination point of view, a sustainable way to develop tourism.

Our hypothesis is twofold:

1. The destination is in a situation of local monopoly. We assume that price is a tool that limits frequentation: high prices based on a high differentiation process limit the flow of tourists as tourism is a superior good (Lanza and Pigliaru, 1995).
2. Considering that tourism firms benefit from a rental situation, local authorities may capture part of the monopoly rent by implementing an eco-tax.

In order to test these hypotheses, we propose a dynamic model in which the price is used as a control variable. We show that in this context, monopoly power tends to deteriorate environmental quality. We study the characteristics of the tax that public authorities have to impose in order to preserve the environment. We show that the tax enables the preservation of both the environment and the profitability of tourism in the long run.

The chapter is organized as follows. The next section presents a tourism economy and the key relationships between investment in tourism infrastructures, frequentation and environmental quality when the destination is the price-taker. In the third section, the economy produces tourism journeys in a context of local monopoly. As we focus on long-run effects, we proceed by comparing the steady-state level of each variable. In the fourth section, we show that a tax on tourism revenue enables the improvement of environmental quality and profit in the long run. I n the last section, we conclude and open up new research perspectives.

3.2   TOURISM SPECIALIZATION, WORLD MARKET COMPETITION AND ENVIRONMENT

We consider a single economy specializing in tourism that we call the destination. It is involved in the competitive world tourism market and its market shares are relatively small. The price of a journey (q) is given at the world level and the destination is price-taker.

The local tourism sector is composed of N firms, where N is large. Each firm looks for the level of investment that maximizes its profit, taking into account environmental constraints.

Here we consider the problem of the tourism industry disconnected from the rest of the economy.

The number of tourists is given by:

$$T_t = q^{-\varepsilon} \left(\alpha K_t + \beta Q_t \right)$$

K is the number of infrastructures aiming at lodging visitors; Q reflects the level of environmental quality that is the stock of environmental assets which characterize the destination, ε is the price elasticity of tourism demand. We choose this iso-elastic form in order to facilitate mathematical treatment but we are aware of the interactions between the two factors.

When K increases by one unit, the number of tourists increase by α units *ceteris paribus*. When Q increases by one unit, the number of tourists increase by β units *ceteris paribus*.

The evolution of infrastructures is given by, where I is the instantaneous level of investment:

$$\dot{K} = I - \delta K \qquad \text{with } \delta \text{ the depreciation of capital.}$$

The evolution of environmental quality is defined as:

$$\dot{Q} = r\left(\bar{Q} - Q\right) - \kappa p^{-\varepsilon} \left(\alpha K + \beta Q \right),$$

where $r(\bar{Q}-Q)$ is the regeneration capacity of natural capital (Cazzavillan and Musu, 2001) and κ is the damage caused to the environment by a supplementary tourist.

The instantaneous profit of firm i is given by:

$$\pi_i = q^{1-\varepsilon}\left(\alpha K_i + \beta Q_i\right) - \frac{\phi}{2}I_i^2.$$

Each firm will solve the following program:

$$\underset{I}{Max}\int_0^\infty q^{1-\varepsilon}\left(\alpha K + \beta Q\right) - \frac{\phi}{2}I^2\, dt$$

s.t.

$$\dot{K} = I - \delta K \tag{3.1}$$

$$\dot{Q} = r\left(\bar{Q} - Q\right) - \kappa q^{-\varepsilon}\left(\alpha K + \beta Q\right) \tag{3.2}$$

The current Hamiltonian is given by:

$$H = q^{1-\varepsilon}\left(\alpha K + \beta Q\right) - \frac{\phi}{2}I^2 + \left(I - \delta K\right) + \mu\left[r\left(\bar{Q} - Q\right) - \kappa q^{-\varepsilon}\left(\alpha K + \beta Q\right)\right].$$

The Maximum Principle gives:

$$\lambda = \phi I,$$

$$\dot{\lambda} = \lambda\left(\rho + \delta\right) + \mu\alpha\kappa q^{-\varepsilon} - q^{1-\varepsilon}\alpha, \tag{3.3}$$

$$\dot{\mu} = \mu\left(\rho + r + \kappa q^{-\varepsilon}\beta\right) - q^{1-\varepsilon}\beta, \tag{3.4}$$

The system (3.1), (3.2), (3.3), (3.4), asymptotically converges toward a steady state given below:[1]

$$K^* = \frac{\left(\rho + r\right)q^{1-\varepsilon}\alpha\kappa}{\left(\rho + r + \kappa q^{-\varepsilon}\beta\right)\left(\rho + \delta\right)\phi\delta},$$

$$Q^* = \frac{r\bar{Q} - \dfrac{\left(\rho + r\right)q^{1-2\varepsilon}\alpha^2\kappa^2}{\left(\rho + r + \kappa q^{-\varepsilon}\beta\right)\left(\rho + \delta\right)\phi\delta}}{r + \kappa q^{-\varepsilon}\beta},$$

$$I^* = \frac{\left(\rho + r\right)q^{1-\varepsilon}\alpha\kappa}{\left(\rho + r + \kappa q^{-\varepsilon}\beta\right)\left(\rho + \delta\right)\phi},$$

$$\mu^* = \frac{q^{1-\varepsilon}\beta}{\left(\rho + r + \kappa q^{-\varepsilon}\beta\right)}.$$

Table 3.1   Comparative statics of the steady state

	α	β	q	κ	ε	r	ρ	δ	ϕ
K^*	+	−	+/−	+	−	+	+/−	−	−
Q^*	+/−	+/−	+/−	+/−	+/−	+/−	+/−	+/−	+/−
I^*	+	−	+/−	+	−	+	+/−	−	−
μ^*	0	+	+/−	−	−	−	−	0	0

We verify that *ceteris paribus* the long-term lodging infrastructure stock increases with the tourists' preference for lodging and with the assimilation capability of the environment. It will decrease with the preference of tourists for the environment, the price elasticity of demand and the depreciation of capital, the investment cost parameter.

3.3   TOURISM DIFFERENTIATION, MARKET POWER AND ENVIRONMENT

We now consider an economy specializing in tourism and exhibiting singular natural and cultural endowments, of an island or an old city for example. This destination differentiates its products on the world tourism market. The tourism industry of the destination is always composed of various firms. Nonetheless we consider that the tourism industry acts as a single firm in the world market as it offers specific and unique tourist products. The destination is no longer price-taker in the world market. It will control the price of the journey,[2] we denote this price *p*.

The number of tourists is given by:

$$T = p^{-\varepsilon}\left(\alpha K + \beta Q\right),$$

p represents the price of a journey for a visitor determined by the tourism industry.

The evolution of infrastructures is always given by:

$$\dot{K} = I - \delta K. \tag{3.1'}$$

The evolution of environmental quality is defined as

$$\dot{Q} = r(\overline{Q} - Q) - \kappa p^{-\varepsilon}(\alpha K + \beta Q). \tag{3.2'}$$

The representative firm now solves the same Hamiltonian than in the previous section but taking the price as a control variable.

The maximum principle leads to completing the system (3.1'), (3.2') with the next two equations.

Investment evolves according to:

$$\dot{I} = (\rho + \delta)I - \frac{p^{1-\varepsilon}\alpha}{\varepsilon\phi}. \tag{3.3'}$$

The journey price will vary over time according to:

$$\dot{p} = (\rho + r)p - \frac{\kappa p^{1-\varepsilon}\beta}{(\varepsilon - 1)}. \tag{3.4'}$$

Considering steady-state values now we obtain:

$$K^M = \frac{p^{*1-\varepsilon}\alpha}{\phi\varepsilon(\rho+\delta)\delta} = \frac{\left[\dfrac{(\varepsilon-1)(\rho+r)}{\kappa\beta}\right]^{\frac{\varepsilon-1}{\varepsilon}}\alpha}{\phi\varepsilon(\rho+\delta)\delta},$$

$$Q^M = \frac{r\overline{Q} - \kappa\alpha^2\dfrac{p^{*1-2\varepsilon}}{\phi\varepsilon(\rho+\delta)\delta}}{r+\kappa p^{-\varepsilon}\beta} = \frac{r\overline{Q} - \kappa\alpha^2\dfrac{\left[\dfrac{(\varepsilon-1)(\rho+r)}{\kappa\beta}\right]^{\frac{2\varepsilon-1}{\varepsilon}}}{\phi\varepsilon(\rho+\delta)\delta}}{r+\kappa p^{-\varepsilon}\beta},$$

$$I^M = \frac{p^{*1-\varepsilon}\alpha}{\phi\varepsilon(\rho+\delta)} = \frac{\left[\dfrac{(\varepsilon-1)(\rho+r)}{\kappa\beta}\right]^{\frac{\varepsilon-1}{\varepsilon}}\alpha}{\phi\varepsilon(\rho+\delta)},$$

$$p^* = \left[\frac{(\varepsilon-1)(\rho+r)}{\kappa\beta}\right]^{\frac{-1}{\varepsilon}}.$$

The basic assumption of this model is that p is the price in the presence of monopoly power, so we know that p is always greater than or equal to q. As long as $p^* \geq q^*$, we can observe that $K^M > K^*$ and $Q^M < Q^*$.

So, in the presence of monopoly power, we are in the long run in a situation characterized by a higher lodging capacity and a poorer environmental quality. Because of the higher level of price, the tourism sector invests more in lodging capacities and it leads to the deterioration of environmental quality. The way out of this problem may be to implement a tax τ on tourism income and then to give an ex-post subsidy S to the tourism sector that equals tax revenue.

3.4   TAXES, SUBSIDIES AND SUSTAINABLE TOURISM

Let us now assume that in this economy there exists another agent, local authorities, the objective of whom is to preserve the environmental quality. The environmental degradation is due in the previous model to the presence of monopoly power.

The profit of the tourism sector is now:

$$\pi = p^{1-\varepsilon}\left(\alpha K + \beta Q\right) - \tau p^{1-\varepsilon}\left(\alpha K + \beta Q\right) - \frac{\phi}{2}I^2 + S,$$

where $S = \tau p^{1-\varepsilon}\left(\alpha K + \beta Q\right)$.

Since in this chapter we are only interested in the long-run behaviour of the economy, we will define the long-run tax.

Local authorities are looking for the level of tax that equals in the long run the lodging capacities in the absence of monopoly power and in the presence of monopoly power.

We are looking for τ^* so that $K^* = K^\tau$.

We find that:

$$\tau^* = 1 - \frac{\varepsilon\left(\rho + r\right)q^{1-\varepsilon}\kappa}{\left[\frac{\left(\varepsilon - 1\right)\left(\rho + r\right)}{\kappa\beta}\right]^{\frac{\varepsilon-1}{\varepsilon}}\left(\rho + r + \kappa q^{-\varepsilon}\beta\right)}.$$

The tax enables local authorities to capture the monopoly rent so that investment decisions are taken as if the sector was in a situation of pure competition.

Here a major difference arises between this situation and the case described in section 3.2.

In this economy, the tourism sector receives a price per journey of q but tourists pay a price per journey of p higher than q.

So in this economy, the level of infrastructures in the long run is:

$$K^* = K^\tau = \frac{(\rho+r)q^{1-\varepsilon}\alpha\kappa}{(\rho+r+\kappa q^{-\varepsilon}\beta)(\rho+\delta)\phi\delta}$$

But the level of environmental assets in the long run is:

$$Q^\tau = \frac{r\bar{Q} - \dfrac{(\rho+r)q^{1-2\varepsilon}\alpha^2\kappa^2}{(\rho+r+\kappa q^{-\varepsilon}\beta)(\rho+\delta)\phi\delta}}{r+\kappa p^{-\varepsilon}\beta}.$$

As long as tourists pay a price higher than q, we see that the level of environmental assets in the long run is higher in the presence of the tax than in the two alternative situations.

$$Q^\tau > Q^* > Q^M.$$

So finally, the implementation of the tax gives:

$$Q^\tau > Q^* > Q^M.$$

$$K^\tau = K^* < K^M.$$

So we can distinguish two situations.

Situation 1	$T^* < T^\tau < T^M$	$\pi^* < \pi^\tau < \pi^M$
$\alpha(K^M - K^\tau) > \beta(Q^\tau - Q^M)$		

Situation 2	$T^* < T^M < T^\tau$	$\pi^* < \pi^M < \pi^\tau$
$\alpha(K^M - K^\tau) < \beta(Q^\tau - Q^M)$		

In the first situation, the implementation of the tax leads to a higher level of environmental quality in the long run but with a fall in the long-run frequentation and also in the long-run profit.

This case arises because tourists are characterized by a strong preference for the lodging capacity K, $\alpha > \beta$.

Conversely, in the second situation the implementation of the tax leads to a higher level of both profit and environmental quality in the long run. This results from the relative preference of the tourists for the stock of environmental assets, $\beta > \alpha$.

Now let us turn to the study of the static properties of the tax rate.

A first interesting feature of the tax is that in the long run it does not depend on the level of α. It means that for a given level of β, polluting tourism (high level of α) and clean tourism (low level of α) are taxed the same.

Table 3.2   Comparative statics of the tax

	β	ε	κ	Q	R	ρ
τ^*	$+/-$	$+$	$-$	$+/-$	$+/-$	$+/-$

We can also state that when the competitive price is weak, the tax increases with β. It reflects the fact that the more tourists are attracted by environmental assets the more tourism should be taxed. But this is true only when the monopoly rent (the difference between p and q) is large.

3.5   CONCLUSION

In this chapter, we investigated the long-run effects of the presence of monopoly power on the behaviour of an economy implementing an 'elite tourism' strategy.

We showed using a simple optimal control framework that monopoly power is associated with a higher level of profit for the tourism sector but this is possible only because of a deterioration of the stock of the environmental assets.

Furthermore, we found that in this local monopoly context, the implementation of a tax that aims at limiting the lodging capacity leads to the preservation of a higher long-run level of environmental assets.

More interestingly, the tax will have different effects depending on tourists' preferences. If tourists are sensitive to the number of infrastructures, the level of profit associated with the tax is lower in the long run than the profit associated with the case of monopoly without tax.

Conversely, if tourists are sensitive enough to the environmental quality, the implementation of a tax in order to correct the perverse effects of monopoly power leads to both environmental preservation and a higher level of profit than in the monopoly without tax.

From that point, we could argue that taxing tourism in eco-destination leads to an improvement of the long-run situation. But this calls for the construction of a more general framework in which this result could be tested.

NOTES

1. See the mathematical appendix for the full solution of the system.
2. Another way to model the phenomenon is to consider that destinations are in a situation of monopolistic competition. A similar approach was developed in Candela and Cellini (2006) but implies a higher degree of formal complexity.

REFERENCES

Brau, R., A. Lanza and F. Pigliaru (2007), 'Tourism specialisation, cross country growth evidence, in African Analyst Quarterly, **2**(2), 61–68

Butler, R. (1980), 'The concept of a tourist area cycle of evolution: implications for the management of natural reserves', *Canadian Geographer*, **24**, 5–12.

Candela, G. and R. Cellini (2006), 'Investment in tourism market: A dynamic model of differentiated oligopoly', *Environmental and Resource Economics*, **35**(1), 41–58.

Casagrandi, R. and S. Rinaldi (1999), 'A theoretical approach to tourism sustainability', Politecnico di Milano Working Paper.

Casagrandi, R. and S. Rinaldi (2002), 'A theoretical approach to tourism sustainability', *Conservation Ecology*, **6**(1).

Cazzavillan, G. and I. Musu (2001), 'Transitional dynamics and uniqueness of the balanced-growth path in a simple model of endogenous growth with an environmental asset', FEEM Working Paper, No. 65.01

Giannoni, S. and M.-A. Maupertuis (2005), 'Environmental quality and long run tourism development: A cyclical perspective for small island tourist economies', FEEM Working Paper, No. 145.05

Kort, P.M, A. Greiner, G. Feichtinger, J.L. Haunschmied, A. Novak and R.F. Hartl (2002), 'Environmental effects of tourism industry investment: An inter-temporal trade-off', *Optimal Control Applications and Methods*, **23**, 1–19.

Lanza, A. and F. Pigliaru (1995), 'The Tourism Sector in the Open Economy', in P. Nijkamp and W. Coccossis (eds), *Tourism and the Environment*, Avebury: Aldershot.

Léon, C., J.M. Hernandez and M. González (2003), 'Endogenous lifecycle and optimal growth in tourism', contribution to CRENoS conference 'Tourism and Sustainable Economic Development', held in Chia, Italy, 19–20 September.

World Tourism Organisation (1995), 'Lanzarote charter for sustainable tourism'.

APPENDIX

A. Solution of the Basic Model

Steady-state values are:

$$K^* = \frac{(\rho+r)q^{1-\varepsilon}\alpha\kappa}{\left(\rho+r+\kappa q^{-\varepsilon}\beta\right)(\rho+\delta)\phi\delta},$$

$$Q^* = \frac{r\overline{Q} - \dfrac{(\rho+r)q^{1-2\varepsilon}\alpha^2\kappa^2}{\left(\rho+r+\kappa q^{-\varepsilon}\beta\right)(\rho+\delta)\phi\delta}}{r+\kappa q^{-\varepsilon}\beta},$$

$$I^* = \frac{(\rho+r)q^{1-\varepsilon}\alpha\kappa}{\left(\rho+r+\kappa q^{-\varepsilon}\beta\right)(\rho+\delta)\phi},$$

$$\mu^* = \frac{q^{1-\varepsilon}\beta}{\left(\rho+r+\kappa q^{-\varepsilon}\beta\right)}.$$

Eigenvalues are:

$$Eig = \left[-\delta, -q^{-\varepsilon}\left(q^{\varepsilon}r+\beta\kappa\right), \delta, \rho+r+q^{\varepsilon}r+\beta\kappa\right].$$

The sign of the eigenvalues alternates and it is enough to say that the system is saddle-point stable.

The complete solution is:

$$\begin{bmatrix} K_t \\ Q_t \\ \lambda_t \\ \mu_t \end{bmatrix} = \exp^{-\delta t} A \begin{pmatrix} -\dfrac{qr-q^{\varepsilon}\delta+\beta^{\varepsilon}\kappa}{\alpha\kappa} \\ 1 \\ 0 \\ 0 \end{pmatrix} + \exp^{-q^{-\varepsilon}\left(q^{\varepsilon}r+\beta\kappa\right)t} B \begin{pmatrix} 0 \\ 1 \\ 0 \\ 0 \end{pmatrix} + \begin{pmatrix} \dfrac{(\rho+r)q^{1-\varepsilon}\alpha\kappa}{\left(\rho+r+\kappa q^{-\varepsilon}\beta\right)(\rho+\delta)\phi\delta} \\ r\overline{Q} - \dfrac{(\rho+r)q^{1-2\varepsilon}\alpha^2\kappa^2}{\left(\rho+r+\kappa q^{-\varepsilon}\beta\right)(\rho+\delta)\phi\delta} \\ \dfrac{\dfrac{}{}}{r+\kappa q^{-\varepsilon}\beta} \\ \dfrac{(\rho+r)q^{1-\varepsilon}\alpha\kappa}{\left(\rho+r+\kappa q^{-\varepsilon}\beta\right)(\rho+\delta)} \\ \dfrac{q^{1-\varepsilon}\beta}{\left(\rho+r+\kappa q^{-\varepsilon}\beta\right)} \end{pmatrix}.$$

B. Solution of the Model with Monopoly Power

The current-value Hamiltonian is:

$$H = p^{1-\varepsilon}\left(\alpha K + \beta Q\right) - \frac{\phi}{2}I^2 + \left(I - \delta K\right) + \mu\left[r\left(\bar{Q} - Q\right) - \kappa p^{-\varepsilon}\left(\alpha K + \beta Q\right)\right].$$

with I and p as control variables.
   The maximum principle gives:

$$\lambda = \phi I,$$

$$\mu = \frac{\left(\varepsilon - 1\right)}{\kappa\varepsilon}p,$$

$$\dot{\lambda} = \lambda\left(\rho + \delta\right) + \mu\kappa p^{-\varepsilon}\alpha - p^{1-\varepsilon}\alpha,$$

$$\dot{\mu} = \left(\rho + r\right) - \frac{\kappa p^{-\varepsilon}\beta}{\left(\varepsilon - 1\right)}.$$

or to put it differently:

$$\dot{I} = \left(\rho + \delta\right)I - \frac{p^{1-\varepsilon}\alpha}{\varepsilon\phi},$$

$$\dot{p} = \left(\rho + r\right)p - \frac{\kappa\beta}{\left(\varepsilon - 1\right)p^{\varepsilon-1}}.$$

The model works under the assumption that $\varepsilon > 1$.
Steady-state values of the system are:

$$p^* = \left[\frac{\left(\varepsilon - 1\right)\left(\rho + r\right)}{\kappa\beta}\right]^{\frac{-1}{\varepsilon}},$$

$$I^* = \frac{\left[\dfrac{\left(\varepsilon - 1\right)\left(\rho + r\right)}{\kappa\beta}\right]^{\frac{\varepsilon-1}{\varepsilon}}\alpha}{\phi\varepsilon\left(\rho + \delta\right)},$$

$$K^* = \frac{\left[\dfrac{\left(\varepsilon - 1\right)\left(\rho + r\right)}{\kappa\beta}\right]^{\frac{\varepsilon-1}{\varepsilon}}\alpha}{\phi\varepsilon\left(\rho + \delta\right)\delta},$$

$$Q^* = \frac{r\overline{Q} - \kappa\alpha^2 \dfrac{\left[\dfrac{\varepsilon(\rho+r)}{\kappa\beta}\right]^{\frac{2\varepsilon-1}{\varepsilon}}}{\phi\varepsilon(\rho+\delta)\delta}}{r+\kappa p^{-\varepsilon}\beta}.$$

Eigenvalues of the Jacobian of the linearized system are:

$$Eig = \left(-\delta, -r - (-1+\varepsilon)(\rho+r), (\delta+\rho), r+\rho + \frac{(r+\rho)(-1+\varepsilon)^2}{\varepsilon}\right).$$

The system is saddle-point stable as long as the sign of the eigenvalues alternates provided $\varepsilon > 1$.

The solution of the completed linearized system is:

$$\begin{bmatrix} K_t \\ Q_t \\ I_t \\ P_t \end{bmatrix} = \exp^{-\delta t} A \begin{pmatrix} -\dfrac{\beta(-\delta-\rho+\varepsilon\rho+\varepsilon r)}{\alpha(-1+\varepsilon)(\rho+r)} \\ 1 \\ 0 \\ 0 \end{pmatrix} + \exp^{[-r-(-1+\varepsilon)(\rho+r)]t} B \begin{pmatrix} 0 \\ 1 \\ 0 \\ 0 \end{pmatrix} + \begin{pmatrix} \dfrac{\left[\dfrac{(\varepsilon-1)(\rho+r)}{\kappa\beta}\right]^{\frac{\varepsilon-1}{\varepsilon}}\alpha}{\phi\varepsilon(\rho+\delta)\delta} \\ \dfrac{r\overline{Q}-\kappa\alpha^2\dfrac{\left[\dfrac{\varepsilon(\rho+r)}{\kappa\beta}\right]^{\frac{2\varepsilon-1}{\varepsilon}}}{\phi\varepsilon(\rho+\delta)\delta}}{r+\kappa p^{-\varepsilon}\beta} \\ \dfrac{\left[\dfrac{(\varepsilon-1)(\rho+r)}{\kappa\beta}\right]^{\frac{\varepsilon-1}{\varepsilon}}\alpha}{\phi\varepsilon(\rho+\delta)} \\ \left[\dfrac{(\varepsilon-1)(\rho+r)}{\kappa\beta}\right]^{\frac{-1}{\varepsilon}} \end{pmatrix}.$$

C. Derivation of the Optimal Tax on Monopoly in the Long Run

The current-value Hamiltonian is:

$$H = p^{1-\varepsilon}(\alpha K + \beta Q) - \frac{\phi}{2}I^2 + (I - \delta K) + \mu\left[r(\overline{Q} - Q) - \kappa p^{-\varepsilon}(\alpha K + \beta Q)\right].$$

We find that capital in the steady-state equals:

$$K^\tau = \frac{\left[\dfrac{(\varepsilon-1)(\rho+r)}{\kappa\beta}\right]^{\frac{\varepsilon-1}{\varepsilon}}\alpha(1-\tau)}{\phi\varepsilon(\rho+\delta)\delta}.$$

We look for τ^* that satisfies:

$$K^\tau = K^* \Leftrightarrow \frac{\left[\dfrac{(\varepsilon-1)(\rho+r)}{\kappa\beta}\right]^{\frac{\varepsilon-1}{\varepsilon}}\alpha(1-\tau)}{\phi\varepsilon(\rho+\delta)\delta} = \frac{(\rho+r)q^{1-\varepsilon}\alpha\kappa}{(\rho+r+\kappa q^{-\varepsilon}\beta)(\rho+\delta)\phi\delta}.$$

And then solving this equation with respect to τ we find:

$$\tau^* = 1 - \frac{\varepsilon(\rho+r)q^{1-\varepsilon}\kappa}{\left[\dfrac{(\varepsilon-1)(\rho+r)}{\kappa\beta}\right]^{\frac{\varepsilon-1}{\varepsilon}}(\rho+r+\kappa q^{-\varepsilon}\beta)}.$$

4. The Economics of Local Tourist Systems

Guido Candela, Paolo Figini and Antonello E. Scorcu

4.1 INTRODUCTION

Tourism has a systemic nature, stemming both from the heterogeneity of goods that comprise the tourist package, and from the existing complex interactions among firms, tourists and residents. The tourist product is comprised of several heterogeneous but complementary goods and services supplied by firms belonging to different industries which are mainly, but not exclusively, located in the tourist destination. Such a systemic nature and the existence of a geographical identification – the destination – calls for the introduction of what can be defined as the Local Tourist System (LTS). This notion has already been recognised by the legislation: for example, the Italian Law introduces the LTS as a policy instrument:

> We call local tourist systems, homogeneous or integrated tourist environments, which comprise territories also belonging to different regions, and which are characterised by the integrated supply of cultural, environmental goods and tourist attractions, including typical agricultural and local handicraft products, or those characterised by a widespread presence of individual or associated tourist firms. (Legge Quadro sul Turismo, *Law 29 March 2001 No. 135*, Our translation)

Because the tourist firm has some specific characteristics which distinguish it from other typologies of firm, public intervention in the sector can support and develop tourist firms but this opens up potential consequences on market competition and equilibrium. The LTS highlights a potential trade-off problem: on the one hand it can increase the effectiveness of the 'tourist system' as a whole, by raising its competitiveness with respect to other destinations; on the other hand, it can also lead to an increase in market power and to a possible increase in prices and a fall in demand. These consequences are due to the fact that the LTS shares some characteristics of both the Industrial District (ID), that complies with firms' tendency to localise in the same region,[1] and the Cultural District (CD), based on the integration in the same region of artistic and cultural activities that acquire their own idiosyncrasy.[2] Each type of district aims to increase the efficiency of supply through external economies (ID) or territorial identification (CD) and promotes the overall development of the local territory (whereas this can be identified with the municipality, the county or the region). However, although there is common ground, relevant differences also emerge.

Our approach aims to identify each district's peculiar characteristics: Marshallian economies enjoyed by production firms for ID;[3] the idiosyncratic nature of local cultural and/or artistic production for CD; complementarities in the composition of the tourist product and Marshallian economies enjoyed by tourist firms in the case of LTS.

With local development, such characteristics might merge in advanced districts: complex cultural districts (e.g., theatres) present external economies (Caves, 2000), industrial districts present cultural dimensions if the product is linked to local culture as in the case of pottery or design (Santagata, 2004); finally, Sacco and Tavano Blessi (2005) identify advanced cultural districts, characterised by cultural production with ancillary services such as tourism, and advanced local tourist systems, characterised by tourism production and compatible industrial production.[4]

A simple model detecting differences and similarities between LTS, ID and CD is unfolded in section 4.2, where the three different districts are analysed in terms of prices, profits and local population welfare. In section 4.3, the reasons for State intervention in the LTS are outlined. The focus is, in particular, on coordination failures, since the tourist good presents an anticommon problem stemming from its systemic nature. Section 4.4 outlines some policy implications and concludes.

4.2 A SIMPLIFIED MODEL OF DISTRICTS

Definitions and Symbols

In order to study the theoretical aspects of industrial districts (IDs), cultural districts (CDs) and Local Tourist Systems (LTSs), it is sufficient to introduce a two region, $k = 1, 2$, and two good, $j = x, y$ model. Moreover, two alternative assumptions concerning the geographical organisation of production are introduced:

a. *non-systemic production*: Region 1 only produces good x, and $y_1 = 0$, while Region 2 only produces good y, and $x_2 = 0$;

b. *system*: the whole Region $(1, 2)$ produces both goods, being defined a system.

If every externality of production has been internalised by the local policy maker, the group of firms, which coincides with the region itself, can be considered a regional monopolist.

In the case of non-systemic production, the local demand for goods x and y, approximated in a linear and separable form, is:[5]

$$x = f(p_x) \approx a - bp_x \qquad \text{demand for good } x, \text{ with price } p_x, \qquad (4.1a)$$

$$y = g(p_y) \approx m - np_y \qquad \text{demand for good } y, \text{ with price } p_y. \qquad (4.1b)$$

If production is organised as a system, the three districts can be described as follows.

A) The Industrial District

In the ID constituted by Region $(1, 2)$, demand functions of goods x and y are represented by equations (4.1). However, in an ID externalities due to Marshallian agglomeration economies occur: they can be internalised into the cost function $C_j(\cdot)$ of firms pertaining to a sector, which also depend on the production level of firms in the other sector. In equations (4.2) we assume the particular specification:[6]

$$C_x = H(x, y) \approx x^2 - y^2, \qquad (4.2a)$$

$$C_y = K(x, y) \approx y^2 - x^2. \qquad (4.2b)$$

B) The Cultural District

If Region $(1, 2)$ constitutes a CD, demand of goods x and y change according to the idiosyncratic 'quality surplus' stemming from the cultural system. Effects on the cost side, on the contrary, can be ignored since externalities are a typical industrial effect, rather than a characteristic of cultural production; by promoting the interaction and competition among artists, the CD increases the quality and creativity of its own artistic good, even though this would not necessarily increase the productivity of the whole district.[7] Therefore, it follows that equations (4.1) can be augmented by a parameter θ in the consumer's reserve price, as in equations (4.3):

$$x = f'(p_x; \theta) \approx \theta a - bp_x, \qquad (4.3a)$$

$$y = g'(p_y; \theta) \approx \theta m - np_y. \qquad (4.3b)$$

where we assume that the effect $\theta > 1$ is common and equal for both goods characterising the CD.

Since we assume that the interaction does not produce any effect on the production side, cost functions in the CD are separated: in equation (4.4) we assume that the cost specifications for both goods x and y are:

$$C_x = H'(x) \approx x^2, \tag{4.4a}$$

$$C_y = K'(y) \approx y^2. \tag{4.4b}$$

C) The Local Tourist System

Tourist demand can be represented by the quantity of goods demanded in the destination by tourists, which is roughly a function of N, the number of nights spent in the destination. Obviously, if there are two separate regions, tourists have at their disposal a 'monotonous' tourist good in each destination, while the tourist product in the LTS includes both goods offered, becoming heterogeneous. Therefore, we have:

a) tourist demand in Region 1 is: $N_x = A - Bv_1$, with $v_1 = hp_x$, since the region offers in its tourist product just h units of good x per night spent;

b) tourist demand in Region 2 is: $N_y = A - Bv_2$, with $v_2 = kp_y$, since the region offers in its tourist product just k units of good y per night spent;

c) tourist demand in the LTS composed of Region (1, 2) is: $N_x^{LTS} = \sigma A - Bv_1$ and $N_y^{LTS} = \sigma A - Bv_2$. As the region offers a diversified tourist product, with more variety compared to the one supplied by the two separate regions, one can assume that:

$$\sigma > 1. \tag{4.5}$$

Since LTS firms produce goods (x and y) that enter into the tourist product, respectively for the amount of h and k,[8] total demand for each good is the sum of (uncorrelated) domestic and tourist demands.[9] Therefore, the overall demand for goods x and y, in Regions 1 and 2 respectively, are the following:

$$X = x + hN_x = f(p_x) + hN_x = (a + hA) - (b + h^2 B)p_x, \tag{4.6a}$$

$$Y = y + kN_y = g(p_y) + kN_y = (m + kA) - (n + k^2 B)p_y. \tag{4.7a}$$

In the LTS composed by the Region (1, 2), because of the higher quality hypothesis, the overall demands are:

$$X = x + hN_x^{LTS} = f(p_x) + hN_x^{LTS} = (a + h\sigma A) - (b + h^2 B)p_x, \tag{4.6b}$$

$$Y = y + kN_y^{LTS} = g(p_y) + kN_y^{LTS} = (m + k\sigma A) - (n + k^2 B)p_y. \tag{4.7b}$$

Since the tourist product is a combination of different goods, local firms enjoy significant Marshallian agglomeration economies; hence, the positive externality effect on production costs occurs in the LTS, as well as within the ID. Total production costs of firms in one sector also depend on the production of the other sector and we assume the same cost structure (4.2a) and (4.2b) of the ID: $H = x^2 - y^2$; $K = y^2 - x^2$.

All the key elements to assess the optimal policy for IDs, CDs and LTSs are at a glance, since regions can be considered as monopolistic firms where the policy maker aims at maximising the overall profit. Moreover, we can also assess the welfare effect on the local community of each of the three cases considered. The simplest way to do so is by introducing the (average) agent's utility function, a Cobb–Douglas function, defined on both goods x and y:

$$U = \Theta x^\alpha y^{1-\alpha}, \tag{4.8}$$

where $0 < \alpha < 1$, and $\Theta > 0$ is a quality parameter which measures the satisfaction that the agent gets from the goods.[10] Given disposable income Z and prices p_x and p_y, the consumer maximises equation (4.8) by allocating a fixed share of his own income to each good, according to the elasticity of the utility function:[11]

$$U = \Theta(\alpha Z/p_x)^\alpha [(1-\alpha) Z/p_y]^{1-\alpha} = \Theta Z(\alpha/p_x)^\alpha [(1-\alpha)/p_y]^{1-\alpha}.$$

To estimate the change in welfare, we compute the total differential of U:

$$dU = (U/\Theta)d\Theta + (U/Z)dZ - \alpha(U/p_x)dp_x - (1-\alpha)(U/p_y)dp_y. \tag{4.9}$$

Industrial Regions and Industrial Districts

We consider model A from the previous section for industrial regions organised or not as industrial districts and compute the market equilibrium and local population's welfare in the different cases.

Referring to the more general case of an Industrial District $(1, 2)$ producing goods x and y, the ID's target coincides with the joint profit maximisation of both firms which, being a district, avoid any market failure by internalising external economies:

$$\begin{aligned}
\max_{p_x, p_y} \Pi_{12} &= xf(p_x) + yg(p_y) - H(x, y) - K(x, y) \\
&= ap_x - bp_x^2 + mp_y - np_y^2 - (x^2 - y^2) - (y^2 - x^2) \quad (4.10a) \\
&= ap_x - bp_x^2 + mp_y - np_y^2.
\end{aligned}$$

If Region 1 supplies only good x (for $y \equiv 0$, $K(\cdot) \equiv 0$) its goal reduces to the profit maximisation of firms producing good x:

$$\max{}_{p_x} \; \varPi_1 = ap_x - bp_x^2 - x^2. \tag{4.10b}$$

If Region 2 produces only good y (for $x \equiv 0$, $H(\cdot) \equiv 0$) its goal reduces to the profit maximisation of firms producing good y

$$\max{}_{p_y} \; \varPi_2 = mp_y - np_y^2 - y^2. \tag{4.10c}$$

From the first-order conditions of equations (4.10) we obtain the equilibrium prices in the different configurations:

- in Region 1: $p_x = a / 2b + x$;
- in Region 2: $p_y = m / 2n + y$;
- in the ID (1, 2): $p_x{}^{ID} = a / 2b$ and $p_y{}^{ID} = m / 2n$.

The emergence of the ID brings a reduction in prices with respect to non-systemic production: $p_x > p_x{}^{ID}$ and $p_y > p_y{}^{ID}$, and an increase in quantity of the two goods supplied by the market. Obviously, such an outcome is the result of the positive externality effect on production costs stemming from geographical agglomeration, an effect that can not be internalised if the two industrial regions are separated and independent.

With respect to the welfare effect, equation (4.9) shows that consumers always gain by the emergence of the ID, since the lower prices and the consequent increase in quantity is a sufficient condition bringing (with $d\varTheta = dZ = 0$) an increase in the consumer indirect utility level, $dU > 0$.

Cultural Regions and Cultural Districts

Let us consider model B mentioned above (for regions which can be organised or not as cultural districts) and compute market equilibrium and welfare of the local population.

In the case of Cultural District (1, 2) producing both goods x and y, the production goal is joint profit maximisation of (cultural) firms with a quality premium θ on their respective products, which are recognised as parts of the same cultural package:

$$\max{}_{p_x \, p_y} \; \varPi_{12} = xf'(p_x) + yg'(p_y) - H(x) - K(y),$$
$$\max{}_{p_x \, p_y} \; \varPi_{12} = \theta ap_x - bp_x^2 + \theta mp_y - np_y^2 - x^2 - y^2. \tag{4.11a}$$

If Region 1 specialises in cultural good x (for $y \equiv 0$, $K(\cdot) \equiv 0$ and $\theta = 1$) the previous expression reduces to:

$$\max{}_{p_x} \; \varPi_1 = ap_x - bp_x^2 - x^2, \tag{4.11b}$$

whereas if Region 2 specialises in good y (for $x \equiv 0$, $H(\cdot) \equiv 0$ and $\theta = 1$) the corresponding expression is:

$$\max{}_{p_y} \; \Pi_2 = mp_y - np_y^2 - y^2. \tag{4.11c}$$

From the first-order conditions of equations (4.11) we obtain the equilibrium prices in the different configurations:

- in Region 1: $p_x = a / 2b + x$;
- in Region 2: $p_y = m / 2n + y$;
- in the CD (1,2): $p_x^{CD} = \theta a / 2b + x$ and $p_y^{CD} = \theta m / 2n + y$.

In this case, the emergence of the CD brings about an increase in prices with respect to non-systemic production, $p_x < p_x^{CD}$ and $p_y < p_y^{CD}$, due to the idiosyncratic effect of the cultural district. In the CD, prices increase as a result of the quality improvement, hence bringing about a reduction in the consumer's utility. However, the quality improvement also leads to an increase in utility, $d\Theta > 0$. Then, if income remains unchanged, $dZ = 0$, consumers gain from the CD only if the following condition is verified:

$$(U / \Theta)\, d\Theta > \alpha(U / p_x)\, dp_x + (1 - \alpha)(U / p_y)dp_y. \tag{4.12}$$

Nevertheless, (4.12) is often the expected outcome, since it is the microeconomic precondition supporting the assumption that the CD 'protects' the market for cultural goods. If (4.12) is not verified, the representative consumer would 'reject' the Cultural District organisation. Therefore, the mere existence of a CD is likely to be related to a higher consumers' welfare.

Tourist-Industrial Destinations and Local Tourist Systems

Consider now model C mentioned above for regions which can be organised or not organised as Local Tourist Systems. The goal of Local Tourist System (1, 2) is profit maximisation of the joint production of goods x and y, supplied to both tourists and residents:[12]

$$\begin{aligned}
\max{}_{p_x\, p_y} \; \Pi_{12} &= Xp_x + Yp_y - H(X, Y) - K(X, Y) \\
&= (a + h\sigma A)p_x - (b + h^2 B)p_x^2 + (m + k\sigma A)p_y + \\
&\quad - (n + k^2 B)p_y^2 - X^2 + Y^2 - Y^2 + X^2 \\
&= (a + h\sigma A)p_x - (b + h^2 B)p_x^2 + (m + k\sigma A)p_y - (n + k^2 B)p_y^2.
\end{aligned} \tag{4.13a}$$

The goal of the Tourist-industrial region 1 ($Y \equiv 0$, $K(\cdot) \equiv 0$) is profit maximisation from the production of good x, supplied to both tourists and residents:

$$\max_{p_x} \Pi_1 = (a + hA)p_x - (b + h^2B)p_x^2 - X^2, \qquad (4.13b)$$

whereas in the Tourist-industrial region 2 ($X \equiv 0$, $H(\cdot) \equiv 0$) the overall goal is profit maximisation from the production of good y, supplied to tourists and residents:

$$\max_{p_y} \Pi_2 = (m + kA)p_y - (n + k^2B)p_y^2 - Y^2 \qquad (4.13c)$$

From the first-order conditions of equations (4.13) we obtain the equilibrium prices in the different configurations:

- in Tourist-industrial region 1: $p_x = [(a + hA) / 2(b + h^2B)] + X$;
- in Tourist-industrial region 2: $p_y = [(m + kA) / 2(n + k^2B)] + Y$;
- in the LTS (1, 2): $p_x^{LTS} = (a + h\sigma A) / 2(b + h^2B)$ and
  $p_y^{LTS} = (m + k\sigma A)/2(n + k^2B)$.

If, compared to the two independent destinations, the LTS does not produce any clear effect on prices: $\sigma > 1$ and the signs of the following differences are not uniquely defined:

$$p_x^{LTS} - p_x = hA(\sigma - 1) / 2(b + h^2B) - X,$$

$$p_y^{LTS} - p_y = kA(\sigma - 1) / 2(n + k^2B) - Y.$$

This conclusion stems from two opposite effects: on the one hand, agglomeration economies reduce the average cost of goods but the quality improvement in the tourist product brought about by its completion increases tourist demand.

Therefore, the LTS shows similarities to both IDs (the tourist good is a bundle of goods that enjoys the advantages of Marshallian economies) and CDs (the tourist good can be assimilated to a cultural good and hence it takes profit from the idiosyncratic image of the destination).[13] The LTS is a complex system: it is not an ID, since the territorial aggregation has an effect on the demand side; it is not a CD, since the aggregation has an effect on the average costs of production. Unsurprisingly, the effect of the LTS on the total welfare of local population is ambiguous and should be studied in a general equilibrium context.

To keep things simple, however, we can distinguish two cases: if the LTS brings about an overall price reduction, the local consumer – as in the ID case – surely takes advantage of it. But in the case of a price increase, the change in the agent's utility depends on whether or not she takes part in the distribution of profits generated by tourism itself; if we assume that the resident of the destination, whose demands are (4.1a) and (4.1b), does not consume the local tourist product, she does not take advantage from its quality improvement, $d\Theta = 0$. Therefore, if the representative agent receives income from the Local Tourist System, $dZ > 0$, she would have an increase in her own indirect utility only if:

$$(U / Z)\, dZ > \alpha(U / p_x)dp_x + (1 - \alpha)(U / p_y)dp_y. \qquad (4.14)$$

Otherwise, if the resident gets a job in some other sector and does not get any income from the Local Tourist System, $dZ = 0$, he suffers a reduction in his welfare, $dU < 0$.

To sum up, while in our framework the ID increases consumers' welfare, and while we may suppose that the CD is likely to produce an increase in welfare, with respect to the LTS the answer is not clear. When the LTS is associated with an increase in prices, the welfare change is not uniquely defined and local households' gain depends on the way income, generated from extra-tourism attracted by the better quality of the destination organised as a LTS,[14] is distributed.

4.3   THE ANTICOMMONS PROBLEM IN THE LTS: COORDINATION OF TOURIST FIRMS

The Role of the Destination Authority

Public policies in the tourist sector can be supported mainly for two reasons: i) to finance those public structures and infrastructures (for which the private market fails) required to complete the tourist product and to increase the destination's competitiveness;[15] ii) to solve a potential coordination problem arising when private firms supply different goods and services comprising the tourist product. This latter issue is analysed in this section, with particular reference to the role that the public authority of the destination may play.

In order to focus on this, we develop a very simple model.[16] In the destination there are just two types of firms: hotels, offering accommodation but not board, and restaurants, offering board but not accommodation. Under these conditions, tourists intending to spend a holiday in the destination have to buy services from both firms, which can individually exclude the tourists by denying them board and/or accommodation. In the tourist sector, whose product combines heterogeneous goods supplied by different firms, this situation occurs easily. Such a phenomenon, known as anticommon, is characterised by property fragmentation[17] and is symmetrical and opposed to the widely known common good.[18]

If p_a and p_b are respectively accommodation and board price, the tourist product, composed by one unit of each service per day, has price p equal to

$p = p_a + p_b$. Tourist demand is expressed by the number of nights spent N and can be written as: $N = \alpha - p = \alpha - p_a - p_b$.

If we assume, by the sake of simplification, that production costs are null, the firms' profit maximisation problems are, respectively:

$$\max{}_{p_a} \Pi_a = p_a N = p_a(\alpha - p_a - p_b), \tag{4.15a}$$

$$\max{}_{p_b} \Pi_b = p_b N = p_b(\alpha - p_a - p_b), \tag{4.15b}$$

from which we get accommodation and board equilibrium prices:

$$p_a = (\alpha - p_b) / 2 , \tag{4.16a}$$

$$p_b = (\alpha - p_a) / 2 . \tag{4.16b}$$

We can solve system (4.16) by substitution and, in the simple linear specification of our example, we get the following equilibrium prices:

$$p_b{}^* = p_a{}^* = \alpha / 3. \tag{4.17}$$

Therefore, a tourist demanding N units of the tourist product supplied by the destination, composed by one unit of accommodation and board per day, pays a total price p equal to:

$$p^* = 2\alpha / 3. \tag{4.18}$$

which implies a quantity level of equilibrium equal to $N^* = \alpha / 3$. In this situation, firms get the following profits:

$$\Pi_a{}^* = \Pi_b{}^* = (\alpha / 3)(\alpha / 3) = \alpha^2 / 9. \tag{4.19}$$

Can there be any improvement from this situation? Let us assume now that there is a 'systemic firm' offering both board and accommodation, with these types of supplies possibly coordinated by a public authority, the policy maker. That is to say that the supply problem can be analysed by focussing on the profit maximisation of the whole destination. By considering the same demand function $N = \alpha - p$ we get:

$$\max{}_v \Pi = pN = p(\alpha - p), \tag{4.20}$$

from which we get the destination equilibrium price:

$$p^{**} = \alpha / 2. \tag{4.21}$$

Comparing equation (4.21) with equation (4.18), we note that $p^* > p^{**}$ whereas $N^{**} = \alpha/2 > \alpha/3 = N^*$. Therefore, without coordination, the price of the tourist product as a whole is higher and tourist nights spent in the destination are lower.

Since we assume that both hotels and restaurants in this example are symmetric as regards costs (both null), the policy maker can impose the optimal price structure for both accommodation and board, $p_a^{**} = p_b^{**} = \alpha/4$. These posted prices imply, by means of equations (4.15), that profits are:

$$\Pi_a^{**} = \Pi_b^{**} = (\alpha/4)(\alpha/2) = \alpha^2/8. \tag{4.22}$$

Profits shown in equation (4.22) are higher that those in (4.19) since $\alpha^2/8 > \alpha^2/9$; in the LTS, when the local government solves the coordination problem by imposing (or proposing) the optimal price structure for each component of the tourist package, each firm increases its profits and, at the same time, tourists gain from lower prices.

Therefore, in the LTS, the policy-maker should: i) coordinate firms producing the goods which enter the tourist package; ii) fix the price of the whole product; iii) impute prices for each component of the tourist product, such as to suggest a coordination of posted prices. Coordination is needed since the tourist good turns out to be an anticommon, in which there is an excess of property rights between firms supplying single parts of the final good. Coordination intervention by the policy maker leads to both an increase in profits for all firms, and to a greater number of overnight stays demanded by tourists.

The Role of the Tour Operator

The positive role in solving the coordination problem is not an exclusive prerequisite of the public authority: if the policy maker refuses the coordination responsibility, the anticommons problem can find a solution in the establishment of a 'coordinating' tourist firm: the tour operator.

The tour operator offers to local firms a free sale contract at the discounted price $(p_j - d)$, with the same discount d applied for simplicity to each firm.[19] The 'full board' package is offered directly by the tour operator at price p. The non-coordinated equilibrium price constitutes the participation constraint to be satisfied. The maximisation problem is therefore:

$$\max_{p,d} \Pi_{to} = pN - (p_a - d)N - (p_b - d)N = (p - p_a - p_b + 2d)N \tag{4.23}$$

s.t. $N = \alpha - p$

$(p_a - d)N \geq \alpha^2/9$ the participation constraint for the accommodation firm;

$(p_b - d)N \geq \alpha^2/9$ the participation constraint for the restaurant;

as $\alpha^2 / 9$ is the profit (4.19) earned by the firms in the case of direct sale to tourists.

Without the tour operator, the equilibrium price (4.17) is $p_a = p_b = \alpha / 3$. As usual in agency models, if we assume that the principal gives the agent the minimum acceptable profit, we get the (provisional) value of d:

$$d = \alpha / 3 - \alpha^2 / 9(\alpha - v). \qquad (4.24)$$

By substituting (4.24) in the tour operator profit function, we obtain:

$$\max_p \Pi_{to} = p(\alpha - p) - 2\alpha^2 / 9. \qquad (4.25)$$

The first order condition of (4.25) defines the solution $p_{to} = \alpha / 2 = p^{**}$, the same optimal offer (4.21) of the policy-maker. However, although the tour operator solution mimics the social optimum, profits for the two local firms are different: the tour operator reaps off the whole increase in profits that would be enjoyed with the policy maker's intervention, fostering a distributive conflict between the (external) tour operator and the two local firms:[20]

$$\Pi_a = \Pi_b = \alpha^2 / 9 \text{ and } \Pi_{to} = 5\alpha^2 / 9 \text{ being } d = 2\alpha / 9.$$

To conclude, the tour operator can play a positive role in the LTS too, by imposing a solution to the anticommons failure. The analogy with the case of common goods, whose ' tragedy' may be avoided by giving property rights to either a public or a private monopoly, is therefore complete.

4.4 CONCLUSIONS

The scope of Industrial, Cultural and Local Tourist Systems is to gain the economic advantages of geographical integration. Nevertheless, the simple framework presented in this chapter suggests the existence of crucial differences with regard to characteristics, effects and strategies.

The ID arises as a consequence of positive externalities in production, in terms of reduction of the average costs sustained by firms located in the same area. Alfred Marshall first identified this effect, which has three dimensions: i) easier access to an efficient and specialised labour market for firms located in the district; ii) more efficient markets for raw materials and intermediate goods needed by the local industry; iii) quicker and easier circulation of ideas, products and process innovations, with the possibility to promptly 'copy' them. Firms perceive the advantage of a common localisation (cost reduction and profit increase) and economic rationality leads them to such industrial agglomeration. In the Marshallian perspective, public intervention is unnecessary, since congestion and decay of the territory (external diseconomies) would replace economies, making the over-localisation in an ID unprofitable. As the ID allows firms to access more efficient production organisations and techniques, it also advantages consumers, who enjoy the average cost reduction by means of a price reduction.

The CD, on the contrary, arises from the need for cultural identification: the territory acknowledges an idiosyncratic aspect in its cultural product; the CD goal is to make the product easily recognisable (and certified) by connoisseurs and cultural consumers, therefore increasing their reservation price.[21]

> One of the institutional conditions that favoured the economic growth of highly integrated territories, has been the assignment of collective property rights on local resources. Collective property rights (territorial, product, as well as cultural labels, etc.) are a way to offer efficient economic incentives and better development perspectives to local producers. Furthermore, these collective rights protect from counterfacting and dumping. In the end, they represent a great contribution to the construction of a site's public perception. (Santagata et al., 2004, p. 60. Our translation)

Nevertheless, the establishment of a CD does not automatically break out as in the ID case. Actually, the CD develops a territorial brand from which all local cultural firms wish to be covered, with the risk of 'playing down' the cultural districts through overproduction and reduced quality: the CD typically presents a common problem.[22] From this point of view, the CD needs public intervention to deal with the distribution of rights to enjoy product brand (Cuccia and Santagata, 2004). The successful CD leads to an increase in consumer surplus, since the positive change in utility induced by a better quality more than compensates for the disadvantages of higher prices.

The tourist product is comprised of a bundle of different goods and services, complementing each other in the tourist destination and, hence, the LTS might solve a problem of production coordination. However, such a combination might not automatically develop, since tourist production presents an anticommon problem; the policy maker intervention is required, although a private intervention (i.e., tour operator) could solve the problem too, even if a profit distribution conflict might arise.

Since the ultimate effect of LTSs on prices – pushed down by agglomeration externalities but pushed up by extra demand in tourism stemming from higher quality – is not uniquely defined, it may happen that total welfare in the destination depends on the way revenue from tourism is locally distributed.

Table 4.1 sums up our conclusions, suggesting that there are more diversities than similarities among the three models of local production presented in this chapter.

Table 4.1   A comparison of industrial, cultural and Local Tourist Systems

Type of district	Reasons for the birth	Need for public intervention	Rationale for public intervention	Local community welfare
Industrial District	Externalities	No	—	Welfare increases
Cultural District	Product idiosyncrasy	Yes	Remedy to the problem of commons	Welfare increases in case of success
Local Tourist System	Goods and services combination	Yes	Remedy to the problem of anticommons	Uncertain result depending on income distribution

ID and CD importance in real world economies has been widely recognised, but LTSs are also gaining importance and highlight the relevance of a policy approach based on the destination. In Italy, a sort of LTS has been introduced in 2001 by the National Tourist Act and is explicitly denominated Sistema Turistico Locale. LTSs represent a policy instrument aimed at favouring the integrated development of tourism, by taking into consideration the heterogeneity and complexity of the phenomenon, and enhancing firms' aggregation and the co-operation between the public and the private sector. From a theoretical point of view, LTSs represent a new way to conceive and administrate the territory aiming at overcoming the existing policy fragmentation of the Italian territory, enhancing integration between tourism and other industries, and by looking endogenously for the optimal size of the destination. With the introduction of LTSs, the policy-maker intends to stimulate tourism development even to the possible detriment of competition or, rather, competition between LTSs is favoured to the detriment of competition between single tourist firms.

ACKNOWLEDGEMENTS

We thank participants in the second international conference: 'Tourism and Sustainable Economic Development: Macro and Micro Issues', held in Laguna Chia, Italy, 16–17 September 2005 and in the 'Second International Conference on Tourism Economics', held in Palma de Mallorca, Spain, 18–20 May 2006 for comments and suggestions on previous versions of the paper. The usual disclaimers apply.

NOTES

1. Among the several works on industrial districts, see Becattini (1989 and 2000). Industrial districts are crucial in the Italian economy, whose industrial organisation is characterised by a high number of small and medium size firms geographically located in narrow hyper-specialised territories. Such a characteristic has been considered one of the successful features of the Italian economic development of the last decades. Footwear in the Marche region, Sassuolo and Carpi pottery, Prato textiles, iron rods in Brescia, furniture in Brianza and eyeglasses in Cadore can be mentioned as a few of the many examples.
2. On this point see Cuccia and Santagata (2004) and Santagata (2004). The development of the cultural filière as a possible (economic) specialisation of a geographical area stems from the Greater London Council case, based upon the integration between cultural activities and relevant sectors of the tourist system. The birth of a CD may be a spontaneous process, as in the West End of London, Greenwich Village in New York or the Rive Gauche in Paris; elsewhere, it is the result of a development program or an urban refurbishment, as in Glasgow or in the Museum Quarter of Vienna (see Candela and Scorcu, 2004).
3. It is not our aim to model the complexity of industrial districts, for which we refer to Maggioni (2004) and related bibliography.
4. An example of the evolution of districts is provided by the Black Country, the region of Birmingham, UK. Born as a typical Marshallian industrial district, based on external economies of scale, when the industrial localisation exhausted its advantages (and after a long period of economic depression), it became a cultural district. Its value added was offered by the local industrial heritage, thus triggering the early tourism demand and evolving into a destination. Now the Black Country is a local tourist system, managed through the coordination and diversification of several tourist goods and services and enjoying new (non-industrial) external economies. See Porter (2003) on the dynamics of districts and Cuccia and Santagata (2004) on public sector intervention.
5. Separability stems from the assumption of non interrelation between goods demands. Moreover, the linear approximation forces the equilibrium to be a local solution.
6. This specification allows us to treat the two equilibrium prices separately.
7. However, in the early days of the market for pictures, in the 17th century in Amsterdam, both quality and productivity increased significantly (Montias, 2002).
8. An example might illustrate this assumption. If the good x is 'board', p_x is daily board price which includes two meals a day. We can assume that tourists consume one meal per day in a restaurant (for instance, in case of a 'half-board' stay, because the other meal is already included in the lodging): the demand $N_x = A - Bv_1$, with $v_1 = hp_x$, takes on, in this case, the value $h = \frac{1}{2}$. The overall demand $X = x + hN_x$ is consequently made up by a local component (x) and by the tourist component given by nights spent N weighted for $h = 1/2$.
9. We do not consider externalities between tourists and residents (see Candela et al., 2005).
10. In this specification we assume no indirect effect on domestic welfare of total (domestic or external) demand through personal incomes. In other words, we consider a partial equilibrium approach. On this issue, see also Section 2.4.
11. The Cobb–Douglas function has constant utility elasticity and the consumer spends for each good a constant income share, respectively equal to α for good x and $(1 - \alpha)$ for good y.
12. Differently from CDs, whose products are not usually consumed by the local population, tourist services (and inputs) are also demanded by residents: this is particularly important for land, water and other natural resources for which there is an explicit trade-off between the demand of hospitality firms and the demand of the local population for residential purposes.
13. Nevertheless, unlike industrial districts, tourism districts also need a widespread supply of cultural and environmental goods, as well as tourist attractions, typical crafts and agricultural products, etc.
14. Such a model can describe the income distribution problems in tourist enclaves. Many local communities in developing countries specialising in tourism do not enjoy the advantages of a tourism multiplier, and they may also suffer damage stemming from the increase in prices

due to tourist arrivals. Nevertheless, this effect may also occur in developed country destinations: families of local workers employed in sectors not connected to tourism do not get any additional income; on the contrary, they may suffer from the increase in prices of, for example, real estate and building lands. LTSs lead us directly to the inequality issue and, from here, to the problem of social sustainability of development paths based on tourist specialisation.

15. See Candela and Figini (2005), chap. 11.
16. Franzoni (2003), from which our model is taken, studies the anticommons issue from a more general perspective.
17. Obviously, this problem is more general and arises when different firms produce 'components' which contribute to the production of the final good.
18. The anticommon has been introduced by Michelman (1982) and has been developed by Heller (1998 and 1999). See Parisi et al. (2000 and 2004). The common good is a good for which property rights are not precisely defined, this way being at everyone's disposal (Hardin 1968).
19. The tour operator signs 'insurance' contracts with hotels, restaurants, air companies, etc., which accept a lower but certain price by transferring the risk of unsold packeges to the tour operator. Firms accept the coordination role of the tour operator if they end up with equal or higher expected profit. On optimal tourist contracts in a stochastic environment, see Mussoni (2004) and Castellani and Mussoni (2004).
20. There is no impact on local development only if the tour operator is domestic. These quantitative results are dependent upon very specific (and ad hoc) assumptions, such as separability, specific functional forms, etc. A natural extension of this framework should be the computation of a general equilibrium model, grounded on strong microeconomic principles. Most of our qualitative results, however, should remain unaffected.
21. See Candela and Scorcu (2004).
22. Common goods (Hardin, 1968) risk depletion if access is not regulated.

REFERENCES

Becattini, G. (1989), *Modelli Locali di Sviluppo*, Bologna: Il Mulino.
Becattini, G. (2000), *Distretti Industriali e Sviluppo Locale*, Turin: Bollati Boringhieri.
Candela, G. and P. Figini (2005), *Economia dei Sistemi Turistici*, Milan: McGraw-Hill.
Candela, G. and A.E. Scorcu (2004), *Economia delle Arti*, Bologna: Zanichelli.
Candela, G., M. Castellani and R. Dieci (2005), 'Technology of the externalities and economic policy', Collana 'Note e ricerche', Biblioteca Centralizzata del Polo Scientifico-Didattico di Rimini, University of Bologna.
Castellani, M. and M. Mussoni (2004), 'An economic analysis of the tourism contracts: free sale and allotment', Collana 'Note e ricerche', Biblioteca Centralizzata del Polo Scientifico-Didattico di Rimini, University of Bologna.
Caves, R.E. (2000), *Creative Industries. Contracts between Art and Commerce*, Cambridge: Harvard University Press.
Cuccia, T. and W. Santagata (2004), 'Adhesion – exit: incentivi e diritti di proprietà collettivi nei distretti culturali', *Studi Economici*, **80**, 5–30.
Franzoni, L.A. (2003), *Introduzione all'Economia del Diritto*, Bologna: Il Mulino.
Hardin, G. (1968), 'The tragedy of the commons', *Science*, **162**, 1243–48.
Heller, M.A. (1998), 'The tragedy of the anticommons: property in the transition from Marx to markets', *Harvard Law Review*, **111**, 621.
Heller, M.A. (1999), 'The boundaries of private property', *Yale Law Review*, **108**, 1163–223.

Maggioni, M.A. (2004), 'Agglomeration economies, geographical competition and industrial synergies: modelling the structure and evolution of industrial districts', in G. Cainelli and R. Zoboli, *The Evolution of Industrial Districts*, Heidelberg and New York: Springer Verlag, pp. 79–113.

Michelman, F.I. (1982), 'Ethics, economics, and the law of property', in J.R. Pennock and J.W. Chapman, *Nomos XXIV: Ethics, Economics and the Law*, New York: New York University Press.

Montias, J.M. (2002), *Art at Auction in Amsterdam in the 17th Century*, Amsterdam: Amsterdam University Press.

Mussoni, M. (2004), 'Il contratto vuoto per pieno: un'analisi economica', *Sistemaeconomico*, **2**, 17–51.

Parisi, F., B. Depoorter and N. Schultz (2000), 'Duality in property: commons and anticommons', Law and Economics Research Paper Series, no. 00-32, University of Virginia School of Law.

Parisi, F., N. Schultz and B. Depoorter (2004), 'Simultaneous and sequential anticommons', *European Journal of Law and Economics*, **17**, 175–90.

Porter, M.E. (2003), 'Building the Microeconomic Foundation of Prosperity: Findings from the Microeconomic Competitiveness Index', in World Economic Forum, *Global Competitiveness Report 2002–2003*, Cambridge: Harvard University Press.

Sacco, P.L., and G. Tavano Blessi (2005), 'Distretti culturali evoluti e valorizzazione del territorio', *Global and Local Economic Review*, **VIII**(1), 7–41.

Santagata, W. (2004), 'Cultural districts and economic development', in V. Ginsburgh and D. Thorsby, *Handbook of the Economics of Art and Culture*, Amsterdam: Elsevier.

Santagata, W., P.L. Scandizzo and P. Valentini (2004), 'Ora ci vogliono i numeri per rimanere nella lista Unesco del patrimonio mondiale', *Il Giornale dell'arte*, Settembre, p. 60.

5. Inbound Tourism and Internal Migration in a Developing Economy

Jean-Jacques Nowak and Mondher Sahli

5.1 INTRODUCTION

In search of remedies for persistent balance of payments deficits and unemployment, international aid agencies and governments in developing countries (henceforth refereed to as DCs) have been attracted to tourism. As a result, this sector is increasingly viewed as one of the best opportunities and most viable options for a strategy of accelerated economic and social development in these countries. However, in order to be able to accurately assess the merits of tourism promotion as part of a development strategy, a thorough knowledge of the mechanisms by which tourism can affect the host economy are needed, in particular sectoral outputs, factor incomes, prices, other sector exports and, most importantly, domestic welfare.

But until recently, the predominant approaches in tourism have been based on incomplete partial-equilibrium frameworks with fixed prices and wages, and unlimited supplies of factors (labour, capital, etc.). For example, techniques such as Keynesian multipliers and input–output analysis are still very commonly used to estimate the economic impacts of an inbound tourism boom (see for example, Flechter, 1994 and Frechtling and Horvath, 1998).

The problem with these approaches is that they ignore the presence in the economy of constraints on resource availability (and, hence, of competition between sectors for scarce resources), the market relationships between sectors, inputs and agents, the role of price adjustments, etc. As a result, indirect and feedback mechanisms are not taken into consideration. The specificity of tourism cannot be captured and an inbound tourism shock is modelled as any other demand shock (on private investment, domestic consumption, etc.). As such a shock always draws previously unemployed resources (labour, capital, etc.) into employment and no potentially negative feedback or indirect effect is considered, this kind of analysis predicts an increase in overall economic activity with no reduction of any sector's output and thus, a positive impact on the economy. Despite the presence of leakages caused by imports and saving, this positive impact is clearly overestimated.[1]

But a real economy is an integrated system in which indirect and feedback mechanisms are important, along with direct mechanisms. In general, resources are limited and allocated by (sometimes imperfect) markets. There is strong competition between sectors, and price effects matter. Any change in tourism demand may have negative impacts which can be as strong as the positive impacts and sometimes even stronger. Therefore, an accurate assessment of the economic effects of an inward tourism boom requires a general equilibrium approach.

This approach is quite recent in tourism analysis and has been applied in both theoretical studies (see for example Copeland, 1991; Nowak et al., 2003 and 2005) and empirical studies (with Computable General Equilibrium (CGE) modelling: see Adams and Parmentier, 1995; Blake et al., 2003 and 2006; Narayan, 2004; Dwyer et al., 2005; Gooroochurn and Sinclair, 2005(. All these studies suggest that an increase in tourism demand may seriously alter the country's patterns of production and specialization, in particular by crowding out internationally traded sectors (i.e. export and import-competing sectors). Moreover, most of these studies support Copeland's view (1991) that the main mechanism by which an inbound tourism boom may change domestic welfare is through an increase in the price of internationally non-traded goods and services bought by foreign tourists. Since their production never leaves the country, these goods and services are internationally non-traded according to standard definitions. But they become partially exportable thanks to foreign tourists who come specifically to the host country to consume them. Thus, any additional foreign tourists cause the price of these goods to rise which amounts to a terms-of-trade improvement for the host country. This usual 'terms-of-trade effect' provides a welfare gain to its residents.

But, as already pointed out by Dwyer and Forsyth (1993) and theoretically illustrated by Nowak et al. (2005), the presence of some distortion in the economy (monopoly, taxation, subsidization, increasing returns to scale in manufacturing, external effects like pollution, etc.) modifies the way by which tourism impacts on domestic welfare by adding other mechanisms. Since an inbound tourism expansion may change the economic cost of such a distortion, it can give rise to an extra welfare change which comes in addition to the usual terms-of-trade gain. Thus, if the cost of the distortion is aggravated, the resulting welfare loss lessens the gain provided by the improvement of terms of trade. This loss can even be superior to the gain, in which case the inbound tourism expansion results in an immiserization of domestic residents.

As all kinds of distortions are present in real economies, much attention has to be paid to such costs when assessing the welfare effect of a tourism expansion. This is especially true for DCs where, as already said above, tourism is viewed as one of the best available tools to promote growth and development (Sinclair, 1998; WTO, 2001). There is an increasing concern nowadays for public policy makers in DCs as to whether mass tourism coastal resorts and other particular tourism activities, such as golf, safaris, etc. play a catalytic role in the overall economic development and truly improve the welfare of their community.

In this chapter, we therefore present a *general equilibrium model* which explicitly takes into consideration specific features of some DCs (dualistic structure of the labour market, sectoral unemployment, inter-regional migrations, competition between agriculture and tourism for labour and land) to analyze the ways by which an inbound tourism boom affects this kind of country, in particular its national welfare. In particular, it highlights a channel specific to some DCs by which a tourism boom impacts on incomes and welfare. We show that, under realistic assumptions, tourism promotion may make DC residents worse off.

The chapter is structured as follows. Section 5.2 describes the theoretical framework of the economy considered. Section 5.3 examines the consequences of an inbound tourism growth on sectors' outputs, relative prices, factor incomes, urban unemployment, internal migrations and domestic welfare. Finally, section 5.4 provides some concluding remarks.

5.2   THE MODEL

In this model, we consider a small open economy that is made up of two regions: an urban region U and a coastal, or natural, area C.

The urban region contains only one sector, called X_N, which includes all modern activities: the manufacturing sector, public and private services (e.g. banking, insurance). Very often in DCs, these activities are non-traded, that is, they are protected from international competition by high costs of transport, domestic regulations and trade protection. Nevertheless we have assumed in this economy that the urban sector X_N produces traded goods and services only, because this simplifies the model considerably by giving it a recursive structure. Moreover whether the urban sector is traded or not does not influence the main results regarding domestic welfare determination.

The coastal/natural area is made up of two sectors: agriculture X_A and tourism X_S. The agricultural sector is an importing sector, whereas the tourism sector exports its entire production. However, the exporting nature of the tourism sector is unusual in the respect that it stems not from the international mobility of the goods and services produced, but from the temporary international mobility of consumers. In fact, its production never leaves the country and is non-traded according to standard definitions. Consumption is by non-residents who come to the host country specifically for these tourism products. Thus it is the foreign consumers who come to the product and not the reverse, giving an international component to the demand faced by this sector. In order to simplify the analysis, two hypotheses are made. First, we assume the absence of domestic and outbound tourism. All the tourism production is consumed by international tourists visiting the country (a likely hypothesis for a DC). The possibility of tourism imports is excluded because residents do not travel outside the country. Introducing outbound tourism or domestic tourism would reduce the welfare gain from the terms of trade improvement. The second simplifying hypothesis is that the goods and services produced by X_N are consumed by all residents, but not by foreign tourists.

The theoretical model chosen to represent this economic structure is based on Harris and Todaro (1970) that focuses attention on the coexistence in DCs of massive urban unemployment and rural–urban labour migrations. For simplicity's sake, this analysis is carried out under the assumption that there are no international migrations or cross-border migrants. If one considers the possibility of additional workers in tourism from other countries, the analysis would have to be modified (for further details, see for example, Hazari and Nowak, 2003 and Chesney and Hazari, 2003).

In the first segment, the labour market is regulated and wages are set by a set of 'institutional' forces (minimum wages, trade unions, public sector pay policies and labour codes) that aim to assure workers an 'adequate' standard of living by keeping the wages above market-equilibrium level. This category generally includes 'modern/formal' manufacturing industries, public services and service industries (banks, insurance companies, etc.), that are regrouped in our model within Sector X_N and located in urban region U.

In the second segment, wages are determined in a very neoclassical way, leading to equality between the supply and the demand of labour. It includes activities described as 'informal' as well as agriculture, where a competitive wage determination predominates. In these sectors, even if labour laws exist, they are rarely respected (one example being the minimum agricultural wage).

In tourism activities, both of these wage structures are used. For example, in many small tourism firms (e.g. independent hotels, restaurants and food services, night clubs, handicrafts trade, etc.), there is a high wage variability and it is well known that unionization is minimal and 'under the table' is common. The labour market here has a competitive structure. However, in large organizations where international chains are concerned, the labour market tends to be organized in the same way as the industrial sector (laws are respected, efficiency wages, etc.). But even if the two segments exist side by side, two reasons lead us to assume that flexibility is, in fact, globally predominant. Firstly, small and mid-sized tourism businesses predominate, both in developing and developed countries (ILO, 2001). Secondly, tourism activities are highly seasonal in nature, thus creating fluctuating labour needs. The International Labour Organization (ILO) has demonstrated that deep similarities exist between agriculture and tourism labour markets in developing countries (ILO, 1989). Consequently, we find it justified to consider the tourism labour market to be competitive.[2]

In this chapter, we set up a framework that incorporates both coastal and urban region. The economy in question produces three goods: X_N in the urban area and X_S and X_A in the coastal region. Migratory flows connect the two regions. There is some unemployment in the urban region whereas full employment prevails in the coastal/natural area.

The Urban Region

In the urban region, firms combine labour L_N and specific capital K to produce the urban good X_N. For the sake of simplicity, we assume that this urban good is traded (e.g. imported) and that the country is small on its international market. So its price P_N is set to its international level P_N^*. This is not a necessary condition to obtain meaningful results regarding the welfare but it considerably simplifies the model.

The urban wage rate is denoted by $\bar{w}_U$ and the rental rate on capital by r. The zero profit condition is:

$$P_N = C_N(\bar{w}_U, r) \tag{5.1}$$

C_j is the unit cost function in sector ($j = A, S, N$). The unit factor requirements in each sector are given by the Shepherd–Samuelson relations: $C_j^i = \partial C_j / \partial i$ with $i = w$; r or t (t is the rental rate on land). P_j is the price of good j ($j = A, S, N$).

For the grounds exposed above, the real wage rate $\bar{w}_U$ is rigid downward and is set above its competitive level. It is expressed in terms of agriculture good X_A which is then chosen as the numéraire.

The flexibility of r ensures full employment of the stock of urban capital:

$$C_N^r \cdot X_N = \bar{K} \tag{5.2}$$

X_j denotes the output of sector j ($j = A, S, N$).

On the contrary, the wage rigidity gives rise to some unemployment in this region:

$$L_N + L_{ch} = L_U \tag{5.3}$$

L_N ($= C_N^w \cdot X_N$) is the amount of labour employed by X_N, L_{ch} is the number of unemployed urban workers and L_U is the total urban labour force.

The urban goods X_N are consumed by all residents, regardless of whether their location is urban or coastal, but not by tourists. Using duality theory, the Hicksian compensated demand function for good N is given by

$$e_{P_N}(P_A, P_N, u) \text{ with } e_{P_j} = \partial e / \partial P_j .$$

$e(P_A, P_N, u)$ is the residents' well-behaved expenditure function and u is the level of residents' utility. Recall that residents consume only goods X_A and X_N, but no tourism products X_S.

Any welfare variation is expressed as:

$$dy \equiv e_u \cdot du \tag{5.4}$$

where $e_u = \partial e / \partial u$ denotes the inverse of the marginal utility of income.

The Coastal/Natural Region

In this region, we assume that agriculture and tourism compete for the same factors of production (labour L_j and land T_j) and produce under constant returns to scale. The hypothesis that agriculture and tourism are in competition for land and labour is corroborated by numerous empirical studies. Bryden (1973) and Weaver (1988) present the example of the Caribbean where the tourism sector exists to the detriment of both export and subsistence agriculture. While sceptical regarding the Caribbean, Latimer (1985) nonetheless affirms that this hypothesis holds true both for Mexico and for Bali. Tyrakowski (1986) for his part states that the development of resorts in some areas of the Spanish Mediterranean coastline has resulted in the loss to the agricultural sector of vast expanses of high-yield land and a large number of workers. Parsons (1989) describes the case of the Canary Islands where this phenomenon is particularly striking. The same can be said of other Mediterranean islands, such as Cyprus, Malta, the Greek islands (Crete, Myconos, Corfu, etc.) and destinations that combine both agriculture and an attractive natural environment since many occupations required in tourism are done by workers who used to work in the agricultural sector (landscaping, gardening, janitorial, maintenance, dishwashing, table bussing, and security services). For instance, the intensive tourism development and accompanying infrastructure of certain coastal areas and inland oases in Tunisia clearly illustrates the widespread loss of agriculture land and the transfer of rural labour from agriculture to tourism activities making farming and tourism an either/or situation in certain regions, such as Nabeul-Hammamet, Sousse-Monastir, and Tozeur.

Let us note here that the term 'land' must be understood to also include water, an essential input for both sectors. The construction of large-scale resorts, swimming pools, golf courses, etc., exerts significant pressure on water resources and thus creates a drain on the reserves available to agriculture, particularly in regions such as the Mediterranean where water resources are scarce. As the high season for tourism often coincides with the dry period, water levels are already low and the shortage is exacerbated (see for example Groupe Huit, 1979 regarding Tunisia and McTaggart, 1988 regarding Bali). Moreover, Northern tourists' behaviour regarding water is very different from that of the local Southern populations and introduces wasteful habits (EEA, 2001). In certain regions this problem has shown such a degree of seriousness that deterioration of natural land and sea vegetation has been observed (see Cocossis and Mexa, 2004 for more details).

The coastal wage rate w_C and the rental rate on land t are perfectly flexible, which ensures full employment of both factors:

$$L_A + L_S = L_C \tag{5.5}$$

$$T_A + T_S = \overline{T} \tag{5.6}$$

where L_C is the total labour employed in the coastal/natural zone. Contrary to the land endowment $\overline{T}$ which is fixed, L_C is endogenous and varies as migratory flows occur between the two regions. $L_j (= C_j^w \cdot X_j)$ and $T_j (= C_j^t \cdot X_j)$ are the amounts of labour and land used by sector j ($j = A, S$).

The competitive profit conditions are expressed in terms of the 'price equals unit cost' equations:

$$P_A = 1 = C_A(w_C, t) \tag{5.7}$$

$$P_S = C_S(w_C, t) \tag{5.8}$$

As agricultural products are homogenous goods and the economy is small on their international market, their price is thus exogenous. In addition, we assume that the country is a net importer of both goods. But, even if its tourist product S has strong similarities to its foreign equivalents, this country has certain unique characteristics (climate, natural and cultural riches, etc.) which differentiate its product. This product consequently has no exact foreign substitute. Therefore, although the country is small on the scale of international tourism activity, the demand for services it faces is never perfectly elastic. The price P_S of its tourism services can thus be different from the price in other countries. It is determined by the confrontation of the country's domestic supply X_S and the foreign tourists' demand D_{FT}:

$$X_S = D_{FT}(P_S, \Delta) \tag{5.9}$$

This foreign tourists' demand D_{FT} depends positively on some exogenous factors (foreign income, fashion, etc.) which are captured by the parameter Δ, and depends negatively on its own price P_S: $\partial D_{FT}/\partial \Delta > 0$ and $\partial D_{FT}/\partial P_S < 0$.[3]

In this model, any inbound tourism boom is captured by an exogenous increase in Δ.

Let us finish the description of this region by noting that it has a Heckcher–Ohlin–Samuelon (HOS) structure, as revealed by the equation system (5.5)–(5.8). Because of this HOS structure, we have to consider the factor intensity of both the agricultural and the tourism sectors (T_S/L_S, T_A/L_A). But unlike the standard HOS model, the labour supply here is variable because of migration flows between the city and the coast (or the natural area). Therefore the supply functions of tourism and agriculture depend not only on the coastal relative price (P_S) but also on the labour supply (L_C) in this region. These supplies are then subject to a traditional price effect and to a Rybczynski quantity effect.

Links Between the Two Regions

The two regions are related by migration flows. Moreover, the agricultural goods and the urban goods are available to all residents, regardless of their location. There is no income transfer (remittances) between urban people and coastal people.

These migration flows are modelled along the lines suggested by Harris and Todaro (1970). As long as the coastal wage differs from the urban expected wage (i.e. the fixed urban wage weighted by the probability of finding a job in the modern sector), there are labour migration flows. This process continues until both wages become equal to each other:

$$w_C = w_U^e = \overline{w}_U \cdot (L_N/L_U)$$
$$= \overline{w}_U/(1 + \kappa) \tag{5.10}$$

w_U^e is the urban expected wage rate and $\kappa = L_{ch}/L_N$ is the ratio of unemployed to employed workers in the urban region and is often called the ratio of urban unemployment. It is easy to show that this ratio is closely related to the urban unemployment rate (L_{ch}/L_U) and thus always moves in the same direction. In the next section, we will use either one or the other to explain the results of a tourism boom.

Labour is the only factor that is completely mobile between the three sectors. The fixed amount of labour available in the economy ($\overline{L}$) is divided as follows (cf. (5.3) and (5.5)):

$$\overline{L} = L_C + L_U = (L_A + L_S) + L_N \cdot (1 + \kappa) \tag{5.11}$$

The residents' budget constraint is:

$$e(P_A, P_N, u) = Y \tag{5.12}$$

where Y is the national income:

$$\begin{aligned} Y &= P_N \cdot X_N + P_A \cdot X_A + P_S \cdot X_S \\ &= \overline{w}_U \cdot L_N + r \cdot \overline{K} + w_C \cdot L_C + t \cdot \overline{T} \end{aligned} \tag{5.13}$$

We have thus defined the general equilibrium of this economy for any given level of the urban good's international price P_N^*, of the urban wage rate $\overline{w}_U$ and of the foreign tourists' demand Δ.

5.3   A CASE OF IMMISERIZING TOURISM

In this section, we present the implications of an inbound tourism boom on relative prices, outputs, factor incomes and resident welfare. As we stated earlier, the tourism boom is captured by change in Δ in equation (5.9).

The mathematic solution of the model leads to the following expression for the change in residents' welfare y.

$$\hat{y} = \underbrace{\eta_S \cdot \hat{P}_S}_{(TT)} \underbrace{-\beta_{ch} \cdot \hat{\tau}}_{(UE)} \tag{5.14}$$

The $^\wedge$ notation denotes relative changes, with $\hat{x} \equiv d \ln(x)$. Where:

- $\eta_S = P_S \cdot D_{FT} / Y$: share of international tourism demand in national income (always > 0).
- $\beta_{ch} = w_C \cdot L_{ch} / Y$: share of national income which would have been paid to unemployed workers had they chosen to continue to work on the coast at the prevailing wage rate (> 0 as long as $L_{ch} \neq 0$).
- $\hat{\tau}$: relative change of the *ratio* of urban unemployment $\tau = L_{ch}/L_N$ ($\hat{\tau}$ could be < 0 or > 0).

From the above equation, we are now able to describe the consequences of an increase in inbound tourism on the key economic variables. The immediate impact of this excess of tourism demand is an increase in its price $\hat{P}_S$ ($\hat{P}_S > 0$). This rise of P_S is at the origin of the double effect on residents' welfare.

On the one hand, this increase brings about a gain in welfare to the resident community because of the country's improved terms of trade. Since the tourism product S is exported through a temporary movement of consumers from their origin countries into the destination, the rise in its price increases domestic welfare, as would be the case in any traditional export product (its value is given by the first term (TT) in equation (5.14), which is unambiguously positive).

On the other hand, the rise in P_S modifies the cost of urban wage distortion. In fact, this increase changes factor incomes (w_C and t) in the coastal region according to the factor intensities of each sector (T_S/L_S, T_A/L_A), thus breaking the equality between the coastal wage and the expected urban wage. This imbalance gives rise to migratory flows between the two areas resulting in an increase or decrease in the urban unemployment rate (its value is reflected by the unemployment effect term (UE) in equation (5.14) which can be positive or negative).

A reduction in unemployment is accompanied by the creation of income which further adds to the gain provided by the appreciation of the real exchange rate (TT). In this case, the net effect of an inbound tourism boom on domestic welfare would be unambiguously positive. However, an increase in unemployment leads to a reduction in available income, which reduces the gain brought about by the first term (TT) and could even eliminate this gain entirely. Therefore, the net effect of an inbound tourism boom on domestic welfare is ambiguous. Welfare increases (falls) if the first (second) term in equation (5.14) determines the direction of the welfare effect.

Note that the second term (UE) is proportional to β_{ch} which represents the portion of national income that would have been paid to unemployed workers had they chosen to continue to work on the coast at the prevailing wage rate ($\beta_{ch} = w_C \cdot L_{ch}/Y > 0$). Recall that τ is the ratio of unemployment to urban employed workers ($\tau = L_{ch}/L_N$) and follows the same evolution as the urban unemployment rate (L_{ch}/L_U).

Ambiguous Net Welfare Effect

The case where a tourism boom can lead to an ambiguous net welfare effect (i.e. welfare gain or immiserization) requires the coastal tourism sector to be relatively more land-intensive than the coastal agricultural sector: (T_S/L_S) > (T_A/L_A). Although this case may seem surprising, studies have shown that it is relevant for some tourist destinations, which are intensive users of coastal land (large-scale resorts, national parks, golf tourism, etc.) and whose agriculture sector is controlled by families working on small farms (Page, 1999; WTO, 2001).

In the presence of a land-intensive tourism sector and in accordance with the Stolper–Samuelson theorem (cf. equations (5.7) and (5.8)), the increase in P_S raises the rental rate on land t and decreases the coastal wage rate w_C which then becomes inferior to the urban expected wage rate ($w_C < w_U^e$, cf. (5.10)). A migration from the coast to the city takes place reducing the total labour available on the coast and increasing the number of urban unemployed workers as well as the ratio of urban unemployment ($\hat{\tau} > 0$ in equation (5.14)). The initial misemployment of human resources due to the presence of wage distortion on the urban labour market is then magnified. This causes a loss of real income in the community of the host country (the term (UE) is unambiguously negative in (5.14)) and weakens the welfare gain provided by the positive terms of trade effect (TT). This loss could be even superior to the gain, in which case tourism's net effect turns out to be negative and results in an immiserization of the resident community $[(TT) + (UE) < 0]$.

Let us analyse the impacts of an inbound tourism boom on tourism and agricultural outputs. The rise in P_S is the cause of two mechanisms. The first is a price effect, the second a quantity effect (or resource movement effect). The increase in the tourism product's price stimulates the output of the tourism sector to the detriment of the output of the agricultural sector. The resource movement effect is a result of migration flows. According to the Rybczynski theorem, the decline in the coastal labour supply following the departure of labours for the city leads to the decline of the more labour-intensive sector, here agriculture, and the expansion of the land-intensive sector, tourism (cf. Table 5.1).

Positive Net Welfare Effect

The case where tourism's net welfare effect is unambiguously positive requires the coastal tourism sector to be more labour-intensive than the coastal agricultural sector $(T_S/L_S) < (T_A/L_A)$. With a labour-intensive tourism sector, the increase in P_S causes the labour remuneration in the coastal zone w_C to rise and the land remuneration t to fall. As urban jobs become less attractive ($w_C > w_U^e$, cf. (5.10)), some unemployed workers decide to return to the coast. This migration from the city towards the coast increases the labour force available on the coast and reduces the number of urban unemployed, and thus the urban unemployment rate ($\hat{\tau} < 0$ in equation (5.14)). This social gain (the term (UE) is positive in (5.14)) comes in addition to the first gain provided by P_S (due to the improvement in terms of trade; i.e. (TT) in (5.14)). The total gain $((TT) + (UE) > 0)$ turns out to be higher than without unemployment.

Just as in the previous situation, the coastal sector outputs are determined by a price effect and a resource movement effect. The increase in the tourism product's price stimulates the output of the tourism sector to the detriment of

Table 5.1 A summary of coastal tourism's economic impacts

Scenarios	Coastal Wage	Rental Rate on Land	Migration	Terms of Trade	Urban Unemployment	Tourism Output	Agriculture Output	Net Welfare Effect
Coastal tourism more land-intensive than agriculture	−	+	Coast → City	+	+	+	−	Ambiguous
Coastal tourism more labour-intensive than agriculture	+	−	City → Coast	+	−	+	−	Positive

Notes: (+) increase (or improvement); (−) decrease (or deterioration) the output of the agricultural sector. The resource movement effect is a result of migration flows. According to the Rybczynski theorem, the arrival of additional workers on the coast, following the migration, brings about an expansion of the more labour-intensive sector, in this case tourism, and a decline of the more land-intensive sector, here agriculture. Thus, the two effects have the same consequences on production so that the coastal outputs follow an unambiguous evolution, i.e. tourism sector expansion and agricultural sector decline (cf. Table 5.1).

Summary of Results

Let us conclude this section by saying that, as these results are based on assumptions which we believe are relevant for some kinds of DCs, they provide numerous insights relevant to tourism development in these economies. Perhaps the most important result is to have shown that in addition to the negative environmental and socio-cultural impacts traditionally recognized in the literature, tourism can also, under certain conditions, be the origin of economic costs in such countries. At times these costs could be so negative that they result in the immiserization of the resident community (i.e. the net welfare effect is negative).

A second significant result of the model is that a tourism policy that encourages land-intensive tourism may be just as unsustainable (from an economic perspective) as a policy that causes excessive environmental costs. In some instances, a policy that promotes large-scale resorts, golf courses, etc. in DCs may result in a loss of welfare to local residents, as compared with a policy that promotes a labour-intensive tourism industry.

5.4   CONCLUSION

There is now an extensive literature on the economic impacts of additional inbound tourism which sets out tools to measure these impacts and includes many case studies. Many of them showed that inbound tourism gives rise to migration flows within the host economy (see for instance, Gössling and Schultz, 2005). However, to our knowledge, no theoretical analysis has examined this phenomenon yet. Our model provides a framework to study the consequences of tourism development on labour flows between coastal/natural regions and cities.

Results obtained in this chapter are not meant to denigrate tourism activity in DCs, but to show that in addition to the environmental, social and cultural costs traditionally recognized in the literature, tourism can also, under certain conditions, be the origin of economic costs. At times these costs could be so high that they result in the immiserization of the resident community. We have seen that in the kind of economy considered here, this result requires a specific configuration of factor intensities, i.e. a tourism sector which is more land-intensive than agriculture. This case, although it cannot be entirely discounted as shown by the examples cited above, does not seem to be the most common situation. However, the demonstration of the existence of these economic costs should encourage governments to give due consideration to the general macroeconomic equilibrium technique and CGE modelling when deciding on a tourism development strategy. They should not, as is customarily the case, limit the discussion of the effects of additional inbound tourism to a simple evaluation of its gross economic impacts and internal and external leakages, often presented as the only negative externalities.

ACKNOWLEDGEMENTS

We would like to thank the participants at the second international conference on 'Tourism and Sustainable Economic Development – Macro and Micro Economic Issues' for their comments. We also wish to thank the participants at the workshop on 'Small Islands' Tourism Economies and Sustainable Development', held on 2–3 December 2005 in Corte, Corsica, for helpful suggestions. A modified version of this chapter was published in *Tourism Economics*, **13**(1), March 2007. Copyright © 2007 IP Publishing Ltd.

NOTES

1. A more detailed discussion is available in Dwyer et al. (2004a; 2004b).
2. A model with a generalized minimum wage in the tourism industry is discussed by Sahli and Hazari (2005) and Sahli and Nowak (2006).
3. A more detailed discussion of modelling tourism in this manner is available in Copeland (1991) and Nowak et al. (2003).

REFERENCES

Adams, P.D. and B.R. Parmentier (1995), 'An applied general equilibrium analysis of the economic effects of tourism in a quite small, quite open economy', *Applied Economics*, **27**(10), 985–94.
Blake, A., T. Sinclair and G. Sugiyarto (2003), 'Tourism and globalization: economic impact in Indonesia', *Annals of Tourism Research*, **30**(3), 683–701.
Blake, A., R. Durbarry, J.L. Eugenio-Martin, N. Gooroochurn, B. Hay, J. Lennon, M.T. Sinclair, G. Sugiyarto and I. Yeoman (2006), 'Integrating forecasting and CGE models: the case of tourism in Scotland', *Tourism Management*, **27**, 292–305.

Bryden, J. (1973), *Tourism and Development: A Case Study of Commonwealth Caribbean*, London: Cambridge University Press.

Chesney, M. and B.R. Hazari (2003), 'Illegal migrants, tourism and welfare: a trade theoretic approach', *Pacific Economic Review*, **8**(3), 259–68.

Cocossis, H. and A. Mexa (2004), *The Challenge of Tourism Carrying Capacity Assessment: Theory and Practice*, Aldershot, UK: Ashgate Publishing Limited.

Copeland, B.R. (1991), 'Tourism, welfare and de-industrialization in a small open economy', *Economica*, **58**, 515–29.

Dwyer, R.L. and P. Forsyth (1993), 'Assessing the benefits and costs of inbound tourism', *Annals of Tourism Research*, **20**(4), 751–68.

Dwyer, L., P. Forsyth and R. Spurr (2004a), 'Evaluating tourism's economic effects: new and old approaches', *Tourism Management*, **25**, 307–17.

Dwyer, L., P. Forsyth and R. Spurr (2004b), 'Inter-industry effects of tourism growth: some implications for destination managers', *Tourism Economics*, **9**(2), 117–32.

Dwyer, L., P. Forsyth, R. Spurr and T. Ho (2005), 'The economic impacts and benefits of tourism in Australia: a general equilibrium approach', Sustainable Tourism CRC, Australia.

European Environmental Agency (EEA) (2001), *Environmental Signals 2001*, Copenhagen: OPOCE.

Flechter, J. (1994), 'Input–output analysis', in S. Witt and L. Moutinho (eds), *Tourism Marketing and Management Handbook*, second edition, UK: Prentice-Hall International, pp. 480–84.

Frechtling, D, and E. Horvath (1998), 'Estimating the multiplier effects of tourism expenditures on a local economy through a regional input–output model', *Journal of Travel Research*, **37**(4), 324–32.

Gooroochurn, N. and M.T. Sinclair (2005), 'Economics of tourism taxation: evidence from Mauritius', *Annals of Tourism Research*, **32**(2), 478–98.

Gössling, S. and U. Schulz (2005), 'Tourism-related migration in Zanzibar, Tanzania', *Tourism Geographies*, **7**(1), 43–62.

Groupe Huit (1979), 'The sociocultural effects of tourism in Tunisia: a case study of Sousse', in E. de Kadt (ed.), *Tourisme: passeport pour le développement?*, Paris: Economica.

Harris, J.R. and M.P. Todaro (1970), 'Migration, unemployment and development: a two-sector analysis', *American Economic Review*, **60**, 126–42.

Hazari, B.R. and J.-J. Nowak (2003), 'Tourism, guest workers and resident immiserization', *The Journal of Developing Areas*, **36**(2), 101–24.

ILO (1989), 'Productivity and training in the hotel, catering and tourism sector', Geneva: Hotel, Catering and Tourism Committee.

ILO (2001), 'Human resources development, employment and globalization in the hotel, catering and tourism sector', Geneva.

Latimer, H. (1985), 'Developing island economies: tourism v. agriculture', *Tourism Management*, **6**, 32–42.

McTaggart, W.D. (1988), 'Hydrologic management in Bali', *Singapore Journal of Tropical Geography*, **9**, 96–111.

Narayan, P.K. (2004), 'Economic impact of tourism on Fiji's economy: empirical evidence from the computable equilibrium model', *Tourism Economics*, **10**(40), 419–33.

Nowak, J.-J., M. Sahli and P. Sgrò (2003), 'Tourism, trade and domestic welfare', *Pacific Economic Review*, **8**(3), 245–58.

Nowak, J.-J., M. Sahli and P. Sgrò (2005), 'Tourism, trade and domestic welfare', in A. Lanza and F. Pigliaru (eds), *Tourism and Sustainable Economic Development*,

Cheltenham, UK and Northampton, MA, USA: Edward Elgar, pp. 87–104.

Page, S. (1999), *Tourism and Development: the Evidence from Mauritius, South Africa and Zimbabwe*, ODI.

Parsons, J.J. (1989), 'The Canary Island search for stability', *Focus*, **35**(2), 22–9.

Sinclair, M.T. (1998), 'Tourism and economic development: a survey', *Journal of Development Studies*, **34**(5), 1–51.

Sahli, M. and B. Hazari (2005), 'Tourism, employment and national welfare', *Asia-Pacific Journal of Accounting & Economics*, **12**(2), 155–64.

Sahli, M. and J.-J. Nowak (2006), 'Tourism, factor intensity and domestic welfare', Proceedings of the 'First International Symposium on Environment Identities and Mediterranean Area', Corte-Ajaccio, France, 10–13 July.

Tyrakowski, K. (1986), 'The role of tourism in land utilization conflicts on the Spanish Mediterranean coast', *Geojournal*, **13**, 19–26.

Weaver, D. (1988), 'The evolution of a plantation tourism landscape on the Carribbean island of Antigua', *Tiddschrift voor Economische en Sociale Geographie*, **79**, 319–31.

WTO (2001), 'The least developed countries and international tourism', in WTO (ed.), *Tourism in the Least Developed Countries*, Madrid.

6. Tourism, Jobs, Capital Accumulation and the Economy: a Dynamic Analysis

Chi-Chur Chao, Bharat R. Hazari, Jean-Pierre Laffargue, Pasquale M. Sgrò and Eden S.H. Yu

6.1 INTRODUCTION

Tourism is a growing and important industry in both developed and developing countries. It is also an important source of earning foreign exchange and provides employment opportunities for domestic labor. Generally, tourist consumption in the receiving country is predominantly of non-traded goods and services. This type of consumption can be very significant in economies suffering a cyclical downturn in their traded-goods sector in times of recession. The recent recovery of the Hong Kong economy is an excellent example of tourism-led growth with job creation. The restructuring and relocation of manufacturing processes to China in the past two decades has resulted in unemployment of unskilled workers in Hong Kong. The Asian financial crisis in 1997 and the SARS outbreak in 2003 had made the situation even worse, with the unemployment rate in Hong Kong exceeding 7 per cent. Since April 2003, China allowed individuals from selected cities to visit Hong Kong; this resulted in tourism growth. About four million Chinese tourists came to Hong Kong, which in turn created job opportunities and substantially reduced unemployment.[1]

Tourism research has concentrated on understanding the effects of tourism on the economy both in distortion and distortion-free models. In the latter models,[2] a tourism boom via a demand push raises the relative price of the non-traded good. Since tourism is essentially exports of services, this gain in the 'tertiary terms of trade' improves residents' welfare. Subsequent research has extended the analysis of the effects of tourism in two directions. The first direction is to examine static economies with distortions. Hazari et al. (2003) and Nowak et al. (2003) are examples of this line of research, where the former analyzes the welfare effect of tourism in a Harris–Todaro (1970) economy, while the latter introduces increasing returns to scale in the economy. The second direction of research is the analysis of tourism in

105

dynamic models of trade. Using a one-sector growth model, Hazari and Sgro (1995) found that tourism without monopoly power in trade is necessarily welfare improving. Recently, Chao et al. (2006) demonstrated that an expansion of tourism may result in capital decumulation, thereby lowering welfare in a two-sector model with a specific type of distortion, namely, capital-generating externality. However, the relationship between tourism and employment remains unexplored in the literature. Does an expansion in tourism create more jobs in the local economy, reduce the unemployment rate and hence improve workers' welfare? We explore this problem in a uniform minimum-wage dynamic economy,[3] and extend the framework by incorporating capital adjustments in the long run. The assumption of a minimum wage is captured by wage indexation. We find that because of the nature of labor intensity of the tourism industry, the expansion of tourism raises demand for labor and increases employment. Nonetheless, the expansion of the tourism sector may lead to capital decumulation in other traded sectors. When the traded sector is strongly capital-intensive relative to the non-traded goods sector, the fall in the capital stock plays a dominant role that can lower economic welfare. Therefore, in evaluating the effectiveness of tourism to the economy, a trade-off exists between the gain in employment and the loss in capital decumulation. German data is used to simulate these results.

The structure of this chapter is as follows. Section 6.2 sets out a dynamic model with capital accumulation to examine the effects of tourism on the relative price of the non-traded good, labor employment, capital accumulation and welfare in the short and long runs. Section 6.3 provides numerical simulations for the effects of tourism on the economy, while section 6.4 outlines the main findings and conclusions.

6.2   THE MODEL

We consider an open economy that produces two goods, a traded good X and a non-traded good Y, with production functions: $X = X(L_X, K_X, V_X)$ and $Y = Y(L_Y, K_Y, V_Y)$. The variables L_i, K_i and V_i denote the allocation of labor and capital and specific factors employed in sector i, $i = X, Y$. While both labor and capital are perfectly mobile between sectors, there are specific factors to each sector.[4] So, the model considered is a hybrid of the Heckscher–Ohlin and the specific-factors model. Commodity X has been chosen as the numeraire. The relative price of the non-traded good Y is denoted by p. The production structure of the model is expressed by the revenue function: $R(1, p, K, L) = \max \{X(L_X, K_X, V_X) + pY(L_Y, K_Y, V_Y): L_X + L_Y = L, K_X + K_Y = K\}$, where L is the actual level of labor employment and K is the stock of capital in the economy. The fixed endowments of specific factors V_i have been suppressed in the revenue function. Denoting subscripts as partial derivatives and employing the envelope property, it follows: $R_p = Y$, being the output of good Y, and $R_{pp} > 0$, expressing the positive supply curve. The stability condition of this system requires that sector Y is labor-intensive relative to sector X.[5] This gives: $R_{pL} > 0$ and $R_{pK} < 0$, by the Rybczynski theorem. The rental on capital r equals R_K. The specificity of factors V_i results in $R_{KK} < 0$ and $R_{KL} > 0$.[6] Let w denote the wage rate, then the level of total employment is determined by

$$R_L(1, p, K, L) = w, \tag{6.1}$$

where $R_{LL} < 0$ due to diminishing returns of labor.[7] Note that the wage rate is set by the government according to the goods prices, i.e., $w = w(1, p)$, with $\partial w / \partial p > 0$ and $(p/w)(\partial w / \partial p) \leq 1$. This real wage indexation results in economy-wide unemployment, measured by $\bar{L} - L$, where $\bar{L}$ is the exogenously given labor endowment in the economy.

We now consider the demand side of the economy. Domestic residents consume both goods, C_X and C_Y, while foreign tourists demand only the non-traded good Y. Let $D_Y(p, T)$ be the tourists' demand for good Y, where T is a shift parameter capturing the tastes and other exogenously given variables, for example, foreign income, with $\partial D_Y / \partial T > 0$. The market-clearing condition for the non-traded good requires the equality of demand (where this consists of domestic and tourist demand) and supply:

$$C_Y + D_Y(p, T) = R_p(1, p, K, L). \tag{6.2}$$

This equation determines the relative price of the non-traded good, p.

In a dynamic setting, domestic savings out of consumption of goods X and Y are used for capital accumulation:

$$\dot{K} = R(1, p, K, L) - C_X - pC_Y, \tag{6.3}$$

where the dot over the variable denotes its time derivative. Note that in exchange for tourism exports, capital is imported at a given world price which is normalized to unity.

Under the budget constraint (6.3), the domestic residents maximize the present value of their instantaneous utility, $U(\cdot)$. The overall welfare W is therefore:

$$W = \int_0^\infty U(C_X, C_Y) e^{-\rho t} dt, \tag{6.4}$$

where ρ represents the rate of time preference. Let λ denote the shadow price of capital in the economy. The first-order conditions with respect to C_X and C_Y are:

$$U_X(C_X, C_Y) = \lambda, \tag{6.5}$$

$$U_Y(C_X, C_Y) = \lambda p. \tag{6.6}$$

where U_X and U_Y denote marginal utilities of consuming good X and Y respectively.

In addition, the evolution of the shadow price of capital is governed by the following dynamic equation:

$$\dot{\lambda} = \lambda[\rho - R_K(1, p, K, L)], \tag{6.7}$$

which is a function of the difference between the subjective rate of time preference and the return to capital.

Using the above framework, we can examine the resource allocation and welfare effects of tourism on the economy in the short and long runs.

Short-run Equilibrium

In the *short*-run equilibrium, the initial amount of capital K is given by K_0 as its shadow price is fixed.[8] For a given value of the tourism parameter T, the system can be solved for L, p, C_X and C_Y by using equations (6.1), (6.2), (6.5) and (6.6) as functions of K, λ and T; $L = L(K, \lambda, T)$; $p = p(K, \lambda, T)$, $C_X = C_X(K, \lambda, T)$ and $C_Y = C_Y(K, \lambda, T)$. An increase in capital, K, raises the productivity of labor and hence labor employment ($\partial L/\partial K > 0$). However, the increase in capital lowers the supply of good Y by the Rybczynski effect, which raises its price ($\partial p/\partial K > 0$). This in turn lowers the demand for good Y by domestic residents ($\partial C_Y/\partial K < 0$). Furthermore, for $U_{XY} > 0$ the decreased consumption of good Y lowers the marginal utility of good X, which reduces the demand for good X ($\partial C_X/\partial K < 0$). Similarly, a rise in the shadow price of capital lowers the demand for labor in production ($\partial L/\partial \lambda < 0$) and the demand for goods in consumption ($\partial C_X/\partial \lambda < 0$ and $\partial C_Y/\partial \lambda < 0$). This results in the fall in the relative price of the non-traded good ($\partial p/\partial \lambda < 0$). In addition, a rise in tourism increases the demand for the non-traded good and hence its price ($\partial p/\partial T > 0$). This leads to an increase in employment in the economy, $\partial L/\partial T > 0$. However, the higher price also reduces the demand for both goods by domestic residents ($\partial C_X/\partial T < 0$ and $\partial C_Y/\partial T < 0$).[9]

Dynamics

We can utilize the short-run comparative-static results to characterize the local dynamics of the model. The dynamics of domestic capital accumulation in equation (6.3) and its shadow prices in equation (6.7) are:

$$\dot{K} = R[1, p(K, \lambda, T), K, L(K, \lambda, T)] - C_X(K, \lambda, T) - p(K, \lambda, T)C_Y(K, \lambda, T), \quad (6.8)$$

$$\dot{\lambda} = \lambda\{\rho - R_K[1, p(K, \lambda, T), K, L(K, \lambda, T)]\}. \quad (6.9)$$

Taking a linear approximation of the above system around the equilibria, we have:

$$\begin{bmatrix} \dot{K} \\ \dot{\lambda} \end{bmatrix} = \begin{bmatrix} A & B \\ M & N \end{bmatrix} \begin{bmatrix} K - \tilde{K} \\ \lambda - \tilde{\lambda} \end{bmatrix}, \quad (6.10)$$

where a tilde (~) over a variable denotes its steady-state level. Note that $A = R_K + R_L(\partial L/\partial K) + D_Y(\partial p/\partial K) - \partial C/\partial K$, $B = R_L(\partial L/\partial \lambda) + D_Y(\partial p/\partial \lambda) - \partial C/\partial \lambda$, $M = -\lambda[R_{KK} + R_{KL}(\partial L/\partial K) + R_{Kp}(\partial p/\partial K)]$ and $N = -\lambda[R_{Kp}(\partial p/\partial \lambda) + R_{KL}(\partial L/\partial \lambda)]$.[10] The signs of A, B, M and N are in general indeterminate. However, for our purposes, $A > 0$, $M > 0$ and $N < 0$ when $R_{Kp} < 0$ and $R_{Lp} > \partial w/\partial p$, i.e., the non-traded good Y is labor-intensive, and $R_{LL}/R_{LK} < R_{pL}/R_{pK} < R_{KL}/R_{KK}$. Furthermore, $B > 0$ when $\eta = -(\partial D_Y/\partial p)(p/D_Y) \geq 1$, i.e., the price elasticity of the demand for good Y by tourists is elastic.

The schedules of $\dot{K} = 0$ and $\dot{\lambda} = 0$ are depicted in Figure 6.1, with the slopes of $d\lambda/dK|_K = -A/B < 0$ and $d\lambda/dK|_\lambda = -M/N > 0$. Under these conditions, the determinant of the above coefficient matrix is negative and the steady-state equilibrium is at point E which is a saddle point with one negative and one positive eigenvalue. For the given initial value of the capital stock K_0, we can obtain from (6.10) the following solutions for the capital stock and its shadow price around their steady-state values:

$$K_t = \tilde{K} + (K_0 - \tilde{K})e^{\mu t}, \quad (6.11)$$

$$\lambda_t = \tilde{\lambda} + \theta(K_t - \tilde{K}), \quad (6.12)$$

where $\theta = (\mu - A)/B < 0$, and μ is the negative eigenvalue in equation (6.10). The stable arm of the relation between K and λ, as shown by equation (6.12) and also depicted by the SS schedule in Figure 6.1, indicates that a decrease in K leads to an increase in its shadow price λ, and vice versa.

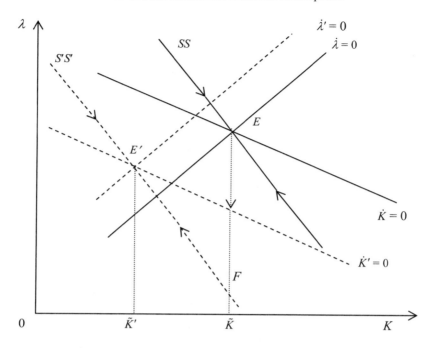

Figure 6.1   An expansion of tourism

Steady State

The long-run equilibrium is obtained by using the short-run equilibrium conditions in equations (6.1), (6.2), (6.4) and (6.5), together with no adjustments in the capital stock and its shadow price in equations (6.3) and (6.7) as:

$$R(1,\ \tilde{p},\ \tilde{K},\ \tilde{L}) - \tilde{C}_X - \tilde{p}\ \tilde{C}_Y = 0, \tag{6.13}$$

$$R_K(1,\ \tilde{p},\ \tilde{K},\ \tilde{L}) = \rho. \tag{6.14}$$

Equations (6.1), (6.2), (6.4), (6.5), (6.13) and (6.14) contain six endogenous variables, $\tilde{L}$, $\tilde{p}$, $\tilde{C}_X$, $\tilde{C}_Y$, $\tilde{K}$ and $\tilde{\lambda}$, along with a tourism parameter, T. This system can be used to solve for the impact of tourism in the long run. An increase in tourism on the long-run price of the non-traded good Y is:

$$d\tilde{p}/dT = S(\partial D_Y/\partial T)(p^2 U_{XX} + U_{YY} - 2pU_{XY})/\Delta > 0, \tag{6.15}$$

where $U_{XX} < 0$, $U_{YY} < 0$, and $\Delta < 0$.[11] Note that $S = R_{KK}R_{LL} - R_{KL}^2 > 0$ by the concavity of the production functions. Hence, an increase in tourism will necessarily improve the tertiary terms of trade.

In addition, from equations (6.1) and (6.14), we can obtain the long-run effects of tourism on the capital stock and labor employment, as follows:

$$d\tilde{L}/dT = [R_{pK}R_{KK}(R_{KL}/R_{KK} - R_{pL}/R_{pK})/S](d\tilde{p}/dT) > 0, \qquad (6.16)$$

$$d\tilde{K}/dT = -[R_{pK}R_{KL}(R_{LL}/R_{LK} - R_{pL}/R_{pK})/S](d\tilde{p}/dT) < 0, \qquad (6.17)$$

where recalling that $R_{LL}/R_{LK} < R_{pL}/R_{pK} < R_{KL}/R_{KK}$ for stability. An increase in tourism will increase employment in the long run, but at the expense of capital accumulation in the economy. The reduction in the capital stock can be seen in Figure 6.1. A boom in tourism shifts both schedules of $\dot{K} = 0$ and $\dot{\lambda} = 0$ to the left.[12] Since the capital stock is given at time 0, the adjustment path takes the system from point E to point F. This immediately leads to a fall in the shadow price of capital,[13] and consequent reductions in capital accumulation from point F to a new equilibrium at point E'.[14]

Welfare

We are now in a position to examine the effect of tourism on overall welfare of the economy. Total welfare in equation (6.4) can be obtained from the sum of the instantaneous utility $Z = U(C_X, C_Y)$. Following Turnovsky (1999, p. 138), the adjustment path of Z is: $Z_t = \tilde{Z} + [Z(0) - \tilde{Z}]e^{\mu t}$, where $Z(0)$ denotes the utility at time 0. Total welfare is $W = \tilde{Z}/\rho + [Z(0) - \tilde{Z}]/(\rho - \mu)$, and the welfare change is: $dW = [dZ(0) - (\mu/\rho)d\tilde{Z}]/(\rho - \mu),$]where $-\mu/\rho$ (> 0) is the discount factor. Utilizing equation (6.13), the change of total welfare by a tourism boom is:

$$dW/dT = [\lambda/(\rho - \mu)]\{D_Y[dp(0)/dT - (\mu/\rho)(d\tilde{p}/dT)] + R_L[dL(0)/dT$$
$$- (\mu/\rho)(d\tilde{L}/dT)] - (\mu/\rho)R_K(d\tilde{K}/dT)\}, \qquad (6.18)$$

where $p(0)$ and $L(0)$ denote the relative price of the non-traded good and labor employment at time 0. Since the capital stock is given at time 0, a tourist boom immediately increases the demand for good Y and hence its price. As a consequence, higher labor demand is needed for producing more good Y. These results can be derived from using equations (6.1), (6.2), (6.5), (6.6) and (6.13) as

$$dp(0)/dT = -(\partial D_Y/\partial T)R_{LL}(2pU_{XY} - p^2U_{XX} - U_{YY})/H > 0, \qquad (6.19)$$

$$dL(0)/dT = -(R_{pL}/R_{LL})[dp(0)/dT] > 0, \qquad (6.20)$$

where $H > 0$.[15]

The welfare effects of tourism in equation (6.18) depend on the changes in the terms of trade, labor employment and capital accumulation. An expansion of tourism increases the initial and steady-state relative price of the non-traded good, Y, which yields a gain in the terms of trade as shown in the first term in the curly bracket in equation (6.18). While the static terms-of-trade effect is well known in the literature, the impact of tourism on labor employment and capital accumulation is generally not mentioned in the literature. These are of critical importance in analyzing economic welfare. As indicated in second term of equation (6.18), tourism can generate more labor employment in the short and the long run via the higher price of the non-traded good. However, the higher price of the non-traded good can reduce the demand for capital, causing a welfare loss as shown by the third term in equation (6.18). Due to these conflicting forces, the welfare effect of tourism is in general ambiguous. To illustrate the strength of our results we will use simulations to ascertain the welfare effects of tourism both in the short and the long run.

6.3   SIMULATIONS

To calibrate the effects of an increase in tourism on the endogenous variables of the economy, we need to specific functional forms for the utility and production functions.

Specifications

We assume that the production of the traded and non-traded goods takes place with the help of Cobb–Douglas production functions:

$$X = A \, L_X^{\alpha_1} K_X^{\alpha_2} V_X^{1-\alpha_1-\alpha_2} , \qquad (6.21)$$

$$Y = B \, L_Y^{\beta_1} K_Y^{\beta_2} V_Y^{1-\beta_1-\beta_2} , \qquad (6.22)$$

where A and B are the constant technology factors, and α_i and β_i are respectively the i-th factor shares in productions of goods X and Y. Total employment for sectors X and Y in the economy is given by

$$L = L_X + L_Y. \qquad (6.23)$$

Similarly, capital allocation between sectors is:

$$K_{-1} = K_X + K_Y. \qquad (6.24)$$

Note that total capital is inherited from the past and is fixed in the short run, but it can be freely allocated between both sectors. This is the reason why total capital is indexed by −1 (it is predetermined in the short-run equilibrium) and capital allocation in each sector is not indexed.

Given the wage rate w, the rental rate r and the relative price of the non-traded good p, the production sector solves the program: Max $X + pY - w(L_X + L_Y) - r(K_X + K_Y)$, subject to $X = A L_X^{\alpha_1} K_X^{\alpha_2}$ and $Y = B L_Y^{\beta_1} K_Y^{\beta_2}$. Here, the specific factors V_X and V_Y are normalized to unity. The first-order conditions with respect to L_i and K_i yield equilibrium allocation of labor and capital between sectors:

$$\begin{aligned} w &= \alpha_1 A (K_X/L_X)^{\alpha_2} L_X^{\alpha_1 + \alpha_2 - 1} \\ &= p\beta_1 B (K_Y/L_Y)^{\beta_2} L_Y^{\beta_1 + \beta_2 - 1}, \end{aligned} \tag{6.25}$$

$$\begin{aligned} r &= \alpha_2 A (L_X/K_X)^{\alpha_1} K_X^{\alpha_1 + \alpha_2 - 1} \\ &= p\beta_2 B (L_Y/K_Y)^{\beta_1} K_Y^{\beta_1 + \beta_2 - 1}. \end{aligned} \tag{6.26}$$

The resulting factor-price frontiers can be deduced from equations (6.25) and (6.26):

$$(w/\alpha_1)^{1-\alpha_2} (r/\alpha_2)^{\alpha_2} L_X^{1-\alpha_1-\alpha_2} = A, \tag{6.27}$$

$$(w/\beta_1)^{1-\beta_2} (r/\beta_2)^{\beta_2} L_Y^{1-\beta_1-\beta_2} = pB. \tag{6.28}$$

In addition, real wage, denoted by w_c, in the economy is assumed to be rigid in the sense that it is indexed to the price of the consumption goods p_c:

$$w_c = w/p_c, \tag{6.29}$$

where p_c is defined in equation (6.32).

On the demand side of the economy, we utilize the CES functional form for the instantaneous utility function of domestic households:

$$U = [b^{1/(1+\sigma)} C_X^{\sigma/(1+\sigma)} + \overline{b}^{\sigma/(1+\sigma)} C_Y^{\sigma/(1+\sigma)}]^{(1+1/\sigma)(1-\gamma)}/(1 - \gamma), \tag{6.30}$$

where $b \in [0, 1]$ and $\overline{b} = 1 - b$ are the parameters, γ expresses the index of relative risk aversion and σ captures the elasticity of substitution between the two goods with $1 + \sigma \geq 0$. From the first-order conditions of utility maximization, we derive

$$bC_Y/\overline{b} C_X = 1/p^{(1+\sigma)}. \tag{6.31}$$

Let $C = [b^{1/(1+\sigma)} C_X^{\sigma/(1+\sigma)} + \bar{b}^{\sigma/(1+\sigma)} C_Y^{\sigma/(1+\sigma)}]^{(1+1/\sigma)}$ denote aggregate consumption. Then by using equation (6.31) we obtain that $C = (C_X/b)(b + \bar{b} \, p^{-\sigma})^{(1+\sigma)/\sigma}$. The relative price of the consumption aggregate is then defined by $p_c C = C_X + p C_Y$, which can be solved for p_c as

$$p_c = (b + \bar{b} \, p^{-\sigma})^{-1/\sigma}. \tag{6.32}$$

Therefore, the current utility of domestic households can be expressed as:
$U(C) = C^{(1-\gamma)}/(1 - \gamma) = [(C_X/b)(b + \bar{b} \, p^{-\sigma})^{(1+\sigma)/\sigma}]^{(1-\gamma)}/(1 - \gamma)$.

The model is closed by using the market-clearing condition for the non-traded good Y:

$$C_Y + D_Y = Y, \tag{6.33}$$

and the demand for the non-traded good by tourists is specified as

$$D_Y = T/p^{\eta}, \tag{6.34}$$

where η measures the price elasticity of demand for good Y by tourists. Tourists spending T, measured in terms of the traded good, is exogenous and tourists consume only non-traded good.

Finally, the budget constraint for each period is:

$$K - K_{-1} + C_X + p C_Y = X + p Y. \tag{6.35}$$

Note that the balance of payments is in equilibrium for each period. From equations (6.33) and (6.35), we can deduce that: $K - K_{-1} + C_X - X = p D_Y$. That is, the excess demand for capital and the traded good is financed by income receipts from tourism.

Total welfare of domestic residents is the discounted sum of the instantaneous utility:

$$W = \Sigma_{t=0}^{\infty} (1 - \rho)^t [C_X(b + \bar{b} \, p^{-\sigma})^{1+1/\sigma}]^{1-\gamma}/(1 - \gamma).$$

This function is maximized relatively to capital and the consumption of the traded good under the series of budget constraints:

$$K - K_{-1} + C_X(b + \bar{b} \, p^{-\sigma})/b = X + p Y = w(L_X + L_Y) + r K_{-1} + v_X V_X + v_Y V_Y.$$

Solving this maximization program with respect to C_X and K, we obtain the first-order conditions:

$$(1 - \rho)^t C_X^{-\gamma} (b + \bar{b} \, p^{-\sigma})^{(1+1/\sigma)(1-\gamma)-1} = \delta/b \text{ and } \delta - \delta_{+1}(1 + r_{+1}) = 0,$$

where δ is the Langrange multiplier. After the elimination of δ and δ_{+1}, we have

$$(1 + r_{+1})(1 - \rho) = (C_X/C_{X,+1})^{-\gamma}[(b + \overline{b}\,p^{-\sigma})/(b + \overline{b}p_{+1}^{-\sigma})]^{(1+1/\sigma)(1-\gamma)-1} \quad (6.36)$$

Calibrations

Equations (6.21)–(6.36) consist of sixteen endogenous variables and a shift parameter of tourist spending T for the economy. We utilize the German data to calibrate the short- and long-run impact of an increase in tourism on the economy. It is assumed that tourists' spending is 0 in the reference steady state. We choose $p = 0.9488$, $X + pY = 1.3909$ and $L = 27.27$, which represent the averages values of these variables for Germany for the period 1996–2002. Units are in trillions of 1995 euros and in millions of persons. We set: $T = 0$, $\sigma = -0.5$, $b = 1/3$, $\rho = 0.05$, $\alpha_1 = 0.30$, $\alpha_2 = 0.50$, $\beta_1 = 0.5$, $\beta_2 = 0.10$, $\lambda = 0.5$ and $\eta = 1$.[16] Note that the labor intensity of good Y is captured by the chosen values of α_i and β_i. The steady-state values of the endogenous variables can be then computed according to:

$D_Y = 0$, $X = (X + pY)/[1 + (\overline{b}/b)p^{-\sigma}]$,

$Y = (X + pY - X)/p$,

$C_Y = Y$, $C_X = X$,

$r = 1/(1 - \rho) - 1$,

$L_Y = [\beta_1 pY/(\alpha_1 X + \beta_1 pY)]L$,

$L = L_X + L_Y$,

$K_Y = \beta_2 pY/r$,

$B = Y/L_Y^{\beta_1} K_Y^{\beta_2}$,

$w = p\beta_1 B^{1/(1-\beta_2)}(p\beta_2/r)^{\beta_2/(1-\beta_2)} L_Y^{-(1-\beta_1-\beta_2)/(1-\beta_2)}$,

$K_X = \alpha_2 X/r$,

$A = X/(L_X^{\alpha_1} K_X^{\alpha_2})$, ,

$U = \left[b^{1/(1+\sigma)}C_X^{\sigma/(1+\sigma)} + \overline{b}^{1/(1+\sigma)}C_Y^{\sigma/(1+\sigma)} \right]^{(1+1/\sigma)(1-\gamma)}/(1 - \gamma)$,

$K = K_X + K_Y$, and

$p_c = (b + \overline{b}\,p^{-\sigma})^{-m-1/\sigma}$.

The reference steady state values are therefore: $C_X = 0.4718$, $C_Y = 0.9687$, $D_Y = 0$, $K = 6.2285$, $K_X = 4.4821$, $K_Y = 1.7464$, $L = 27.27$, $L_X = 6.4212$, $L_Y = 20.8488$, $p = 0.9488$, $p_c = 0.9657$, $r = 0.0526$, $U = 2.4003$, $w = 0.02204$, $X = 0.4718$ and $Y = 0.9687$.

There is one anticipated variable C_{X+1} and one predetermined variable K_{-1} in the system. The eigenvalues in the neighbourhood of the reference steady state are equal to 0.9717 and 1.092. So the local condition of existence and uniqueness are satisfied (one of the eigenvalues must be less than one and the other larger than one to get the existence and uniqueness of a solution). As we will compare sums of discounted utilities when the convergence speed to the steady state is slow, we simulated the model over 250 periods.[17]

As for reference simulations, we let tourist spending T to increase from 0 to 0.01 (which means by 10 billions euros, the German value-added in non-tradable goods being 982 billion euros). We obtain the short- and long-run impacts of tourism on the economy, as plotted in Figure 6.2:

1. C_X and C_Y immediately increase above their reference values, and then progressively decrease but C_Y ends with a level lower than its reference value.
2. L_X immediately falls and then slightly increases, while L_Y immediately rises and then slightly decreases. This gives that total employment L to rise initially and progressively decreases but stays above its reference level.
3. K_X immediately declines and continuously falls, while K_Y immediately rises and then declines. However, total K progressively decreases to a lower level.
4. X immediately decreases and then progressively decreases to a lower level, while Y immediately rises and then progressively decreases to a level which is higher than its reference value.
5. p immediately increases above its reference value, and then progressively decreases but stays above its reference value.
6. U immediately increases above its reference value, and then progressively decreases to a value that is above its reference value. The sum of discounted utilities increases from 343.6305 to 344.0061. Hence, a rise in tourism improves total welfare in the long run.

Consider next the case that the non-traded sector Y is *strongly* labor-intensive relative to the traded sector X. For this case, we choose $\beta_2 = 0.001$ and leave the other parameters the same as before. The consequent eigenvalues are 0.9683 and 1.093, and the reference steady-state values are the same as in the previous case but for: $K = 4.4996$ and $K_Y = 0.0175$. Consider reference simulations by increasing tourist spending T from 0 to 0.01. We obtain the short- and long-run impacts of tourism, as plotted in Figure 6.3. Compared to the results in Figures 6.2 and 6.3, the patterns of

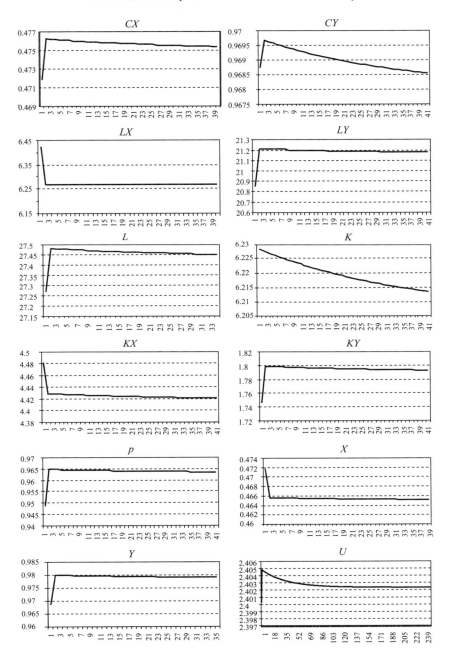

Figure 6.2   Effects of tourism (β₂ = 0.10)

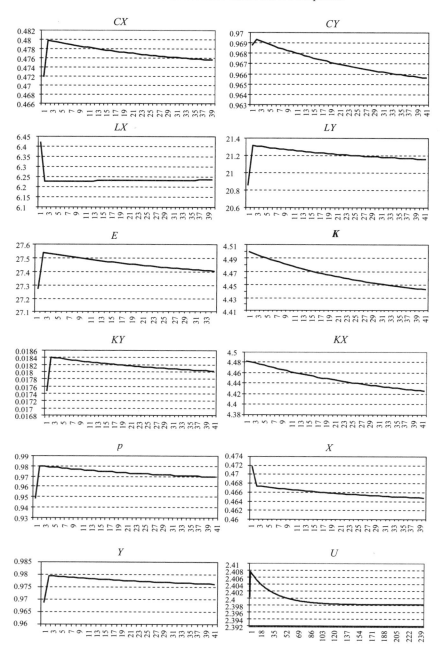

Figure 6.3   Effects of tourism ($\beta_2 = 0.001$)

changes in all the endogenous variables are the same. However, in Figure 6.3, the rise in total employment L is smaller but the fall in capital K is larger. These differences render a different effect of tourism on utility and welfare: although U immediately increases above its reference value, it progressively decreases and reaches a value below its reference value. Therefore, the sum of discounted utilities decreases from 343.6305 to 343.5839. Thus, owing to the fall in the capital stock, a rise in tourism can lower total welfare when the traded sector is strongly capital-intensive relative to the non-traded tourism sector.

6.4   CONCLUSIONS

Using a dynamic general-equilibrium framework, this chapter has examined the short- and long-run effects of tourism on labor employment, capital accumulation and resident welfare for an open economy with unemployment via wage indexation. A tourism boom improves the terms of trade, increases labor employment, but lowers capital accumulation if the non-traded tourism sector is labor-intensive relative to the other traded sector. Nonetheless, this reduction in the capital stock depends on the degree of factor intensity. When the traded sector is not strongly capital-intensive, the fall in capital would not be so severe and the expansion of tourism improves welfare. However, when the traded sector is strongly capital-intensive, the fall in capital can be a dominant factor and total welfare falls. This immiserizing result of tourism on resident welfare is confirmed by the German data.

ACKNOWLEDGEMENTS

The authors would like to thank the participants at the Second International Tourism and Sustainable Development conference organized by CRENoS, Universities of Cagliari and Sassari, Fondazione Eni Enrico Mattei and World Bank, Sardinia 16–17 September, 2005 for useful comments. The work described in this chapter was supported by a grant from the Research Grants Council of the Hong Kong Special Administrative Region, China (Project No. CUHK4603/05H).

NOTES

1.   The economic doldrums were halted and the GDP growth was 8.2 per cent in 2004, well above the average 4.8 per cent over the previous 20 years. The details can be found in the Budget Speech by the Hong Kong Financial Secretary on March 16, 2005. The simulations

in this chapter have been done on the basis of German data. Hong Kong data is not easily accessible. Moreover, the results are robust with regard to the choice of the country.

2. See Copeland (1991) and Hazari and Sgro (2004).
3. See Brecher (1974) for the minimum wage model in a Heckscher–Ohlin setting.
4. See Jones (1971), Neary (1978) and Khan (1982) for the specific-factor model, and Beladi and Marjit (1992) for related applications. Also see Batra and Beladi (1990) and Chao and Conlon (1993) for the specific-factor model with unemployment.
5. The stability analysis is provided in the Appendix.
6. Letting $c^i(\ \cdot\ )$ be the ith sector unit cost function, by perfect competition we have: $c^X(w, r, v_X) = 1$ and $c^Y(w, r, v_Y) = p$, where w is the fixed minimum wage and v_i are the rates of return on the specific factors V_i. Owing to the existence of the specific factors, the capital return r depends on the good price p and the factor suppliers L and K.
7. A recent study on a generalized minimum wage model can be found in Neary (1985) and Kreickemeier (2005). Also see Hatzipanayoyou and Michael (1995) and Michael and Hatzipanayoyou (1999) for endogenous labor supply.
8. See Sen (1990) and Turnovsky (1999, p. 108) for the definition of a short-run equilibrium.
9. Mathematical derivations of the comparative-static results are provided in the Appendix.
10. Following Brock (1996), we use $\partial C/\partial K = \partial C_X/\partial K + p(\partial C_Y/\partial K)$, $\partial C/\partial \lambda = \partial C_X/\partial \lambda + p(\partial C_Y/\partial \lambda)$ and $\partial C/\partial T = \partial C_X/\partial T + p(\partial C_Y/\partial T)$.
11. Note that $\Delta = R_{pK}R_{KK}(R_{KL}/R_{KK} - R_{pL}/R_{pK})\{(U_{XY} - pU_{XX})[R_{1L} - p(\partial w/\partial p)](U_{XY} - pU_{XX}) + (U_{YY} - pU_{XY})(R_{pL} - \partial w/\partial p)\} + R_{pK}R_{LK}(R_{pL}/R_{pK} - R_{LL}/R_{LK})[R_{1K}(U_{XY} - pU_{XX}) + R_{pK}(U_{YY} - pU_{XY})] - (U_{XY} - pU_{XX})(R_KR_{LK} - R_LR_{KK})(\partial w/\partial p) - (R_{LL}R_{KK} - R_{LK}^2)Q < 0$, where $Q = \lambda + D_Y(\eta - 1)(U_{XY} - pU_{XX}) - (\partial D_Y/\partial p)(pU_{XY} - U_{YY}) + R_{pp}(2pU_{XY} - p^2U_{XX} - U_{YY}) > 0$ by the stability conditions: $\eta \ge 1$, $R_{pL} > \partial w/\partial p$, $R_{pK} < 0$ and $R_{LL}/R_{LK} < R_{pL}/R_{pK} < R_{KL}/R_{KK}$.
12. Holding λ fixed, the shifts of $\dot{K} = 0$ and $\dot{\lambda} = 0$ in Figure 6.1 are:
$dK/dT|_K = -[R_L(\partial L/\partial T) + D_Y(\partial p/\partial T) - (\partial C/\partial T)]/A < 0$ and
$dK/dT|_\lambda = \lambda[R_{LK}(\partial L/\partial T) + R_{pK}(\partial p/\partial T)]/M < 0$, where
$R_{LK}(\partial L/\partial T) + R_{pK}(\partial p/\partial T) = (\partial D_Y/\partial T)R_{pK}R_{LK}[R_{pL}/R_{pK} - R_{LL}/R_{LK} - (\partial w/\partial p)/R_{pK}](U_{XX}U_{YY} - U_{XY}^2)/J < 0$.
13. From (6.1), (6.2), (6.5), (6.6) and (6.13), we can obtain: $d\lambda(0)/dT = (\partial D_Y/\partial T)\{[D_YR_{LL} - R_L(R_{pL} - \partial w/\partial p)](U_{XX}U_{YY} - U_{XY}^2) + \lambda R_{LL}(U_{XY} - pU_{XX})]\}/H < 0$, where $H = -R_{LL}Q - R_{pL}[R_{1L}(U_{XY} - pU_{XX}) + R_{pL}(U_{YY} - pU_{XY})] + R_L(U_{XY} - U_{XX})(\partial w/\partial p) > 0$.
14. The change in the steady-state value of λ depends on the relative shifts of the schedules of $\dot{\lambda} = 0$ and $\dot{K} = 0$; specifically, $d\bar{\lambda}/d\alpha = (\partial D_Y/\partial T)\{(R_{LL}R_{KK} - R_{LK}^2)[D_Y + \lambda(U_{XY} - pU_{XX})] + (U_{XX}U_{YY} - U_{XY}^2)R_{pK}[R_KR_{LK}(R_{pL}/R_{pK} - R_{LL}/R_{LK} - (\partial w/\partial p)/R_{pK}) + R_LR_{KK}(R_{LK}/R_{KK} - R_{pL}/R_{pK} + (\partial w/\partial p)/R_{pK})]\}/\Delta > $ or < 0.
15. See footnote 13 for the positive sign of H.
16. Allowing the price elasticity to be different to 1 would not change the results qualitatively.
17. The model was simulated and its eigenvalues computed with the software Dynare, which was run under Matlab. Dynare was developed by Michel Juillard, and can be unloaded from the website http://www.cepremap.cnrs.fr/dynare.

REFERENCES

Batra, R.N. and H. Beladi (1990), 'Pattern of trade between underemployed economies', *Economica,* **57**, 485–93.

Beladi, H. and S. Marjit (1992), 'Foreign capital and protectionism', *Canadian Journal of Economics*, **25**, 233–8.

Brecher, R.A. (1974), 'Minimum wage rates and the pure theory of international trade', *Quarterly Journal of Economics*, **88**, 98–116.

Brock, P.L. (1996), 'International transfers, the relative price of non-traded goods, and the current account', *Canadian Journal of Economics*, **29**, 161–80.

Chao, C.C. and J. Conlon (1993), 'Unemployment, wage indexation and commercial policies', *Journal of Macroeconomics*, **15**, 165–74.

Chao, C.C., B.R. Hazari, J.P. Laffargue, P.M. Sgro and E.S.H. Yu (2006), 'Tourism, Dutch disease and welfare in an open dynamic economy', *Japanese Economic Review*, **57**, 501–15.

Copeland, B.R. (1991), 'Tourism, welfare and de-industrialization in a small open economy', *Economica*, **58**, 515–29.

Harris, J.R. and M. Todaro (1970), 'Migration, unemployment and development: a two-sector analysis', *American Economic Review*, **60**, 126–42.

Hatzipanayoyou, P. and M.S. Michael (1995), 'Tariffs, quotas and voluntary export restraints with endogenous labor supply', *Journal of Economics*, **62**, 185–201.

Hazari, B.R. and P.M. Sgro (1995), 'Tourism and growth in a dynamic model of trade', *Journal of International Trade and Economic Development*, **4**, 243–52.

Hazari, B.R. and P.M. Sgro (2004), *Tourism, Trade and National Welfare*, Amsterdam: Elsevier.

Hazari, B.R., J.-J. Nowak, M. Sahli and D. Zdravevski (2003), 'Tourism and regional immiserization', *Pacific Economic Review*, **8**, 269–78.

Jones, R.W. (1971), 'A three factor model in theory, trade, and history', in J.N. Bhagwati, R.A. Mundell, R.W. Jones and J. Vanek (eds), *Trade, Balance of Payments and Growth*, Amsterdam: North-Holland.

Khan, M.A. (1982), 'Social opportunity costs and immiserizing growth: some observations on the long run versus the short', *Quarterly Journal of Economics*, **97**, 353–62.

Kreickemeier, U. (2005), 'Unemployment and the welfare effects of trade policy', *Canadian Journal of Economics*, **38**, 194–210.

Michael, M.S. and P. Hatzipanayoyou (1999), 'General equilibrium effects of import constraints under variable labor supply, public goods and income taxation', *Economica*, **66**, 389–401.

Neary, J.P. (1978), 'Short-run capital specificity and the pure theory of international trade', *Economic Journal*, **88**, 488–510.

Neary, J.P. (1985), 'International factor mobility, minimum wage rates, and factor price equalization, a synthesis', *Quarterly Journal of Economics*, **100**, 551–70.

Nowak, J.-J., M. Sahli and P.M. Sgro (2003), 'Tourism, trade and domestic welfare', *Pacific Economic Review*, **8**, 245–58.

Sen, P. (1990), 'Terms-of-trade shocks and the current account in a monetary economy', *Economica*, **57**, 383–94.

Turnovsky, S.J. (1999), *International Macroeconomic Dynamics*, Cambridge, MA: The MIT Press.

APPENDIX

Short-run Comparative Statics

From (6.1), (6.2), (6.5) and (6.6), the comparative-static results in the short run are:

$$\partial L/\partial K = -\{[R_{pK}(R_{pL} - \partial w/\partial p) + R_{LK}(\partial D_Y/\partial p - R_{pp})](U_{XX}U_{YY} - U_{XY}^2) + \lambda R_{LK}U_{XX}\}/J > 0,$$

$$\partial C_X/\partial K = \lambda U_{XY}R_{LK}R_{pK}(R_{pL}/R_{pK} - R_{LL}/R_{LK})/J < 0,$$

$$\partial C_Y/\partial K = -\lambda U_{XX}R_{LK}R_{pK}(R_{pL}/R_{pK} - R_{LL}/R_{LK})/J < 0,$$

$$\partial p/\partial K = -R_{LK}R_{pK}(R_{pL}/R_{pK} - R_{LL}/R_{LK})(U_{XX}U_{YY} - U_{XY}^2)/J > 0,$$

$$\partial L/\partial \lambda = -(R_{pL} - \partial w/\partial p)(U_{XY} - pU_{XX})/J < 0,$$

$$\partial C_X/\partial \lambda = \{R_{pL}(R_{pL} - \partial w/\partial p)(U_{YY} - pU_{XY}) + R_{LL}[\lambda + (\partial D_Y/\partial p - R_{22})(U_{YY} - pU_{XY})]\}/J < 0,$$

$$\partial C_Y/\partial \lambda = \{R_{pL}(R_{pL} - \partial w/\partial p)(pU_{XX} - U_{XY}) + R_{LL}(\partial D_Y/\partial p - R_{pp})(pU_{XX} - U_{XY})\}/J < 0,$$

$$\partial p/\partial \lambda = R_{LL}(U_{XY} - pU_{XX})/J < 0,$$

$$\partial L/\partial T = (R_{pL} - \partial w/\partial p)(\partial D_Y/\partial T)(U_{XX}U_{YY} - U_{XY}^2)/J > 0,$$

$$\partial C_X/\partial T = \lambda R_{LL}U_{XY}(\partial D_Y/\partial T)/J < 0,$$

$$\partial C_Y/\partial T = -\lambda R_{LL}U_{XX}(\partial D_Y/\partial T)/J < 0,$$

$$\partial p/\partial T = -R_{LL}(\partial D_Y/\partial T)(U_{XX}U_{YY} - U_{XY}^2)/J > 0,$$

where $J = [R_{pL}(R_{pL} - \partial w/\partial p) + R_{LL}(\partial D_Y/\partial p - R_{pp})](U_{XX}U_{YY} - U_{xy}^2) + \lambda R_{LL}U_{XX} > 0$. We obtain the above signs when the stability condition, $R_{LL}/R_{LK} < R_{pL}/R_{pK} < R_{KL}/R_{KK}$, is imposed.

Using the above results, we can obtain:

$$B = R_L(\partial L/\partial \lambda) + D_Y(\partial p/\partial \lambda) - \partial C/\partial \lambda = \{(U_{XY} - pU_{XX})[R_{LL}D_Y(1 - \eta) - (R_{Lp} - \partial w/\partial p)(R_L - pR_{Lp})] - [R_{pL}(R_{pL} - \partial w/\partial p) + R_{LL}(\partial D_Y/\partial T)](U_{YY} - pU_{XY}) + R_{pp}R_{LL}(U_{YY} - 2pU_{XY} + p^2U_{XX})\}/J > 0,$$

$$M = -\lambda[R_{KK} + R_{KL}(\partial L/\partial K) + R_{Kp}(\partial p/\partial K)] = -\lambda R_{Kp}(\partial p/\partial K) - \lambda\{R_{pK}R_{KK}(R_{pL} - \partial w/\partial p)(R_{pL}/R_{pK} - R_{LK}/R_{KK})(U_{XX}U_{YY} - U_{XY}^2) + (R_{LL}R_{KK} - R_{LK}^2)[(\partial D_Y/\partial p - R_{pp})(U_{XX}U_{YY} - U_{XY}^2) + \lambda U_{XX}]\}/J > 0,$$

$$N = -\lambda[R_{Kp}(\partial p/\partial\lambda) + R_{KL}(\partial L/\partial\lambda)] = -\lambda R_{pK}R_{LK}[R_{LL}/R_{LK} - R_{pL}/R_{pK} +$$
$$(\partial w/\partial p)/R_{pK}](U_{XY} - pU_{XX})/J < 0,$$

where the condition that $\eta \geq 1$ is imposed in the sign of B. Furthermore, $R_L - pR_{Lp} = R_{L1} < 0$ because R_L is homogeneous of degree one in prices, and the subscript 1 denotes the price of the traded good X, which is relatively capital-intensive (i.e., $R_{L1} < 0$ and $R_{Lp} > 0$). In addition, for stability, we need $R_{pL} > \partial w/\partial p > 0$.

PART II

Measuring and Assessing the Economic
Sustainability of Tourism

7. The Volatility of Growth and Tourism Earnings

Anil Markandya and Suzette Pedroso-Galinato

7.1 INTRODUCTION

Research during the last few years on the determinants of long-run growth has looked at a new factor: the volatility of that growth and the links between volatility and development. It is undeniable that the more volatile countries (by many macroeconomic measures) are the developing ones. One also finds, among developing countries, a negative correlation between the degree of volatility (measured by the standard deviation of GDP growth or the standard deviation of the 'output gap'[1]) and the average level of GDP growth (Hnatkovska and Loayza, 2005). This relation does not, however, hold as clearly for developed countries, where the correlation is much weaker and, for some time periods, even positive.[2]

Hnatkovska and Loayza (2005) argue there are good reasons to think that the two variables are jointly determined. Countries that take higher risks in their investment strategies will achieve higher rewards, but also a greater variance in those rewards. But for this to work, mechanisms for risk sharing have to be well developed – something that is more likely to be the case in developed countries. Another argument for a positive relationship is that volatility, which is partly a manifestation of business cycles in the economy, results in 'creative destruction' (Schumpeter, 1939) of the less productive firms and, thereby, higher long-run growth. This, too, needs well developed financial markets and strong legal and government institutions of the kind not always found in developing countries.

On the other hand, a negative link between volatility and growth will occur if recessions cause reductions in government and private sector capital spending. It is this link, and the causal implications of higher volatility arising from political insecurity, macroeconomic instability and institutional weakness that has been studied by Rodrik (1991); Alesina et al. (1996); Judson and Orphanides (1996); Serven (1997); Hnatkovska and Loayza (2005), among others. The most recent findings of Hnatkovska and Loayza

(2005) show that the causality is from volatility to growth and the impact of the latter on the former is greater the more institutionally underdeveloped the country and the less able it is to conduct counter-cyclical policies. It is also greater when the country is undergoing intermediate stages of financial development. Furthermore, the impact of volatility, which is found in data going back to 1960, has become stronger over time, especially since 1980.

The papers cited above do not look at the reasons for the volatility in a systematic fashion. The variables mentioned above (institutional development, etc.) are introduced as control variables in regressions in which the growth rate of GDP is the dependent variable and volatility is the key explanatory variable. In trying to determine the causal effect of volatility on growth, however, some studies use instrumental variables. Hausman-type tests of whether volatility and growth are jointly endogenous result in a strong rejection of the hypothesis of exogenous volatility, which implies the need for instrumental variables as the appropriate method of estimation. The variables they use to instrument volatility are real exchange rate misalignment, frequency of banking crises, price volatility and volatility of terms of trade shocks.

In this chapter, we take a closer look at the determinants of volatility of GDP, and extend the discussion on this topic to measures of volatility of export earnings from different sources, including tourism. There is a debate, for example, on whether volatility of aid flows is a source of volatility in income and growth (Collier, 1999; Bulir and Hamann, 2003). One can also ask whether the structure of the economy, in terms of its share of GDP, affects volatility. And, for economies specializing in tourism, does that degree of specialization help them reduce the volatility of GDP growth? Brau et al. (2005) show quite convincingly that specialization in tourism has helped the growth performance of countries choosing that option. But it is also pertinent to ask whether it has reduced the volatility of that growth performance.

Volatility is a factor of interest, not only because of its effects on economic growth, but in its own right. Large fluctuations in earnings result in instability of employment, changes in government budgets and uncertainty about the degree to which resources will be utilized in the future. All this has welfare consequences. Hence, it is important to understand what measures can be taken to reduce the volatility and what (if any) are the costs of such measures.

This chapter addresses these questions with a focus on tourism. In section 7.2, data on growth, volatility of growth and the major associated factors (volatility of inflation, volatility of terms of trade, frequency of banking crises, exchange-rate misalignment structure of the economy in terms of shares of GDP from services and agriculture, volatility of aid flows, and tourism) are examined. Data are taken from 1980 to 2003 for 144 countries. In this, we are taking forward the work of Hnatkovska and Loayza (2005) and others. In section 7.3, using the same dataset, we compare the volatility of foreign earnings from a number of sources: aid, workers' remittances, exports of raw agricultural products, exports of food products, exports of fuels, exports of manufactures and receipts from tourism. What is of interest here is not only the relative volatility of these different sources, but also the correlation between them; a negative correlation points to sectors that are complementary in terms of reducing overall volatility. Since this chapter is focused on tourism, section 7.4 is devoted to understanding better the volatility of earnings in that sector. Factors that are examined include: volatility of inflation, volatility of terms of trade, exchange-rate stability, financial development, and a host of indicators that measure institutional development (bureaucracy, corruption, accountability), the presence of conflict (internal and external), and law and order. Section 7.5 provides some concluding remarks.

7.2   GROWTH AND VOLATILITY OF GROWTH

The data on growth and volatility of growth show, as others have found, a negative relationship between the two. Figures 7.1–7.5 and Table 7.1 give the correlations between the two variables and others of interest.[3]

The variability of macroeconomic fluctuations is measured by the standard deviation of per capita GDP gap (or output gap), which is the dependent variable. It involves estimating the trend of each country's per capita GDP data series, obtaining the gap between the actual and trend per capita GDP and calculating the standard deviation of the gap series. The explanatory variables include each country's total population every six years (TOTPOP), as well as observations that correspond to six-year averages per country for the institutional variables (bureaucracy quality (AVEBUR), corruption (AVECOR),

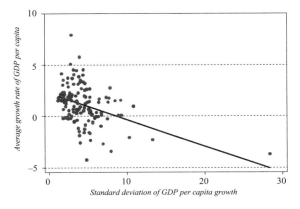

Figure 7.1   Growth and volatility (1980–2003): all countries

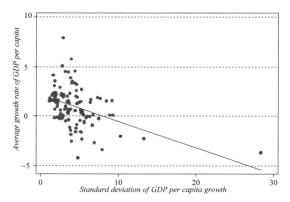

Figure 7.2 Growth and volatility (1980–2003): large countries

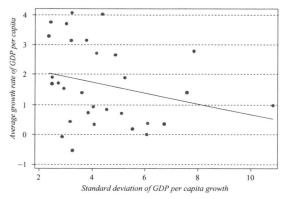

Figure 7.3 Growth and volatility (1980–2003): small countries

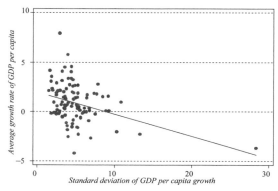

Figure 7.4 Growth and volatility (1980–2003): less developed countries

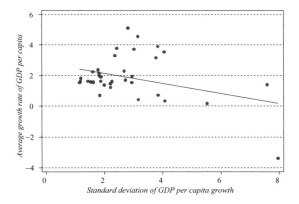

Source: World Bank (2005)

Figure 7.5 Growth and volatility (1980–2003): more developed countries

external conflicts (AVEECO) and internal conflicts (AVEINCO), and law and order (AVELAW), tourism receipts (AVETOUR), contribution of the services (AVESERV) and agricultural sectors (AVEAGR) to the economy. Also included are the volatility of inflation (SDINF), of the terms of trade (SDTOT), of international aid (SDAID) and of private capital flows (SDPCF). These are obtained by calculating the annual growth rates of these variables and then, the standard deviation of the growth rates for every six-year period. The sample used in the estimation consists of 133 countries, of which 35 are high-income countries. Data covered are from 1980 to 2003 and were divided into four phases, corresponding to 1980–1985, 1986–1991, 1992–1997, and 1998–2003. The list of variables is shown in Appendix Table 7.1A.

The heterogeneity across countries is captured by the income group classification of each country – low income (LOWI), lower middle income (LOWMI), upper middle income (UPMI) and high income, where the first three groups are represented by dummy variables and the last group is the base. Interaction variables were generated between two institutional variables (law and order, bureaucracy) and the income group dummies, because the income level of a country is highly correlated with the institutional variables. Table 7.1 shows the pairwise correlations of the variables. In terms of the correlation coefficients that are statistically significant at the 5 percent significance level, the results are as follows:

• There is a negative relationship between the volatility of growth and: volatility of private capital flows, share of services in the economy, average per capita income and the institutional variables. On the other

Table 7.1 Pairwise correlation of the variables

	OGAP	SDINF	SDTOT	AVETOUR	SDAID	TOTPOP	SDPCF	AVESERV	AVEAGR	AVEBUR	AVECOR	AVEECO	AVEICO	AVELAW	AVEINC
OGAP	1.00														
SDINF	0.07	1.00													
SDTOT	0.07	0.18*	1.00												
AVETOUR	-0.02	-0.05	-0.31*	1.00											
SDAID	0.10	0.07	-0.04	0.26*	1.00										
TOTPOP	0.14*	-0.03	0.00	-0.12*	-0.08	1.00									
SDPCF	-0.14*	0.08	0.03	-0.05	0.00	-0.05	1.00								
AVESERV	-0.22*	-0.20*	-0.45*	0.23*	0.11*	-0.15*	0.02	1.00							
AVEAGR	0.04	0.19*	0.36*	-0.15*	-0.26*	0.10*	-0.04	-0.58*	1.00						
AVEBUR	-0.15*	-0.18*	-0.43*	0.14*	0.20*	0.06	0.06	0.46*	0.60*	1.00					
AVECOR	-0.17*	-0.20*	-0.37*	-0.03	0.08	-0.04	0.00	0.43*	0.51*	0.71*	1.00				
AVEECO	-0.25*	-0.04	-0.32*	0.12*	0.09	-0.02	0.05	0.29*	0.40*	0.42*	0.35*	1.00			
AVEICO	-0.16*	-0.10*	-0.39*	0.17*	0.16*	0.02	0.05	0.38*	0.47*	0.58*	0.54*	0.68*	1.00		
AVELAW	-0.11*	-0.13*	-0.46*	0.12*	0.20*	0.01	0.05	0.44*	0.52*	0.73*	0.69*	0.53*	0.79*	1.00	
AVEINC	-0.13*	-0.09	-0.36*	0.08	0.36*	-0.03	0.12*	0.48*	0.55*	0.66*	0.58*	0.32*	0.48*	0.64*	1.00

Notes:
* Statistically significant at the 5 percent level.
Legends: OGAP – output gap; SDINF – volatility of inflation; SDTOT – volatility of terms of trade; AVETOUR – average tourism receipts as percentage of GDP; SDAID – volatility of aid; TOTPOP – total population; SDPCF – volatility of private capital flows; AVESERV – services as percentage of GDP, on average; AVEAGR – agriculture as percentage of GDP, on average; AVEBUR – average index of bureaucracy quality; AVECOR – average index of corruption; AVEECO – average index of external conflict; AVEICO – average index of internal conflict; AVELAW – average index of law and order; AVEINC– average per capita GDP.

hand, a positive correlation is found between the volatility of growth and the size of the economy, which is measured by the total population.

- The volatility measures of inflation, terms of trade and aid flows, as well as the respective shares of agriculture and tourism in the economy, do not have a statistically significant correlation with the volatility of growth.
- The institutional variables and income level have positive and significant correlations, indicating that a high institutional performance is strongly correlated with higher income *per capita*.

An OLS regression was carried out to estimate the impact of the explanatory variables on the output gap (OGAP). The regression model is given by[4]

$$
\begin{aligned}
OGAP_{it} = {} & \alpha + \beta_1 SDINF_{it} + \beta_2 SDTOT_{it} + \beta_3 SDAID_{it} + \beta_4 SDPCF_{it} \\
& + \varphi_1 TOTPOP_{it} + \delta_1 AVETOUR_{it} + \delta_2 AVESERV_{it} + \delta_3 AVEGR_{it} \\
& + \delta_3 AVEBUR_{it} + \delta_4 AVECOR_{it} + \delta_5 AVECO_{it} + \delta_6 AVEINCO_{it} \\
& + \delta_7 AVELAW_{it} + \theta_1 LOW * AVELAW_{it} + \theta_2 LOWMI * AVELAW_{it} \\
& + \theta_3 UPMI * AVELAW_{it} + \theta_4 LOWI * AVEBUR_{it} + \theta_5 LOWMI * AVEBUR_{it} \\
& + \theta_6 UPMI * AVEBUR_{it} + \varepsilon_{it}
\end{aligned}
\tag{7.1}
$$

where the subscript i refers to the corresponding country, and t denotes the time periods (six-year phases). The regression results and the corresponding elasticity estimates are shown in Table 7.2. Key findings show the following:

- Size matters. The larger the country (in terms of population), the more volatile is the growth. The elasticity estimate infers that a 1 percent increase in the total population leads to an increase in the volatility of growth by 0.02 percent;
- An increase in the volatility of aid by one percent is associated with a reduction in the volatility of growth by 0.15 percent. This is surprising but may be explained on the basis that aid volatility is anti-cyclical and designed in part to reduce the volatility of growth.
- Although the share of tourism receipts in the economy is not statistically significant, the share of services is. An increase in the share of services of one percent reduces the volatility of growth by 0.72 percent;
- Finally, some of the institutional variables also have a statistically significant impact in terms of lessening the volatility of growth. An improvement in the institutional strength and quality of the bureaucracy, less corruption and higher degree of law and order leads to a decline of growth volatility by 2.61 percent, 0.39 percent and 1.57 percent, respectively.

Table 7.2   Marginal effects and elasticity estimates of the control variables on the volatility of growth

Variable	Marginal effects		Elasticity estimates	
	Coef.	Std. error	Elasticity	Std. error
Intercept	0.094*	0.024		
SDINF	0.007	0.004	0.092	0.061
SDTOT	0.053	0.035	0.091	0.060
AVETOUR	0.001	0.001	0.070	0.056
SDAID	−0.020*	0.006	−0.155*	0.047
TOTPOP	4.66E−12*	2.17E−12	0.021*	0.010
SDPCF	−0.006**	0.003	−0.106**	0.060
AVESERV	−0.001*	0.000	−0.721*	0.272
AVEAGR	−7.27E−06	0.000	−0.002	0.106
AVEBUR	0.074*	0.008	−2.618*	0.160
AVECOR	−0.007*	0.003	−0.395*	0.156
AVEECO	0.000	0.001	−0.055	0.259
AVEICO	−0.002	0.001	−0.291	0.234
AVELAW	−0.031*	0.005	−1.570*	0.173
Interaction variables				
LOWI*AVELAW	0.034*	0.006		
LOWMI*AVELAW	0.038*	0.005		
UPMI*AVELAW	0.051*	0.006		
LOWI*AVEBUR	−0.072*	0.009		
LOWMI*AVEBUR	−0.076*	0.009		
UPMI*AVEBUR	−0.087*	0.009		
R-squared	0.26			
No. of countries	133			
No. of observations	201			

Notes:
Standard errors are heteroskedasticity-consistent. The elasticity calculations are based on mean values of the variables.
(*) Statistically significant at the 5 percent level of significance.
SDINF – volatility of inflation; SDTOT – volatility of terms of trade; AVETOUR – average tourism receipts as percentage of GDP; SDAID – volatility of aid; TOTPOP – total population; SDPCF – volatility of private capital flows; AVESERV – services as percentage of GDP, on average; AVEAGR – agriculture as percentage of GDP, on average; AVEBUR – average index of bureaucracy quality; AVECOR – average index of corruption; AVEECO – average index of external conflict; AVEICO – average index of internal conflict; AVELAW – average index of law and order; low income (LOWI), lower middle income (LOWMI), upper middle income (UPMI).

7.3 VOLATILITY OF FOREIGN EARNINGS FROM DIFFERENT SOURCES

In this section, we look at the volatility of external source earnings from different sources. All countries, but especially developing ones, are at the mercy of sharp changes in their export revenues and their capital flows. How do the major sources of these flows compare in terms of their stability? Table 7.3 provides a description of this volatility in terms of the coefficient of variation and the correlations between the flows. The sources examined are: tourism, remittances from workers, official aid, and export revenues from raw agricultural products, food products, energy fuels and manufacturers.

A number of interesting observations emerge from that table regarding the role of tourism. The earnings from tourism are less volatile than remittances or aid or energy fuels, but are slightly more volatile than earnings from exports of raw agricultural products and manufactures.[5] Earnings from exports of food products are the most stable. Of course volatility will vary considerably from country to country, and in the next section we look at the factors underlying the volatility of tourism earnings in greater detail.

The other data in Table 7.3 look at the correlation between the volatility from these different sources. Again, as in Table 7.1, we focus on the significant correlations. One interesting finding here is that volatility from tourism has a weak correlation with all other sources. So countries that have a high volatility of tourism do not also have a high volatility of other exports or

Table 7.3   Variations in foreign source earnings by source and pairwise correlation

	Tourism	Remit.	Aid	Raw Ag.	Food	Fuel	Manuf.
Tourism	1.00	0.07	−0.13[a]	0.02	−0.11	−0.08	0.03
Remit.	0.07	1.00	−0.08	0.13	−0.07	−0.11	−0.16[a]
Aid			1.00	−0.06	0.01	0.22[b]	0.02
Raw Ag.				1.00	0.33[b]	0.22	0.30
Food					1.00	−0.03	0.40[b]
Fuel						1.00	0.15
Manuf.							1.00
Coeff. Var.	0.65	1.17	1.10	0.55	0.38	0.76	0.59

Notes: Except for the last row, the numbers are pairwise correlations. The last row refers to the average coefficient of variation by foreign source; [a]Statistically significant at the 1 percent level; [b]Statistically significant at the 5 percent level.

Source: Own calculations based on World Bank data.

of remittances or aid. In that way, increasing the scale of tourism may help reduce the volatility of overall earnings. On the other hand, volatility in the earnings from raw agricultural products and that from food are significantly correlated as is that between manufacturing and food; and between fuel and aid. Interestingly, there are virtually no cases of significant negative correlations, i.e., where a high volatility in one source is associated with a lower volatility of another source.

Finally, if we look at the overall volatility of earnings from all sources, we find little correlation with the size of the respective sectors. The share of tourism has a slightly significant positive correlation with overall volatility – the greater the share, the more volatile are total earnings. The shares of earnings from other sources, however, are not significantly correlated with the overall volatility of earnings.

7.4   VOLATILITY OF TOURISM EARNINGS

In this section, we will look at the sources of the volatility of tourism earnings. The variability of tourism earnings is measured by its coefficient of variation. The sample consists of 129 countries, of which 35 are high-income countries.

The data are divided into four six-year phases, corresponding to the periods 1980–1985, 1986–1991, 1992–1997, and 1998–2003. The dependent variable is the *volatility of tourism earnings* (CVTOUR). For each country, the explanatory variables correspond to six-year averages of the population (AVEPOP), exchange rate misalignment (AVEERATEMIS) and institutional variables (bureaucracy quality, corruption, external and internal conflicts and law and order). Also included are the total frequency of financial crisis (TOTFIN), total number of deaths and injuries related to natural disasters (TOTKI), and the volatility measures of: inflation (SDINF), terms of trade (SDTOT) and private capital flows (SDPCF) every six years. There is also a dummy variable for the developing countries (DC) in the model to further capture the heterogeneity between the groups of developed and developing countries. Appendix Table 7.2A gives the definition and data sources of the variables used in this section, in addition to some of the variables listed in Appendix Table 7.1A. The regression equation is as follows:

$$CVTOUR_{it} = \chi_0 + \chi_1 SDINF_{it} + \chi_2 SDTOT_{it} + \chi_3 SDPCF_{it} + \varphi_1 TOTFIN_{it} +$$
$$\varphi_2 TOTKI_{it} + \delta_1 AVEPOP_{it} + \delta_2 AVEBUR_{it} + \delta_3 AVECO_{it} + \delta_4 AVEINCO_{it} + \quad (7.2)$$
$$\delta_5 AVELAW_{it} + \delta_6 AVEERATEMIS_{it} + \varphi_1 DC_i + \mu_{it}$$

where the subscript i refers to a particular country, and t refers to the four time periods. Table 7.4 shows that CVTOUR is positively and statistically

Table 7.4 Pairwise correlations between the volatility of tourism earnings and key variables

	CVTOUR	SDINF	SDTOT	SDPCF	AVEBUR	AVECOR	AVEECO	AVEICO	AVELAW	TOTFIN	AVEERATEMIS	TOTKI	AVEPOP
CVTOUR	1.00												
STDINF	0.20*	1.00											
STDTOT	0.35*	0.19*	1.00										
STDPCF	0.02	0.08	0.03	1.00									
AVEBUR	−0.43*	−0.18*	−0.43*	0.05	1.00								
AVECOR	−0.34*	−0.19*	−0.37*	0.00	0.72*	1.00							
AVEECO	−0.32*	−0.05	−0.34*	0.06	0.44*	0.37*	1.00						
AVEICO	−0.35*	−0.11*	−0.40*	0.05	0.58*	0.55*	0.69*	1.00					
AVELAW	−0.39*	−0.13*	−0.45*	0.05	0.73*	0.70*	0.55*	0.80*	1.00				
TOTFIN	0.12*	0.17*	0.16*	0.02	−0.05	−0.10*	−0.03	−0.14*	−0.16*	1.00			
AVEERATEMIS	0.41*	0.15*	0.33*	0.03	−0.17*	−0.14*	−0.22*	−0.15*	−0.15*	0.13*	1.00		
TOTKI	−0.02	−0.04	0.04	−0.05	−0.07	−0.11*	−0.03	−0.05	−0.03	0.22*	0.03	1.00	
AVEPOP	−0.09	−0.03	0.01	−0.05	0.05	−0.05	−0.02	0.01	0.00	0.14*	−0.04	0.67*	1.00

Notes:
* Statistically significant at the 5 percent level.
Legends: CVTOUR – volatility of tourism earnings; SDINF – volatility of inflation; SDTOT – volatility of terms of trade; SDPCF – volatility of private capital flows; AVEBUR – average index of bureaucracy quality; AVECOR – average index of corruption; AVEECO – average index of external conflict; AVEICO – average index of internal conflict; AVELAW – average index of law and order; TOTFINb– total frequency of financial crises; AVEERATEMIS – average exchange rate misalignment; TOTKI – total number of people killed and injured caused by natural disasters; AVEPOP – average population.

correlated (at the 5 percent significance level) with the volatility of inflation, volatility of terms of trade, frequency of financial crisis and exchange rate misalignment. It is, on the other hand, negatively and statistically correlated with all of the institutional variables.

An OLS regression was carried out on equation (7.2) to estimate the magnitude of each explanatory variable's impact on the volatility of tourism earnings, and test its statistical significance. The estimated marginal effects of each variable are presented in Table 7.5. The quantitative assessments of

Table 7.5   Marginal effects of key variables on the volatility of tourism earnings

Variable	Marginal effects		Elasticity estimates	
	Coef.	Std. error	Elasticity	Std. error
Intercept	0.293*	0.074		
SDINF	0.024	0.028	0.068	0.078
SDTOT	0.616*	0.306	0.213*	0.105
AVEPOP	−1.05E−10	5.59E−11	−0.020*	0.010
SDPCF	−0.004	0.013	−0.015	0.058
AVEBUR	−0.014	0.014	−0.138	0.147
AVECOR	−0.023**	0.014	−0.357**	0.214
AVEECO	−0.005	0.006	−0.205	0.271
AVEICO	0.005	0.007	0.186	0.273
AVELAW	−0.013	0.014	−0.205	0.224
TOTFIN	0.020*	0.008	0.069*	0.030
AVEERATEMIS	0.001*	0.000	0.171*	0.056
TOTKI	5.73E−08	2.04E−07	0.002	0.008
DC	−0.040**	0.040	−0.144	0.115
R-squared	0.26			
No. of countries	133			
No. of observations	201			

Notes:
*Statistically significant at the 5 percent level of significance; **Statistically significant at the 10 percent level of significance.
SDINF – volatility of inflation; SDTOT – volatility of terms of trade; AVEPOP – average population; SDPCF– volatility of private capital flows; AVEBUR – average index of bureaucracy quality; AVECOR – average index of corruption; AVEECO – average index of external conflict; AVEICO – average index of internal conflict; AVELAW – average index of law and order; TOTFIN – total frequency of financial crises; AVEERATEMIS – average exchange rate misalignment; TOTKI – total number of people killed and injured caused by natural disasters; DC – dummy variable for developing countries.

these effects are best reported as an elasticity of CVTOUR with respect to the relevant variables, which gives the percentage by which the coefficient of variation of tourism earnings changes when there is a 1 percent increase in the explanatory variable (see also Table 7.5).

Considering the statistically significant estimates, it can be observed that the volatility of tourism earnings is inversely related to the average population and corruption index, where a higher value of the latter denotes less corruption. Conversely, for every percentage increase in the volatility of terms of trade, frequency of financial crisis and exchange rate misalignment, the volatility of tourism earnings increases by 0.21 percent, 0.07 percent and 0.17 percent, respectively.

7.5 CONCLUSIONS AND POLICY IMPLICATIONS

This chapter has explored a line of reasoning that is gaining currency in the macroeconomics literature – that volatility in economic performance has negative consequences for the level of economic performance – and has applied that to the tourism sector. The observation that higher volatility is causally related to lower growth should make us want to look more closely at the causes of higher volatility. When we do that, we find a number of factors that are important. These include some financial variables (volatility in the flow of private capital and in the flow of official aid, in the case of developing countries); some structural variables (larger countries have greater growth volatility and those that have smaller service sectors); and some institutional variables (with higher levels of law and order and bureaucracy quality, and lack of corruption, the volatility of growth is lower). These results suggest that measures which reduce fluctuations of capital flows and that shift GDP to a more service-sector-oriented society will reduce variability of growth. It is also important to note that other institutional variables (i.e., external and internal conflicts), which could a priori be considered relevant, were tried and not found to be significant.

As far as tourism is concerned, it can contribute to an expanded service sector, which helps reduce volatility. We also note that earnings from tourism are less volatile than a number of other sources of foreign exchange, such as remittances or aid or exports of energy fuels. They are, however, surprisingly more volatile than earnings from exports of raw agricultural products or manufactures. Of course this is an average observation across nearly 100 countries and the degree of tourism volatility can be reduced by appropriate measures, some of which are examined in section 7.4. We also note that the volatility of tourism is not strongly correlated with the volatility from sources such as remittances and aid. In this way, an economy that diversifies through tourism can expect to reduce overall earnings volatility.

When we examine the factors behind the volatility of tourism earnings, we find the following: volatility in the terms of trade, exchange rate misalignment, and frequency of financial crises all increase the volatility of tourism earnings. On the other hand, we observe a reduction in the volatility of tourism earnings when there is less corruption and when bureaucracy quality and law and order are strong. We also find that developing countries' tourism earnings are more volatile than those of more developed countries. The results suggest that, to make tourism a more reliable and stable sector, we must pay attention to the degree of exchange rate misalignment and to reducing the volatility in the terms of trade. We also need to address the problems of financial crises and focus on strengthening .

The results in this chapter are the first in this area and should be tested for robustness through other studies. Nevertheless, they point to some important factors that could be important in determining the role of tourism in economic growth and stable development.

ACKNOWLEDGEMENTS

We would like to thank Soonhwa Yi for help and advice. Any errors that remain are ours.

NOTES

1. The *output gap* is measured as the difference between the log of actual GDP and the log of trend GDP. This measure allows for stable growth not to influence the measure of volatility and is thus a better measure.
2. Hnatkovska and Loayza (2005) find a significant positive correlation between volatility and growth for the period 1960–2000 for 'high-income' economies – i.e., those with a per capita GNI of $9076 or more in 2002. For middle income countries, they find no significant correlation. Working with a shorter and overlapping period (1980–2003), we find a non-significant negative correlation between these two variables for the same set of countries.
3. 'Small countries' refer to those with a total population less than 1 million. 'Less developed countries' refer to the World Bank classification of low and middle income economies (with GNI per capita of $875 or less and $875–$10 725, respectively; also called developing countries); while 'more developed countries' refer to countries that belong to the high income group (with $10 726 GNI per capita or more).
4. Dummy variables of the income groups and other interaction variables were initially included. They were eventually excluded in the model because by doing so, the statistical significance of the coefficients of the remaining variables improved.
5. Manufactures comprise commodities in SITC sections 5 (chemicals), 6 (basic manufactures), 7 (machinery and transport equipment), and 8 (miscellaneous manufactured goods), excluding division 68 (non-ferrous metals) (World Bank 2005).

REFERENCES

Alesina, A., S. Ozler, N. Roubini and P. Swagel (1996), 'Political instability and economic growth', *Journal of Economic Growth*, **1**(2), 189–213.

Brau, R., A. Lanza and F. Pigliaru (2005), 'How fast are the tourism countries growing? The cross country evidence', in A. Lanza, A. Markandya and F. Pigliaru (eds), *The Economics of Tourism and Sustainable Development*, Cheltenham, UK and Northampton, MA, USA: Edward Elgar.

Baxter, M. and R.G. King (1999), 'Measuring business cycles: Approximate band-pass filters for economic time series', *The Review of Economics and Statistics*, **81**(4), 575–93.

Bulir, A. and A.J. Hamann (2003), 'Aid volatility: an empirical assessment', *IMF Staff Papers*, **50**(1), 64–89.

Centre for Research on the Epidemiology of Disasters (CRED) (2005), 'EM-DAT: The international disaster database', available at: http://www.em-dat.net/.

Collier, P. (1999), 'Aid dependency: A critique', *Journal of African Economies*, **8**(4), 528–45.

Hnatkovska, V. and N. Loayza (2005), 'Volatility and growth', in J. Aizenman and B. Pinto (eds), *Managing Volatility and Crises: A Practitioner's Guide*, New York: Cambridge University Press.

Judson, R. and A. Orphanides (1996), 'Inflation, volatility and growth', *Finance and Economics Discussion Series*, **19**, 1–29.

Rodrik, D. (1991), 'Policy uncertainty and private investment in developing countries', *Journal of Development Economics*, **36**(2), 229–242.

Schumpeter, J. (1939), *Business Cycles: A Theoretical, Historical and Statistical Analysis of the Capitalist Process*, New York: McGraw Hill.

Serven, L. (1997), 'Irreversibility, uncertainty and private investment: analytical issues and some lessons for Africa', *Journal of African Economies*, **6**(3), 229–68.

The PRS Group Inc. (2005), 'International country risk guide', available at: http://www.prsgroup.com/icrg/icrg.html.

World Bank (2005), *World Development Indicators*, Washington, DC: World Bank.

APPENDIX

*Table 7.1A   Definitions and sources of variables used in the regression
analysis for the volatility of growth*

Variables	Definition	Source
OGAP*	Standard deviation of per capita GDP gap. This was derived by obtaining the difference between log(per capita GDP) and log(trend of per capita GDP). For each country, the trend was estimated using the bandpass filter that was developed by Baxter and King (1999).	World Bank (2005)
SDINF	Standard deviation of the inflation, which is measured by the rate of change of the consumer price index	
SDTOT	Standard deviation of the log difference of the terms of trade	
AVETOUR*	International tourism receipts as percentage of GDP, on average over the period	
SDAID*	Standard deviation of the log difference of international aid	
TOTPOP	Total population	
SDPCF	Standard deviation of the log difference of the private capital flows	
AVESR*	Services as percentage of GDP, on average over the period	
AVEAG*	Agriculture as percentage of GDP, on average over the period	
AVEBUR	Average index of bureaucracy quality over the period. This index refers to the institutional strength and quality of the bureaucracy is a shock absorber that tends to minimize revisions of policy when governments change. In low-risk countries, the bureaucracy is somewhat autonomous from political pressure (maximum 4 points).	The PRS Group, Inc. (2005)**
AVECOR	Average index of corruption over the period. The index is a measure of corruption within the political system that is a threat to foreign investment by distorting the economic and financial environment, reducing the efficiency of government and business by enabling people to assume positions of power through patronage rather than ability, and introducing inherent instability into the political process (maximum 6 points).	

Table 7.1A　(continued)

Variables	Definition	Source
AVEECO	Average index of external conflict over the period. This index measures the risk to the incumbent government and to inward investment, ranging from trade restrictions and embargoes through geopolitical disputes, armed threats, border incursions, foreign-supported insurgency and full-scale warfare (maximum 12 points).	
AVEICO	Average index of internal conflict over the period. This index is a measure of political violence and its actual or potential impact on governance, taking into consideration such factors as whether threats exist, whether they have political objectives, the size and strength of support, and the geographic nature of the conflict (maximum 12 points).	
AVELAW	Average index of law and order over the period. There are two measures comprising this index. Each sub-component equals half of the total. The 'law' sub-component assesses the strength and impartiality of the legal system, and the 'order' sub-component assesses popular observance of the law (maximum 6 points).	
LOWI	Dummy variable for low income countries	
LOWMI	Dummy variable for low middle income countries	
UPMI	Dummy variable for upper middle income countries	

Notes:
*The raw data are in real US dollars.
**See the website: http://www.prsgroup.com/icrg/icrg.html. The highest number of points indicate the lowest potential risk for that variable, while the lowest number (0) indicates the highest potential risk. In brief, the higher the index, the more affirmative the institutional variable. Each variable covers four periods of six-year phases: 1980–1985; 1986–1991; 1992–1997; and 1998–2003.

Table 7.2A　Definitions and sources of variables used in the regression analysis for the volatility of tourism earnings

Variables	Definition	Source
CVTOUR*	Coefficient of variation of tourism earnings over the period	World Bank (2005)
TOTFIN	Total frequency of financial crises over the period	Hnatkovska and Loayza (2005)
AVEERATEMIS	Exchange rate misalignment, measuring the absolute deviation of the real exchange rate from the equilibrium rate	Author's estimates
TOTKI	Total number of people killed and injured due to natural disasters	CRED (2005)**
DC	Dummy variable for developing countries	

Notes:
*The raw data are in real US dollars.
** See the website: http://www.em-dat.net/.
Each variable covers four periods of six-year phases: 1980–1985; 1986–1991; 1992–1997; and 1998–2003.

8. Managing Value-at-Risk in Daily Tourist Tax Revenues for the Maldives

Michael McAleer, Riaz Shareef and Bernardo da Veiga

8.1 INTRODUCTION

International tourism is widely regarded as the principal economic activity in Small Island Tourism Economies (SITEs) (see Shareef, 2004) for a comprehensive discussion). Historically, SITEs have been dependent on international tourism for economic development, employment, and foreign exchange, among other economic indicators. A unique SITE is the Maldives, an archipelago of 1190 islands in the Indian Ocean, of which 200 are inhabited by the indigenous population of 271 101, and 89 islands are designated for self-contained tourist resorts. The Maldivian economy depends substantially on tourism, and accounts directly for nearly 33 percent of real GDP. According to the Ministry of Planning and National Development (2005) of the Government of the Maldives, transport and communications are the second largest economic sector, contributing 14 percent, while government administration accounts for 12 percent of the economy. Fisheries are still the largest primary industry, but its contribution to the economy has gradually declined to 6 percent in 2003. Employment in tourism accounts for 17 percent of the working population, while tourism accounts for 65 percent of gross foreign exchange earnings.

Any shock that would adversely affect international tourist arrivals to the Maldives would also affect earnings from tourism dramatically, and have disastrous ramifications for the entire economy. An excellent example is the impact of the 2004 Boxing Day tsunami, which sustained extensive damage to the tourism-based economy of the Maldives and dramatically reduced the number of tourist arrivals in the post-tsunami period. Therefore, it is vital for the Government of the Maldives, multilateral development agencies such as the World Bank and the Asian Development Bank who are assisting the Maldives in the tsunami recovery effort, and the industry stakeholders, namely the resort owners and tour operators, to obtain accurate estimates of international tourist arrivals and their variability. Such accurate estimates would provide vital information for government policy formulation, international development aid, profitability and marketing.

A significant proportion of research in the literature on empirical tourism demand has been based on annual data (see Shareef, 2004), but such analyses are useful only for long-term development planning. An early attempt to improve the short-term analysis of tourism was undertaken by Shareef and McAleer (2005), who modelled the volatility (or predictable uncertainty) in monthly international tourist arrivals to the Maldives. Univariate and multivariate time series models of conditional volatility were estimated and tested. The conditional correlations were estimated and examined to determine whether there was specialization, diversification or segmentation in the international tourism demand shocks from the major tourism source countries to the Maldives. In a similar vein, Chan, Lim and McAleer (2005) modelled the time-varying means, dynamic conditional variances and constant conditional correlations of the logarithms of the monthly arrival rate for the four leading tourism source countries to Australia.

This chapter provides a template for the future analysis of earnings from international tourism, particularly tourism taxes for SITEs, discusses the direct and indirect monetary benefits from international tourism, highlights tourism taxes in the Maldives as a development financing phenomenon, and provides a framework for discussing the design and implementation of tourism taxes.

Daily international arrivals to the Maldives and the number of tourists in residence are analyzed for the period 1994–2003. The data are obtained from the Ministry of Tourism of the Maldives. In the international tourism demand literature to date, there does not seem to have been any empirical research using daily tourism arrivals data. One advantage of using daily data, as distinct from monthly and quarterly data, is that volatility clustering in the number of international tourist arrivals and their associated growth rates can be observed and analyzed more clearly using standard financial econometric techniques. Therefore, it is useful to analyze daily tourism arrivals data, much like financial data, in terms of the time series patterns, as such an analysis would provide policy makers and industry stakeholders with accurate indicators associated with their short-term objectives.

In virtually all SITEs, and particularly the Maldives, tourist arrivals or growth in tourist arrivals translates directly into a financial asset. Each international tourist is required to pay USD 8 for every tourist bed-night spent in the Maldives. This levy is called a 'tourism tax' and comprises over 30 percent of the current revenue of the government budget (Ministry of Planning and National Development, 2005). Hence, tourism tax revenue is a principal determinant of development expenditure. As a significant financial asset to the economy of SITEs, and particularly for the Maldives, the volatility in tourist arrivals and their growth rate is conceptually identical to the volatility in financial returns, which is interpreted as financial risk.

This chapter models the volatility in the number of tourist arrivals, tourists in residence and their growth rates. The purpose of this analysis of volatility is to present a framework for managing the risks inherent in the variability of total tourist arrivals, tourists in residence, and hence government revenue, through the modelling and forecasting of Value-at-Risk (VaR) thresholds for the number of tourist arrivals, tourists in residence and their growth rates. Thus, the chapter provides the first application of the VaR portfolio approach to manage the risks associated with tourism revenues.

The structure of the chapter is as follows. The economy of the Maldives is described, followed by an assessment of the impact of the 2004 Boxing Day tsunami on tourism in the Maldives. The concept of Value-at-Risk (VaR) is analyzed, the data are discussed, the models of volatility are presented, the empirical results are examined, forecasting is undertaken, and finally some concluding remarks are given.

8.2   THE TOURISM ECONOMY OF THE MALDIVES

The Maldives is an archipelago in the Indian Ocean, was formerly a British protectorate, and became independent in 1965. It stretches approximately 700 kilometres north to south, about 65 kilometres east to west, and is situated south-west of the Indian sub-continent. The Exclusive Economic Zone of the Maldives is 859 000 square kilometres, and the aggregated land area is roughly 290 square kilometres.

With an average growth rate of 7 percent per annum over the last two decades, the Maldives has shown an impressive economic growth record. This economic performance has been achieved through growth in international tourism demand. Furthermore, economic growth has enabled Maldivians to enjoy an estimated real per capita GDP of USD 2261 in 2003, which is considerably above average for small island developing countries, with an average per capita GDP of USD 1500. The engine of growth in the Maldives has been the tourism industry, accounting for 33 percent of real GDP, more than one-third of fiscal revenue, and two-thirds of gross foreign exchange earnings in recent years. The fisheries sector remains the largest sector in terms of employment, accounting for about one-quarter of the labour force, and is an important but declining source of foreign exchange earnings. Due to the high salinity content in the soil, agriculture continues to play a minor role. The government, which employs about 20 percent of the labour force, plays a dominant role in the economy, both in the production process and through its regulation of the economy.

Tourism in the Maldives has a direct impact on fiscal policy, which determines development expenditure. More than one-fifth of government revenue arises from tourism-related levies. The most important tourism-related revenues are the tourism tax, the resort lease rents, resort land rents, and royalties. Except for the tourism tax, the other sources of tourism-related revenues are based on contractual agreements with the Government of the Maldives. Tourism tax is levied on every occupied bed night from all tourist establishments, such as hotels, tourist resorts, guest houses and safari yachts. Initially, this tax was levied at USD 3 in 1981, and was then doubled to USD 6 in 1988. After 16 years with no change in the tax rate, the tax rate was increased to USD 8 on 1 November 2004. This tax is regressive as it does not take into account the profitability of the tourist establishments. Furthermore, it fails to take account of inflation, such that the tax yield has eroded over time.

Tourism tax is collected by tourist establishments and is deposited at the Inland Revenue Department at the end of every month. This tax revenue is used directly to finance the government budget on a monthly basis. As the tax is levied directly on the tourist, any uncertainty that surrounds international tourist arrivals will affect tourism tax receipts, and hence fiscal policy. Any adverse affect on international tourist arrivals may also result in the suspension of planned development expenditures.

The nature of tourist resorts in the Maldives is distinctive as they are built on islands that have been set aside for tourism development. Tourism development is the greatest challenge in the history of the Maldives, and has led to the creation of distinctive resort islands. Domroes (1985, 1989, 1993, 1999) asserts that these islands are deserted and uninhabited, but have been converted into 'one-island–one-hotel' schemes. The building of physical and social infrastructure of the resort islands has had to abide by strict standards to protect the flora, fauna and the marine environment of the islands, while basic facilities for sustainability of the resort have to be maintained. The architectural design of the resort islands in the Maldives varies profoundly in their character and individuality. Only 20 percent of the land area of any given island is allowed to be developed, which is imposed to restrict the capacity of tourists. All tourist accommodation must face a beachfront area of five metres. In most island resorts, bungalows are built as single or double units. Recently, there has been extensive development of water bungalows on stilts along the reefs adjacent to the beaches. All tourist amenities are available on each island and are provided by the onshore staff.

8.3 DATA ISSUES

The data used in this chapter are total daily international tourist arrivals from 1 January 1994 to 31 December 2003, and were obtained from the Ministry of Tourism of the Maldives. As can be seen in Table 8.1, there were over four million tourists during this ten-year period, with Italy being the largest tourist source country, followed by Germany, the United Kingdom and Japan. The top four countries accounted for over 60 percent of tourist arrivals to the Maldives. Furthermore, tourists from Western Europe accounted for more than 80 percent of tourists to the Maldives, with Russia seen as the biggest emerging market.

A significant advantage of using daily data, as distinct from monthly and quarterly data, is that volatility clustering in the number of international tourist arrivals and their associated growth rates can be observed and analyzed more clearly using standard financial econometric techniques.

There exists a direct relationship between the daily total number of tourists in residence and the daily tourism tax revenue. Modelling the variability of daily tourist arrivals (namely, the number of international tourists who arrive in the Maldives, predominantly by air) can be problematic as institutional factors, such as predetermined weekly flight schedules, lead to excessive variability and significant day-of-the-week effects. This problem can be resolved in one of two ways. Weekly tourist arrivals could be examined, as this approach removes both the excess variability inherent in daily total arrivals and day-of-the-week effects. However, this approach is problematic as it leads to substantially fewer observations being available for estimation and forecasting.

An alternative solution, and one that is adopted in this chapter, is to calculate the daily tourists in residence, which is the total number of international tourists residing in the Maldives on any given day. This daily

Table 8.1   Composition of tourist arrivals, 1994–2003

Source Country	Head Count	% Share
1. Italy	852 389	20.78
2. Germany	730 453	17.81
3. UK	603 501	14.72
4. Japan	381 374	9.30
5. France	238 638	5.82
6. Switzerland	237 245	5.79
7. Austria	118 324	2.89
8. The Netherlands	60 011	1.46
Total International Tourist Arrivals	*4 101 028*	*100.00*

total of tourists in residence is of paramount importance to the Government of the Maldives as it has a direct effect on the tourism tax revenues. The tourists in residence series are calculated as the seven-day rolling sum of the daily tourist arrivals series, which assumes that tourists stay in the Maldives for seven days, on average. This is a reasonable assumption as the typical tourist stays in the Maldives for approximately seven days (Ministry of Planning and National Development, 2005).

The graphs for daily tourist arrivals, weekly tourist arrivals and tourists in residence are given in Figures 8.1–8.3, respectively. All three series display high degrees of variability and seasonality, which is typical of tourist arrivals data. As would be expected, the highest levels of tourism arrivals in the Maldives occur during the European winter, while the lowest levels occur during the European summer. The descriptive statistics for each series are given in Tables 8.2 and 8.3, respectively. The daily tourist arrivals series display the greatest variability, with a mean of 1122 arrivals per day, a

Table 8.2   Descriptive statistics

Statistics	Daily Arrivals	Weekly Arrivals	Tourists in Residence
Mean	1 122	7 833	7 699
Median	1 007	7 510	7 430
Maximum	4 118	14 942	15 517
Minimum	23	3 316	3 145
Std. Dev.	627	2 351	2 293
Skewness	1.087	0.535	0.593
Kurtosis	4.436	2.784	2.981
CoV	0.559	0.300	0.298
Jarque-Bera	1 033	25 808	201 597

Table 8.3   Descriptive statistics for growth rates

Statistics	Daily Arrivals	Weekly Arrivals	Tourists in Residence
Mean	0.010	0.163	5.24e-12
Median	−7.66	−0.027	−0.039
Maximum	368.23	50.37	26.34
Minimum	−412.57	−38.45	−20.64
Std. Dev.	81.19	11.66	3.21
Skewness	0.143	0.344	0.283
Kurtosis	3.01	4.95	8.76
CoV	8 119	71.53	6.12e11
Jarque-Bera	12.44	92.61	4 799.9

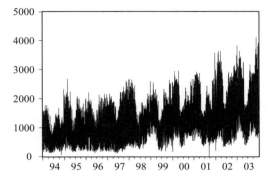

Figure 8.1   Daily tourist arrivals

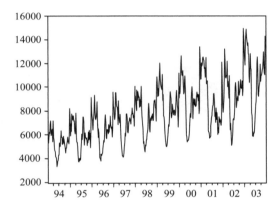

Figure 8.2   Weekly tourist arrivals

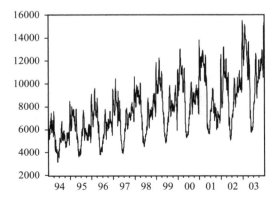

Figure 8.3   Daily tourists in residence

maximum of 4118 arrivals per day, and a rather low minimum of 23 arrivals per day. Furthermore, the daily arrivals series have a coefficient of variation (CoV) of 0.559, which is nearly twice the CoV of the other two series. The weekly arrivals and tourists in residence series are remarkably similar, with virtually identical CoV values of 0.3 and 0.298, respectively, and the normality assumption of both being strongly rejected.

As the focus of this chapter is on managing the risks associated with the variability in tourist arrivals and tourist tax revenues, the chapter focuses on modelling the growth rates, namely the returns in both total tourist arrivals and total tourists in residence. The graphs for the returns in total daily tourist arrivals, total weekly tourist arrivals and total daily tourists in residence are given in Figures 8.4–8.6, respectively. Daily tourist arrivals display the greatest variability, with a standard deviation of 81.19 percent, a maximum of

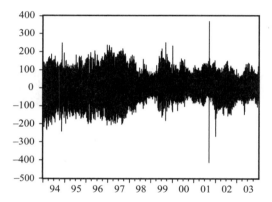

Figure 8.4   Growth rates in daily tourist arrivals

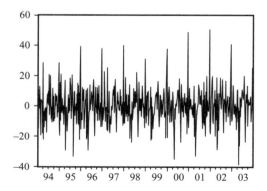

Figure 8.5   Growth rates in weekly tourist arrivals

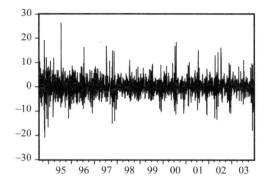

Figure 8.6   Growth rates in daily tourists in residence

368.23 percent, and a minimum of –412.57 percent. Based on the Jarque-Bera Lagrange Multiplier test statistic for normality, each of the series is found to be non-normal. Such non-normality can, in practice, change the critical values to obtain more precise VaR threshold forecasts (for further details, including a technical discussion of issues such as bootstrapping the distribution to obtain the dynamic critical values, see McAleer et al., 2005).

8.4   VOLATILITY MODELS

Risk evaluations are at the heart of research in financial markets, so much so that any assessment of the volatility of financial asset returns without such evaluations cannot be taken seriously. Engle (1982) developed the Autoregressive Conditional Heteroskedasticity (ARCH) model for undertaking risk evaluations by assuming that the conditional variance of the random error depends systematically on its past history. In this context, volatility clustering is taken to mean that large (small) shocks in the current period are followed by large (small) fluctuations in subsequent periods. There are two components of the ARCH specification, namely a model of asset returns and a model to explain how risk changes over time.

Subsequent developments led to the extension of ARCH by Bollerslev (1986) to the Generalized ARCH (GARCH) model. The main feature of GARCH is that there is a distinction made between the short and long run persistence of shocks to financial returns. A serious limitation of GARCH is the assumption that a positive shock (or 'good news') to daily tourist arrivals, tourists in residence, or their respective growth rates, has the same impact on their associated volatilities as does a negative shock (or 'bad news') of equal magnitude. It is well known that a negative shock to financial returns tends to have a greater impact on volatility than does a positive shock. This phenomenon was first explained by Black (1976), who argued that a negative shock increases financial leverage through the debt–equity ratio, by decreasing equity which, in turn, increases risk. Although there is not necessarily a comparable interpretation of leverage that applies to international tourist arrivals, there is nevertheless a significant difference in terms of positive and negative shocks, which make a tourist destination more and less appealing, respectively. Therefore, positive and negative shocks would be expected to have differential impacts on volatility in daily tourist arrivals, tourists in residence, and in their respective growth rates.

In order to incorporate asymmetric behaviour, Glosten et al. (1992) (GJR) extended the GARCH model by incorporating an indicator variable to capture the differential impacts of positive and negative shocks. Several alternative models of asymmetric conditional volatility are available in the literature (see McAleer, 2005 for a comprehensive and critical review).

There have been only a few applications of GARCH models in the tourism research literature to date. Through estimation of ARCH and GARCH models, Raab and Schwer (2003) examine the short- and long-run impacts of the Asian financial crisis on Las Vegas gaming revenues. Shareef and McAleer (2005) model univariate and multivariate conditional volatility in monthly international tourist arrivals to the Maldives. Chan, Lim and McAleer (2005) investigate the conditional mean and variance in the GARCH framework for international tourist arrivals to Australia from the four main tourist source countries, namely Japan, New Zealand, UK and USA. Chan et al. (2005) show how the GARCH model can be used to measure the conditional volatility in monthly international tourist arrivals to three SITEs. Hoti et al. (2005) provide a comparison of country risk ratings, risk returns and their associated volatilities (or uncertainty) for six SITEs where monthly data compiled by the International Country Risk Guide are available (see Hoti and McAleer (2004, 2005) for further details). Their results also show that the GARCH(1,1) and asymmetric GJR(1,1) models provide an accurate measure of the uncertainty associated with country risk returns for the six SITEs. Nicolau (2005) investigates the variations in the risk of a hotel chain's performance derived from opening a new lodging establishment.

The primary inputs required for calculating a VaR threshold are the forecasted variance, which is typically obtained as a conditional volatility, and the critical value from an appropriate distribution for a given level of significance. Several models are available for measuring and forecasting the conditional volatility. In this chapter, two popular univariate models of conditional volatility will be used for estimating the volatilities and forecasting the corresponding VaR thresholds. These specifications are the symmetric GARCH model of Bollerslev (1986), which does not distinguish between the impact of positive and negative shocks to tourist arrivals (that is, increases and decreases in tourist arrivals), and the asymmetric GJR model of Glosten et al. (1992), which does discriminate between the impact of positive and negative shocks to tourist arrivals on volatility.

The asymmetric GJR(p,q) model is given as:

$$Y_t = E(Y_t \mid F_{t-1}) + \varepsilon_t,$$

$$\varepsilon_t = h_t^{1/2} \eta_t,$$

$$h_t = \omega + \sum_{l=1}^{p} \left[\alpha_l \varepsilon_{t-l}^2 + \gamma_l I(\eta_{t-l}) \varepsilon_{t-l}^2 \right] + \sum_{l=1}^{q} \beta_l h_{t-l},$$

$$I(\eta_t) = \begin{cases} 1, \ \varepsilon_t \leq 0 \\ 0, \ \varepsilon_t > 0 \end{cases},$$

where F_t is the information set available at time t, and $\eta_t \sim iid(0,1)$. The four equations in this asymmetric model of conditional volatility state the following:

1. the growth in tourist arrivals depends on its own past values (namely, the conditional mean);
2. the shock to tourist arrivals, ε_t, has a predictable conditional variance (or risk) component, h_t, and an unpredictable component, η_t;
3. the conditional variance depends on its own past values, h_{t-l}, and previous shocks to the growth in the tourist arrivals series, ε_{t-l}^2; and
4. the conditional variance is affected differently by positive and negative shocks to the growth in tourist arrivals, as given by the indicator function, $I(\eta_t)$.

In this chapter, $E(Y_t \mid F_{t-1})$ is modelled as a simple AR(1) process. For the case $p = q = 1$, $\omega > 0$, $\alpha_1 \geq 0$, $\alpha_1 + \gamma_1 \geq 0$ and $\beta_1 \geq 0$ are the sufficient conditions to ensure a strictly positive conditional variance, $h_t > 0$. The ARCH (or $\alpha_1 + \frac{1}{2}\gamma_1$) effect captures the short-run persistence of shocks (namely, an indication of the strength of the shocks to international tourist arrivals in the short run), and the GARCH (or β_1) effect indicates the contribution of shocks to long run persistence or (or $\alpha_1 + \frac{1}{2}\gamma_1 + \beta_1$) (namely, an indication of the strength of the shocks to international tourist arrivals in the long run). For the GJR(1,1) model, $\alpha_1 + \frac{1}{2}\gamma_1 + \beta_1 < 1$ is a sufficient condition for the existence of the second moment (that is, a finite variance), which is necessary for sensible empirical analysis. Restricting $\gamma_1 = 0$ in the GJR(1,1) model leads to the GARCH(1,1) model of Bollerslev (1986). For the GARCH(1,1) model, the second moment condition is given by $\alpha_1 + \beta_1 < 1$.

In the GJR and GARCH models, the parameters are typically estimated using the maximum likelihood estimation (MLE) method. In the absence of normality of the standardized residuals, η_t, the parameters are estimated by the Quasi-Maximum Likelihood Estimation (QMLE) method (for further details see, for example, Li et al. 2002 and McAleer, 2005). The second moment conditions are also sufficient for the consistency and asymptotic normality of the QMLE of the respective models, which enables standard statistical inference to be conducted.

8.5   EMPIRICAL RESULTS

The variable of interest for the Maldivian Government is the number of tourists in residence on any given day as this figure is directly related to tourism revenue. As mentioned previously, every tourist is obliged to pay the tourism tax of USD 8 for every occupied bed night. In this section, the tourists in residence series are used to estimate the GARCH(1,1) and GJR(1,1) models described above. Estimation is conducted using the EViews 5.1 econometric software package, although similar results can be obtained using the RATS 6 econometric software package. The QMLE of the parameters are obtained for the case $p = q = 1$.

The estimated GARCH(1,1) equation for the tourists in residence series for the full sample is given as follows:

$$\hat{Y}_t = \underset{(0.054)}{0.001} + \underset{(0.017)}{0.1561Y_{t-1}},$$

$$h_t = \underset{(0.058)}{0.598} + \underset{(0.009)}{0.149\varepsilon_{t-1}^2} + \underset{(0.012)}{0.799h_{t-1}},$$

where the figures in parentheses are standard errors.

The estimated GJR(1,1) equation for the tourists in residence series for the full sample is given as follows:

$$Y_t = \underset{(0.054)}{0.001} + \underset{(0.017)}{0.1561Y_{t-1}},$$

$$h_t = \underset{(0.058)}{0.592} + \underset{(0.011)}{0.121\varepsilon_{t-1}^2} + \underset{(0.015)}{0.048I(\eta_{t-1})\varepsilon_{t-1}^2} + \underset{(0.012)}{0.803h_{t-1}}.$$

All the parameters are estimated to be positive and significant, which indicates that both models provide adequate explanation of the data. As γ_1 is estimated to be positive and significant, volatility is affected asymmetrically by positive and negative shocks. In this sense, the asymmetric GJR model dominates its symmetric GARCH counterpart empirically. It is found that negative shocks (or a decrease in tourist arrivals) have a greater impact on volatility than do positive shocks (or an increase in tourist arrivals) of a similar magnitude. Furthermore, as the respective estimates of the second moment conditions,

$$\hat{\alpha}_1 + \frac{1}{2}\hat{\gamma}_1 + \hat{\beta}_1 = 0.948,$$

for GJR(1,1) and $\hat{\alpha}_1 + \hat{\beta}_1 = 0.948$ for GARCH(1,1), are satisfied, the QMLE are consistent and asymptotically normal. This means that the estimates are statistically adequate and sensible for purposes of interpretation.

8.6   FORECASTING

A rolling window is used to forecast the 1-day ahead conditional variances and VaR thresholds for the tourists in residence, with the sample ranging from 7 January 1994 to 31 December 2003. In order to strike a balance between efficiency in estimation and a viable number of rolling regressions, the rolling window size is set at 1000, which leads to a forecasting period from 3 May 1997 to 31 December 2003. A rolling window is a moving sub-sample within the entire sample data set. In the empirical example presented here, estimation starts from observations 1 to 1000 of the data set, which corresponds to the period 7 January 1994 to 7 May 1997. Then, rolling the sample to observations 2 to 1001, which corresponds to the period 8 January 1994 to 8 May 1997, estimation is undertaken again, followed by observations 3 to 1002, and so on until the last rolling sample is reached.

Using the notation developed above, the VaR threshold forecast for the growth rate of tourists in residence at any given time t is given by:

$$VaR_t = E(Y_t \mid F_{t-1}) + z\sqrt{h_t},$$

where $E(Y_t \mid F_{t-1})$ is the forecasted expected growth rate of total tourists in residence at time t, h_t is the forecasted conditional variance of the growth rate in total tourist arrivals, and $z = -2.33$ is the negative critical value from the normal distribution at the one-sided 1 percent level of significance.

Figures 8.7 and 8.8 give the forecasted variances for both models. As can be seen from the figures, the forecasts are quite similar, with a correlation coefficient of 0.98. The forecasted VaR thresholds are given in Figures 8.9 and 8.10, respectively. As discussed above, the forecasted VaR threshold represents the maximum expected negative growth rate that could be expected given a specific confidence level. As is standard in the finance literature, where many of these techniques were developed and refined, this paper uses a 1 percent level of significance to calculate the VaR. In other words, growth rates smaller than the forecasted VaR should only be observed in 1 percent of all forecasts, which is referred to as the correct 'conditional coverage'.

The empirical results show that, in using the GJR (GARCH) model, we observe 32 (30) instances where the actual daily growth rate is smaller than the forecasted VaR threshold. Based on a Likelihood Ratio test, both models display the correct conditional coverage. In addition, Figures 8.11 and 8.12 give the second moment conditions for each rolling window of both models.

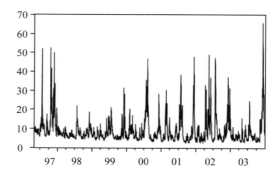

Figure 8.7   GJR variance forecasts for tourist in residence

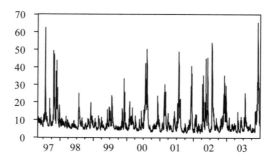

Figure 8.8   GARCH variance forecasts for tourist in residence

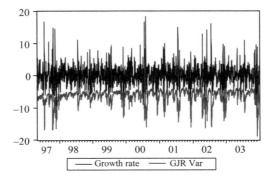

Figure 8.9   Growth rates for tourist in residence and GJR VaR thresholds

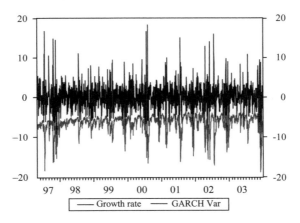

Figure 8.10   Growth rates for tourist in residence and GARCH VaR thresholds

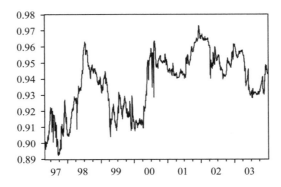

Figure 8.11   Rolling second moment condition for GJR

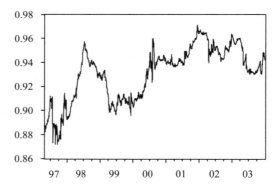

Figure 8.12   Rolling second moment condition for GARCH

As the condition is satisfied for every rolling window, this provides greater confidence in the statistical adequacy of the two estimated models. Finally, both models lead to the same average VaR at –6.59 percent, which means that the lowest expected daily growth rate in tourists in residence, and hence in tourist tax revenues, is –6.59 percent, given a 99 percent level of confidence. In other words, it can be stated with a 99 percent degree of confidence that the daily growth rate will exceed –6.59 percent.

8.3   CONCLUSION

In the Maldives, tourist arrivals and the growth in tourist arrivals translate directly into a financial asset for the government, as each international tourist is required to pay USD 8 for every tourist bed-night. This levy is called a tourism tax and enters directly into government revenue. Thus, tourism tax revenue is a principal determinant of development expenditure. As a significant financial asset to the economies of SITEs, and particularly so in the case of the Maldives, the volatility in tourist arrivals and in their growth rates are conceptually equivalent to the volatility in financial returns, which is widely interpreted as financial risk.

   This chapter provided a template for the future analysis of earnings from international tourism, particularly tourism taxes for SITEs, discussed the direct and indirect monetary benefits from international tourism, highlighted tourism taxes in the Maldives as a development financing phenomenon, and provided a framework for the quantification of the risks associated with tourism tax receipts, which should facilitate the future design and implementation of tourism taxes in SITEs.

   Daily international arrivals to the Maldives and their associated growth rates were analysed for the period 1994–2003. This seems to be the first analysis of daily tourism arrivals and growth rates data in the tourism research literature. The primary purpose for analysing volatility was to model and forecast the Value-at-Risk (VaR) thresholds for the number of tourist arrivals and their growth rates. This would seem to be the first attempt in the tourism research literature to apply the VaR portfolio management approach to manage the risks associated with tourism revenues.

The empirical results based on two widely-used conditional volatility models showed that volatility was affected asymmetrically by positive and negative shocks, with negative shocks to the growth in tourist arrivals having a greater impact on volatility than previous positive shocks of a similar magnitude. The forecasted VaR threshold represented the maximum expected negative growth rate that could be expected given a specific confidence level. Both conditional volatility models led to the same average VaR at –6.59 percent, which meant that the lowest possible growth rate in daily tourists in residence, and hence in tourist tax revenues, was expected to be –6.59 percent at the 99 percent level of confidence. This should be useful information for the Maldivian Government and private tourism service providers in the Maldives.

In the Maldives Tourism Act (Law No: 2/99), it is stated that the tourism tax is USD 8 and is to be paid in USD, which increases foreign exchange reserves directly. Tourist establishments also typically hold large quantities of USD, which encourages the general public to follow suit, and causes the economy to become highly 'dollarized'. Such dollarization substantially changes the way in which a country conducts monetary policy. In the case of the Maldives, in the event of a contraction of USD inflows, the authorities will have to change the way in which they conduct monetary policy. Therefore, understanding the extent to which tourism tax receipts, and hence foreign exchange reserves, can vary will aid the Maldivian Government in planning the conduct of future monetary policy operations.

Tourism taxes also have a significant influence on the Maldivian Government's budget. There are three main components of government expenditure, namely: (1) direct government expenditure on public projects; (2) transfer payments; and (3) debt servicing. In turn, these have to be funded by: (i) tax receipts; (ii) government borrowing; or (iii) money creation. The analysis presented in this chapter shows that tax receipts in the Maldives are highly variable. Therefore, if the Maldivian Government wishes to maintain a relatively constant level of government expenditure, it must compensate reductions in tax receipts with government borrowing or increases in the money supply. Hence, the analysis presented in this chapter should assist the Maldivian Government in quantifying the extent to which they may have to borrow funds in the future. Such knowledge will be useful in aiding the Government in undertaking sustainable development projects that do not have to be interrupted, thereby improving the efficiency of government development projects.

This is precisely what has happened in the post-tsunami period. According to the Ministry of Tourism of the Government of the Maldives, international tourist arrivals declined by 44 percent during the first eight months of 2005 as compared with the same period in the preceding year. Furthermore, the average capacity utilization or occupancy rate was only 58 percent from January through to August 2005, as compared with the first eight months of 2004. The World Bank (2005) has recently stated that there would be a budget shortfall of USD 96 million due to the decline in tourism, of which one-half would have to be raised locally, with the rest to be raised by international donors and development banks.

The analysis presented in this chapter also quantified the potential fall in daily government tax receipts, which affects the ability of the Maldivian Government to service its debt obligations. Hence, potential creditors can use the analysis presented here to decide what should be the appropriate interest rate on loans to the Maldivian Government. Furthermore, VaR thresholds for tourism tax receipts could be incorporated into loan covenants to provide a greater level of protection for financial institutions that might provide loans to the Maldivian Government.

The commercial stability of the tourist resorts owned by local and foreign investors depends significantly on the tourists in residence figures, which will also determine the capacity utilization rate. Working capital, as obtained in the form of an overdraft facility, is required for the smooth operation of these facilities. An extremely large negative shock, such as the 2004 Indian Ocean tsunami, would reduce the asset value of some resorts below the constant debt level, which is the total amount borrowed to finance the purchase of the asset. Following the 2004 tsunami, 19 resorts in the Maldives were closed completely due to extensive damage. In order to recover their asset value, certain occupancy or capacity utilization rates would have to be achieved.

The VaR analysis presented in this chapter could be used by resort operators in a 'Real Options' framework. Resort operators have the option to shut down, either wholly or in part, as this choice can help to minimize losses. Therefore, VaR thresholds have value and can be priced using identical principles as in the case of financial options. In pricing financial options, a crucial input is the volatility of the underlying asset which, in the case of tourist resorts, is the number of tourists in residence. Hence, modelling the conditional volatility of tourists in residence will aid resort operators in deciding whether to remain open, shut down a portion of the resort, or shut down operations in their entirety. Therefore, managing Value-at-Risk should assist significantly in achieving optimal risk management strategies.

ACKNOWLEDGEMENTS

The first author acknowledges the financial support of the Australian Research Council, the second author wishes to thank the financial assistance of the School of Accounting, Finance and Economics at Edith Cowan University and the third author is most grateful for the financial support of an International Postgraduate Research Scholarship and University Postgraduate Award at UWA. The authors wish to thank Clive Granger, Matteo Manera and Juerg Weber for helpful comments and suggestions. An earlier version of this chapter was presented at the Second International Conference on Tourism and Sustainable Development: Macro and Micro Economic Issues, Cagliari, Sardinia, Italy, September 2005.

REFERENCES

Black, F. (1976), 'Studies of stock market volatility changes', *Proceedings of the American Statistical Association, Business and Economics Statistics Section*, pp. 177–81.

Bollerslev, T. (1986), 'Generalized autoregressive conditional heteroscedasticity', *Journal of Econometrics*, **31**, 307–27.

Chan, F., S. Hoti, M. McAleer and R. Shareef (2005), 'Forecasting international tourism demand and uncertainty for Barbados, Cyprus and Fiji', in A. Lanza, A. Markandya and A. Pigliaru (eds), *The Economics of Tourism and Sustainable Development*, Cheltenham, UK and Northampton, MA, USA: Edward Elgar, pp. 30–55.

Chan, F., C. Lim and M. McAleer (2005), 'Modelling multivariate international tourism demand and volatility', *Tourism Management*, **26**, 459–71.

Domroes, M. (1985), 'Tourism resources and their development in maldives islands', *GeoJournal*, **10**, 119–26.

Domroes, M. (1989), 'Tourism in the Maldives: The potential of its natural attraction and its exploitation', *Applied Geography and Development*, **36**, 61–77.

Domroes, M. (1993), 'Maldivian tourist resorts and their environmental impact', in P.P. Wong (ed.), *Tourism vs Environment: The Case for Coastal Areas*, Dordrecht, The Netherlands: Kluwer Academic Publishers, pp. 69–82.

Domroes, M. (1999), 'Tourism in the Maldives: the resort concept and tourist related services', *Insula: International Journal of Island Affairs*, **8**, 7–14.

Engle, R.F. (1982), 'Autoregressive conditional heteroscedasticity with estimates of the variance of United Kingdom inflation', *Econometrica*, **50**, 987–1007.

Glosten, L.R., R. Jagannathan and D.E. Runkle (1993), 'On the relation between the expected value and volatility of the nominal excess return on stocks', *Journal of Finance*, **46**, 1779–801.

Hoti, S. and M. McAleer (2004), 'An empirical assessment of country risk ratings and associated models', *Journal of Economic Surveys*, **18**(4), 539–88.

Hoti, S. and M. McAleer (2005), *Modelling the Riskiness in Country Risk Ratings*, Contributions to Economic Analysis, Vol. 273, Amsterdam: Elsevier.

Hoti, S., M. McAleer and R. Shareef (2005), 'Modelling country risk and uncertainty in small island tourism economies', *Tourism Economics*, **11**(2), 159–83.

Li, W.K., S. Ling and M. McAleer (2002), 'Recent theoretical results for time series models with GARCH errors', *Journal of Economic Surveys*, **16**, 245–69, reprinted in M. McAleer and L. Oxley (eds), *Contributions to Financial Econometrics: Theoretical and Practical Issues*, Oxford: Blackwell, pp. 9–33.

McAleer, M. (2005), 'Automated inference and learning in modelling financial volatility', *Econometric Theory*, **21**, 232–61.

McAleer, M., R. Shareef and B. da Veiga (2005), 'ST@R: a model of sustainable Tourism@Risk', unpublished paper, School of Economics and Commerce, University of Western Australia.

Ministry of Planning and National Development (2005), '25 Years of Statistics – Maldives', Government of Maldives, pp. 447.

Nicolau, J.L. (2005), 'Leveraging profit from the fixed-variable cost ratio: the case of new hotels in Spain', *Tourism Management*, **26**(1), 105–11.

Raab, C. and R.K. Schwer (2003), 'The short- and long-term impact of the Asian financial crisis on Las Vegas Strip baccarat revenues', *International Journal of Hospitality Management*, **22**(1), 37–45.

Shareef, R. (2004), 'Modelling the volatility in international tourism demand and country risk in small island tourism economies', Unpublished PhD Dissertation, University of Western Australia, Perth, Australia, pp. 440.

Shareef, R. and M. McAleer (2005), 'Modelling the uncertainty in international tourist arrivals to the Maldives', *Tourism Management*, **28**(1), 23–45.

World Bank (2005), 'Maldives: Tackling a Budget Crisis', http://web.worldbank.org/ WBSITE/EXTERNAL/NEWS/0,,contentMDK:20668908~pagePK:64257043~piPK: 437376~theSitePK:4607,00.html (last access: July, 2007).

9. Uncovering the Macrostructure of Tourists' Preferences: a Choice Experiment Analysis of Tourism Demand to Sardinia

Rinaldo Brau and Davide Cao

9.1 INTRODUCTION

This chapter examines the application of stated preference techniques (in particular discrete choice modelling) into the debate on designing policy commonly thought to be best suited to achieving 'sustainable tourism development'.

From a long-run economic perspective, the role of tourism is dubious. The literature has outlined some possible negative effects, such as dependence to foreign capital and to a volatile demand (Sinclair, 1998), disturbances in the labour market (Nowak et al. 2005), Dutch disease effects (Nowak and Sahli, 1999 and see chapter 5 in this book), land competition and speculation (e.g. Giannoni and Maupertius, 2005). However, several theoretical studies (e.g. Lanza and Pigliaru, 1994; Lonzano et al., 2005; Cerina, 2006) have pointed out that these negative effects can be outweighed through a cautionary management of natural resources, not only in ensuring the long-run exploitation of resources, but also in increasing tourists' willingness to pay, and ultimately tourism receipts.

In fact, the focus on the dynamics of tourists' expenditure is central for the debate on the growth potentials of the tourism sector which, on the one hand, is characterised (on the supply side) by a lower-than-average rate of productivity growth; but, on the other hand, can experience high rates of revenue growth thanks to the role (on the demand side) of 'terms of trade' (Lanza and Pigliaru, 1994) and 'high demand elasticity to income' effects.[1] In the theoretical literature on the dynamics of tourism economics, a 'cautionary management' may take place whether by policies for the preservation of environmental quality, or for the limitation of tourists' arrivals.

However, these views appear in sharp contrast with how the tourism industry often is being developed in 'practice' in many areas, where the main focus of attention has been the setting up of infrastructure, residential buildings and services, whose construction often negatively affects the original features of the very natural resources that made a given area attractive as a tourist destination.

A key issue is how to assess whether such transformation of tourist sites and destinations is the result of a rational attempt to respond to tourist preferences, or an undesirable consequence of market failures that have led to a non-optimal exploitation of natural resources. If the second supposition is true, many tourism economies are currently on a sub-optimal path of economic development due to their failure to adequately satisfy consumer preferences as regards the quality of environment. Unfortunately, this 'demand-led' path to economic and physical sustainability lacks substantial empirical evidence, given that it is difficult to verify it by means of the data sets on international tourist demand currently available. It is perhaps for this reason that empirical analyses of tourist demand have usually been carried out only at the aggregate level on less specific issues.

It is customary to say that tourism economies relying on natural resources 'supply their territory' to the international market. However, this is a rather generic expression that encompasses a set of characteristics ranging from the environmental state of a given natural attraction, to man-made facilities such as recreational services and, at least to some extent, the ease of access to a particular natural resource. In other words, tourism is a typical composite good, whose appeal clearly depends on how well balanced the mix of component characteristics is.

An empirical research method suited to the analysis of the relationship between product characteristics and consumer behaviour is the discrete choice modelling technique. In the last 15 years, literature on tourism economics has shown growing interest in stated preference approaches applied to the analysis of tourism demand (e.g. see the survey by Crouch and Louvière, 2000). Some studies have focused on very specific subjects, such as identifying the effects on WTP by selected characteristics that an accommodation facility or a single site should possess (e.g. Morimoto, 2005, studies tourist behaviour in the locality of Luang-Prabang, Laos); or estimating price responsiveness of 'single origin–single destination' flows of international tourist demand (e.g. Morley, 1994). A slightly different approach, in line with a long tradition in transportation studies, has been that of applying discrete choice modelling to destination choice, both for international tourist demand (Huybers, 2003b; Huybers and Bennett, 2000), and for modelling factors that determine inbound tourism flows for short trips (Huybers, 2003a).

In fact, as Huybers (2004) remarks, the use of discrete choice modelling in tourism has appealing properties from a scholarly perspective, as a useful research method applicable to empirically testing some theoretical hypotheses on tourist–consumer behaviour (e.g., think of price sensitivity and 'green preference' effects), and from a more policy-oriented viewpoint, as a tool which policy makers and promotion agencies can use in order to analyse the attractiveness of their existing products or tailor 'tourism products' to existing and new target markets.

We consider both perspectives very important, and therefore we endorse choice modelling as an analytical basis for an empirical analysis of the recent debate on tourism and sustainability. What information can we really infer from current demand, in particular in order to design an accurate 'destination profile' for elaborating local and/or regional policies? Moreover, are current development projects consistent with the actual needs of demand? Also, are 'sustainable tourism policies' an optimal, or at least a satisfying strategy for areas with important (and potentially marketable) natural resources?

With regard to the specifics of this study, which is based on the analysis of a sample of tourists interviewed in Sardinia's airports, tourist preferences are elicited by means of the choice experiment technique, where respondents are asked to indicate their first choice among a series of available alternatives (technically, the 'choice set'). In particular, by means of our choice experiment survey, carried out on a sample of tourists on completion of their holiday in Sardinia, we examine how tourist preferences are differentially affected by high or low degrees of accessibility to the tourist attraction, by the existence of protected areas in the vicinity of the accommodation, by the quality of the natural resources as well as by the overcrowding of tourist destinations. The use of standard econometric techniques for the analysis of discrete choice data enables us to generate estimates of the relative importance of these attributes. We also use the estimation results to simulate the effects on the likelihood that some hypothetical destinations (as defined by the various combination of the aforementioned attributes) are chosen over others. Finally, monetary evaluation of these characteristics are estimated and presented.

The structure of the chapter is as follows. In the next section, we briefly describe the econometric procedures used for analysing the data. In section 9.3, we describe the structure of the study carried out in order to analyse tourism flows in Sardinia and the resulting dataset. Section 9.4 contains the main results of the analysis, and section 9.5 concludes by focusing on the main policy implications of the results.

9.2   ECONOMETRIC TOOLS FOR MODELLING TOURISTS' CHOICES

In this section we briefly summarize the analytical tools used for our empirical application based on the technique of choice experiments. We only recall the basic expressions used for carrying out the estimates, given that discrete choice techniques are nowadays well established.[2] In fact, after being initially developed in transportation and marketing literature, in more recent years the technique has also found several applications in environmental economics and health economics studies.[3]

As we said in the introduction, one interesting application of choice modelling to inbound tourism has been that of studying how the probability of one destination being preferred to another one depends on the different combinations of certain basic characteristics (e.g. Morley, 1995). As a step forward, here we aim to assess the importance (in relative terms) of some 'characteristics which support sustainability', such as lack of overcrowding and preservation of quality in a natural environment vs. locating lodgings near to beaches and/or leisure services.

We want to stress that stated preference approaches are often the only empirical methodology available, given the absence of detailed data and the need to evaluate new policies and interventions. Moreover, a stated preference analysis gets rid off simultaneity problems which would characterize a study based on real markets data (as a simple example, think of the bi-directional link between overcrowding and tourist demand).

The theoretical basis for the application of stated preferences (in particular of choice modelling methods) to the demand of composite products is the Lancasterian approach to consumer analysis, in which utility for each good is defined as a weighted sum of a set of basic characteristics. When applied to tourism, these characteristics can be simply defined as the set of attractions and facilities which concur to define a holiday as a pleasant experience. Hence, when a choice experiment is carried out, the choice by the respondent should reflect, *ceteris paribus*, the combination of attribute levels which offers the highest utility for a given set of choice possibilities (the 'choice set').

Although many complex estimation procedures are now available,[4] in this chapter we base our empirical analysis on the estimates arising from a standard discrete choice multinomial logit model (henceforth, MNL).[5] As is well known, the MNL model enables us to relate the choice made by an individual in a real or hypothetical context to some characteristics which vary across his or her choice set.

More specifically, the data arising from the $j = 1, 2, ..., J$ alternative choices which are observed, and taken by a sample of $h = 1, 2, ..., H$ respondents, are described according to a random utility specification such as the following:

$$U_j^h = V_j^h + \varepsilon_j^h = \boldsymbol{\beta'}\mathbf{x}_j^h + \varepsilon_j^h, \qquad (9.1)$$

where the vector $\mathbf{x}_j^h$ may refer to characteristics of both the choice alternatives and of the respondent. Therefore, the index structure $\boldsymbol{\beta'}\mathbf{x}_j^h$ implies a linear additive specification of indirect utility functions V_j. If an element of $\mathbf{x}_j^h$ is common to all alternatives of the choice set, the variable is termed generic; otherwise it is alternative specific. Intuitively, only the latter may affect a choice probability, unless generic variables are artificially 'made' alternative-specific by associating them only with certain alternatives of the choice set.

The individual random components ε_j^h are assumed to be independently and identically distributed[6] (IID) with an extreme value type 1 (Gumbel) distribution with mean $\eta + \gamma/\mu$ and variance $\sigma^2 = \pi^2/6\mu^2$.[7] The IID assumption across alternatives of the unobservables leads to the well known property of independence of irrelevant alternatives (IIA). The property states that the odds ratio of an alternative k being chosen over alternative l is independent of the availability of attributes or alternatives other than k and l (e.g., McFadden, 1984). Therefore, the exclusion of some alternatives in estimation does not affect the consistency of the estimator, and the odds computed with a dataset related to a limited number of choice alternatives is still a reliable statistic for the market behaviour, even in cases where more choice possibilities are feasible.

One advantage of the above assumptions regarding the functional form is that the MNL model provides a particularly simple close form to estimate. Namely, the likelihood that household h chooses alternative k is:

$$P[y_h = i] = \frac{1}{\sum_{j=1}^{J} \exp[-(V_i - V_j)]}. \qquad (9.2)$$

The previous expression also makes clear that individual specific variables are cancelled out by the difference $V_i - V_j$.

Rearranging and using the index $\boldsymbol{\beta'}\mathbf{x}_j^h$ instead of V_i we get:

$$P[y_h = i] = \frac{\exp(\boldsymbol{\beta'}\mathbf{x}_i^h)}{\sum_{j=1}^{J} \exp(\boldsymbol{\beta'}\mathbf{x}_j^h)}, \qquad (9.3)$$

where y_h is an index of the choice made by household h.

Equation (9.3) can be directly employed to estimate choice probabilities. From these, the market shares for the problems involved are directly obtained. The IIA hypothesis is crucial, here. In fact, if analysts believe it is valid, a choice between two alternatives can be enough for enlarging analysis to a case scenario with many possible choices (e.g. see Train, 2003, pp. 53–4). Otherwise, what needs to be done would be to build choice experiments with a number of alternatives as far as possible similar to those an individual faces in real life. This of course would expose the choice experiment to dramatic increases in task complexity for the respondent.

By estimating the previous model, we obtain an estimate of the relative weight of an attribute for each individual utility function. Substitution rates between the attributes can then be easily computed. In the case of continuous attributes, these rates translate into marginal effects and, with straightforward modifications, into elasticities. When the attribute to be evaluated is discrete, what can be actually computed is a 'value of level change'.

A very useful kind of substitution rate to use is the 'implicit price', which can be computed when there is an attribute expressed in monetary terms. In this case, given the linear specification of the indirect utility function, welfare effects of a level change are measured as follows:

$$WTP = -\frac{1}{\beta_p}\left(V_0^h - V_1^h\right). \tag{9.4}$$

The subscripts $(0,1)$ in equation (9.4) define the indirect utility functions before and after the policy change, whilst β_p is an approximation of the inverse of marginal utility of income, which is usually given by the estimated coefficient associated with the attribute expressed in monetary terms. Alternatively, an estimate of the marginal utility of income can be obtained from the coefficient of a regressor defined as the difference between a respondent's income and the cost of the alternative.

As is explained, for example, in Louvière et al. (2000, p. 337), with the expression (9.4) we get the compensating variation in a case where an individual chooses a particular alternative (destination) with certainty. Alternatively, it can be seen as an appropriate measure for cases where a quality variation applies to all the alternatives of the choice set (Haab and McConnell, 2002). Moreover, even though it is widely acknowledged that the marginal utility of income actually varies with income, the use of the expression is justified by hypothesising that the marginal utility of income is constant over the range of implicit income changes involved by a given policy intervention. This would be quite feasible in cases where the cost difference of a choice alternative is small relative to individual income.

In addition to pointwise estimates, confidence intervals should be computed. Generally, the Krinsky–Robb technique or bootstrap methodologies are used. However, when one aims to evaluate the value of a single level change of a categorical attribute i, so that equation (9.4) reduces to the negative of the ratio of the associated parameter $-\beta_i/\beta_p$, a more immediate approximate estimate of the standard error can also be computed, where an orthogonal experimental design is used.[8] In particular, following Bateman et al. (2002), we have that:

$$\text{var}(WTP) \equiv \text{var}\left(\frac{\beta_i}{\beta_p}\right) = \left(\frac{\beta_i}{\beta_p}\right)^2 \left[\frac{\text{var}(\beta_i)}{\beta_i^2} + \frac{\text{var}(\beta_p)}{\beta_p^2} - \frac{2\text{cov}(\beta_i,\beta_p)}{\beta_i\beta_p}\right] (9.5)$$

In the case of an orthogonal design, the covariance term is zero, so that the previous expression reduces to:

$$\text{var}(WTP) \equiv \text{var}\left(\frac{\beta_i}{\beta_p}\right) = \left(\frac{\beta_i}{\beta_p}\right)^2 \left[\frac{\text{var}(\beta_i)}{\beta_i^2} + \frac{\text{var}(\beta_p)}{\beta_p^2}\right]. \quad (9.6)$$

9.3 AN OUTLINE OF THE SURVEY AND RESULTING DATABASE

The survey was carried out between June and October 2005 by means of personal interviews in three major airports of Sardinia. It aimed to collect comprehensive information sets encompassing the personal characteristics of tourists, their chosen holiday location and average daily expenditure, and a series of opinions and observations concerning their experience of the 'Sardinian tourist product'. The survey included a choice experiment questionnaire designed to obtain original data on the tourists' perception of certain features (particularly with regard to the environment) of a standardized (and hypothetical) range of Sardinian destinations based on hotel accommodation.

The interviews were carried out on people leaving Sardinia, after holidaying in the island. Therefore, they were familiar with the kind of destinations proposed in the questionnaire. We are aware that the elicitation of individuals' preferences after making their choice of destination might involve the risk of self-selection bias, if these preferences concern the estimation of choice probabilities for different destinations. However, stated choices by 'experienced tourists' rather than by prospective ones have the advantage of providing information by an 'informed' sample of people who properly know the nature of the product in question. Moreover, no bias effects occur when the focus is on the characteristics of existing tourist demand flows to Sardinia, rather than on the estimation of the probability of attracting additional flows. Of course, a policy intervention aimed at better matching and responding to the preferences of existing tourists is also likely to have an impact on destination choices at a more general level.[9]

With a view to collecting the required information, the survey was organized as follows. The questionnaire consisted of two main parts, one focusing on socio-demographic characteristics such as age, sex, and provenance (Italian region or country). Also, respondents were asked to give information about their mode of booking, the kind of accommodation, the main motivation for the holiday, etc. Finally, the personal daily expenditure was collected, for purposes of comparison with other existing studies. Most of these variables can be employed to check for the representativeness of the sample and perform some comparisons between subsets of the final demand (see tables 9.2 and 9.3 below). The second part of the questionnaire introduced the choice experiment by means of short descriptions of the purpose of the survey and of a basic scenario (the 'fixed' characteristics). The last part of the questionnaire asked some check questions to verify the quality of data collected and asked respondents to indicate their net personal annual income.[10]

As a basic scenario for carrying out the choice experiments, tourists had to choose between various alternatives for a week's holiday (six nights) in a good quality three star hotel. The holiday scenario considered was a mainly 'beach and seaside' vacation, with accommodation in the vicinity of a seaside resort. This would not of course exclude the possibility of taking excursions to inland areas of the island. However, the primary tourist attraction was the sea.

The description of the hypothetical scenario was followed by presentation of the 'attributes' to be considered. These dealt with characteristics that varied in the choice set of the experiment according to our experimental design. Each attribute could assume different levels in each profile presented for choice; and in order to make the following choice process easier (in addition to the textual and oral explanation of different attribute levels) the interview showed respondents the illustrative choice set shown in Figure 9.1.

We defined and categorized the six attributes on the basis of several rounds of 'expert opinion' meetings carried out in February and March 2005, of a previous survey carried out in 2003 by CRENoS (where tourists were asked to indicate what characteristics they considered Sardinia lacked in terms of tourist services), and a first pre-test consisting of about 50 interviews carried out during the period of the Easter holidays, when the first sizeable tourism flows usually come to Sardinia. The pre-test was particularly useful for assessing if the attributes were presented in a clear and understandable manner, i.e. whether the attribute labels and the wording of each attribute level were valid.[11]

The description of attributes and their levels are shown in Table 9.1. We think that some additional explanation is needed at least for the first two attributes. Namely, since the main attraction of Sardinia is its sea and coast, we needed a measure of the disutility of the distance of accommodation from the main 'attraction site', i.e. the beaches and/or the seaside scenery. Ten

Questionnaire type 1;   Card n° 1

Assuming that the only two possible choices are the following, which would you choose?

Features of holiday	Type A holiday	Type B holiday
Proximity of main tourist attraction	High	Low
Risk of overcrowding in main point of attraction	High	Low
An uncontaminated natural environment	Maximum	Minimum
Availability of additional services	Good availability	Low availability
A nature reserve in the vicinity of your holiday location	Yes	No
Daily cost per person per night	80	65
18. Preference (Tick one box only)	☐	☐

Figure 9.1   An illustrative show-card used in the choice experiment

minutes by car or public transport on a tourist route cover a distance of about 2 km. Given that building accommodation inland rather than on coastal areas reduces environmental impact, detecting tourist aversion to distance is important for municipal and regional territorial planning policy.

The second attribute aimed to capture aversion to overcrowding, which clearly constitutes a difficult task. Rather than trying to find an exact definition of a 'perceived' carrying capacity, we considered that what tourists particularly dislike is the 'risk of overcrowding', which occurs when the availability of the main tourist attraction (access to the beach and the sea) is not guaranteed since it must be contended for with other visitors. The most immediate way to elicit a valuation of this effect was to envisage the possibility of 'preferential access' associated with the accommodation. Where this preferential access is not guaranteed, tourists were faced with the risk of overcrowding (involving the need to find a place to park the car, to go ahead of time to the beach, etc.).

The explanation of the scenario, of the attributes and corresponding levels may be quite time-consuming. This is one of the critical points of the choice modelling method because an inaccurate definition of attributes would make the detection of preferences less precise. But since a proper description requires time, interviewers were at risk of having to abandon the interview. Overall, the average length of the interviews was slightly less than 15 minutes.[12]

In theory, the full factorial arising from all the possible combinations would yield 512 profiles, but in order to keep the number of the required stated choices at a manageable size, we varied the level of the attributes

Table 9.1   Description of the attributes and attribute levels of the choice experiment

1. Proximity of main tourist attraction (principal motivation for holiday choice)	• High: The main attraction (the beach) is easily reachable on foot from your accommodation • Low: From your accommodation, it requires about ten minutes by public transport or by car to reach the main attraction.
2. Risk of overcrowding in main point of attraction	• Low: Your hotel guarantees easy access to the main tourist attraction (e.g. parking and sunshades reserved for hotel guests) • High: Your hotel does not guarantee easy access to the main attraction (tourists rely on their own means)
3. An uncontaminated and untouched natural environment as a primary attraction	• Maximum: a site only reachable on foot, and leaving your car in a place not visible from the beach, and where there are no information and bar/restaurant services, and no buildings in the vicinity • Good: a site only reachable on foot, and leaving your car in a place not visible from the beach, but with some tourist information signs and basic services, around which there are some buildings which are, however, scarcely visible. • Discrete: a site with a nearby parking facility as well as information points and bars/restaurants available; buildings clearly visible. • Minimum: a site with ample parking and adjacent buildings; no lack of shops and kiosks or bar/restaurant services.
4. Availability of recreational services (e.g. guides, entertainment/ organised activities, shopping areas, pubs and night spots).	• Ample availability: A wide variety of all kinds of additional/complementary services in the location chosen. • Good availability: A reasonably good choice and variety of additional/complementary services in the location chosen. • Low availability: A low choice and variety of additional/complementary services in the location chosen. • Minimal availability: A scarce or total lack of additional/complementary services in the location chosen.
5. A natural reserve in the vicinity of your holiday location	• Yes: A nature reserve is within 30 minutes reach of your accommodation (for example, a marine park, a local nature reserve). • No: There are no nearby nature reserves, or at least 30 minutes is needed to reach one.
6. Daily cost per person per night (half board accommodation in a 3 star hotel)	• 50 euros • 65 euros • 80 euros • 95 euros

according to an orthogonal fractional factorial design which yielded 32 profiles. The choice sets were then built by means of a 'shifted pairs' technique (see Louvière et al., 2000). Accordingly, these 32 choice sets were divided into four groups made up of eight choice cards similar to the one presented in Figure 9.1. Each tourist was asked to provide answers to one group of choice cards (i.e. to make eight choices). Finally, with the purpose of limiting order bias, the eight choice sets administered to each respondent were rotated sequentially.

We did not include any 'none of these two alternatives' options in the choice cards. This is a debated issue. In our case, the main argument against inserting this third option was that respondents might have simply indicated this third option in those cases where it was difficult to make a choice between the two alternatives, or they did not like the alternatives proposed. On the contrary, giving respondents the option not to choose any profile would make sense when the possibility of preferring not to go on holiday is made explicit (e.g., as in Huybers, 2003b). In this study, however, we were not interested in estimating the probability or not of coming to Sardinia, but rather how tourists might distribute according to the characteristics of the locations. Moreover, introducing the 'no choice' option often leads to very high values of the alternative specific constants, which then become the main components of the willingness to pay estimates (e.g. Adamowicz et al., 1998).[13]

Sample Representativity

The survey was planned so as to respect a simple stratification of the sample according to two characteristics of a tourist's universe: nationality (mainland Italy or foreign tourist) and type of accommodation (hotel and other categories). We based our survey plan on 2003 tourist flows (overnights), aiming also to respect the seasonality for the distribution of questionnaires. A total of 715 questionnaires were successfully completed.[14] The main characteristics of the sample are shown in Box 9.1.

Over half the respondents were male, aged on average 40, with a good cover of all demographic classes. The average education level is very high, in particular for foreign tourists of which over 50 percent are graduates, *vis à vis* 39 percent of national tourists.

The most striking of the descriptive statistics we obtained is the very high average income, especially for foreign tourists (€ 50 788) but also for the Italians (€ 39 053),[15] relative to the national average income. In fact, the average per capita disposable income in Central and Northern Italy (the areas from which the vast majority of Italian tourists originate) is about € 16 000. This might be due to the high number of interviews with tourists staying in high quality hotels, due to the fact that the interviews were mainly conducted in the airport located in the South of island, where the hotel quality is generally high, but in fact, even tourists not lodging in 4 and 5 star hotels

BOX 9.1   MAIN SOCIO-DEMOGRAPHIC
            CHARACTERISTICS

Gender		Age	
Male	57%	Average (years)	40.1
Female	43%	Median	39.0
Total	*100%*	15–30 years	26%
		31–45 years	43%
		46–60 years	23%
		Over 60 years	8%
		Total	*100%*

Education by nationality

actually declared a quite high income (mean € 35 662; median € 25 000).

In Box 9.2 below, we also report the average daily expenditures by income class declared by respondents. According to expectations, the average expenditure is higher for high classes of income and generally higher for foreign tourists.

Finally, in Box 9.3 we have summarised some of the information about respondents' holidays. We can see that over half of the respondents indicated that they had made use of hotel facilities, in particular 4 or 5 star hotels (34 percent of sample).

One fifth of respondents stayed in rented houses for their own vacation or at a friend's/relative's home. Not considering the category 'friends and relatives' (which is not recorded in official statistics), nor the quota of rented villa not registered,[16] the sample distribution is generally in line with the distribution of tourist flows according to nationality and kind of accommodation. Only the 3 star hotel category quota in the sample is underrepresented compared to official flows. The majority of respondents indicated that they did not use a tour operator to book or purchase their

BOX 9.2   SUMMARY STATISTICS FOR INCOME AND DAILY TOURIST EXPENDITURE

Average per capita daily expenditure by nationality and income classes

Income	National	Foreign	Total
< € 20 000	53.7	112.4	66.2
€ 20 000–€ 40 000	68.8	112.1	84.6
€ 40 000–€ 60 000	114.8	105.6	110.6
€ 60 000–€ 100 000	116.6	134.0	121.9
≥ € 100 000	135.0	200.6	167.2

Income classes by nationality

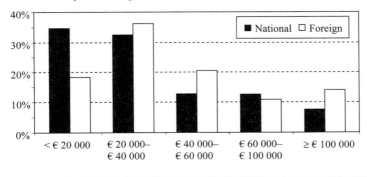

accommodation and travel, preferring a self-made holiday We also asked tourists if they made use of low cost companies to reach the island. Over 50 percent of respondents had chosen this kind of carrier. The low cost customers, as the chart above shows, were relatively more distributed in the lower income classes. Still, mean and median values indicate that even 'low cost flight travellers' arriving in Sardinia represent on average a rich niche market.

BOX 9.3   SUMMARY OF INFORMATION
REGARDING RESPONDENTS' HOLIDAYS

Official flows and sample distribution	Sample (excluding VFR and Farmhouse)			Official data (ISTAT, 2003)		
	National	Foreign	Total	National	Foreign	Total
5 and 4 stars	17	17	34	22	9	31
3 stars and holiday residence	16	8	24	30	10	40
2 and 1 stars	1	1	2	3	2	5
Camping or village resort	9	3	12	13	6	20
Rented villa or 2nd home	12	8	20	3	1	3
B&B and other accommodation	7	1	8	0	0	1
Total	*62*	*38*	*100*	*72*	*28*	*100*

	Tour Operator Use			Use of Low Cost Flight		
	Total	National	Foreign	Total	National	Foreign
Yes	36	38	33	32	21	55
No	64	62	67	68	79	45
Total	*100*	*100*	*100*	*100*	*100*	*100*

Use of low cost flight and income	National		Foreign		Total	
	Yes	No	Yes	No	Yes	No
Average	36 725	39 595	41 999	61 127	39 865	44 449
Mean	20 500	28 000	30 000	40 000	25 000	30 000

Use of low cost by income classes

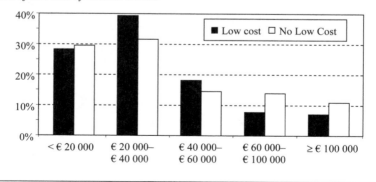

9.4   THE MAIN EMPIRICAL RESULTS

In this section we present and comment on the main results of our analysis and report some summary descriptive statistics and the econometric estimates obtained by the application of the MNL model on the data described in section 9.2.

As can be seen in Table 9.2 below, we have made use of two samples. The first one encompasses all the observations arising from the 715 completed questionnaires, and the second one involves only tourists who had not stayed in 4 or 5 star hotels. The reason for sampling out the high-spending tourists was to measure a potential different sensitivity to the accommodation costs used in the choice experiment, which referred to half board accommodation in a 3 star hotel.

The estimates based on the entire sample are reported in the first half of the table. All attribute levels are inserted as dummies. The cases excluded so as to avoid any singularity in the variance–covariance matrix are 'low proximity of the accommodation to the main attraction', 'low risk of overcrowding', 'maximum level for the quality of natural environment', 'minimal availability of recreational services', and 'absence of a nature reserve in the vicinity of the holiday location'. Finally, an alternative specific constant (ASC) was inserted, in order to ensure that the MNL was able to reproduce observed market shares, and check for the stability of the results. In fact, no changes occur when the ASC is excluded. The 'z statistics' values indicate the general high significance of most attribute levels. Moreover, in all cases the signs agree with economic intuition.

In discrete choice models, commenting on the absolute values would be misleading since all utility parameters are actually multiplied by a common unobservable scale parameter related to the variance of the unobservables. However, having a model with only categorical variables (apart from the cost attribute), the estimated coefficients make it easily viable to carry out an evaluation of the importance of the single attribute and attribute levels in relative terms, that is of the characteristics of the 'tourist product' with each other.

For example, if we set the parameter regarding the availability of hotel accommodation near the sea as being equal to one, we get a value of –1.50 for risk of overcrowding and of 1.16 for the existence of a protected area, of –0.89 for a shift in environmental quality to a discrete level (–1.71 in the case of the lowest level), and of 0.94 for a shift from minimal to good availability of recreational services (1.05 for an ample availability).

We can surmise that what the sample of interviewed people mostly dislikes is a high risk of overcrowding and a shift from maximum to minimal environmental quality. An interesting observation on this latter attribute is

Table 9.2   Multinomial logit estimation

Variable	MNL model with all observations			MNL model without people in 4 and 5 star hotels		
	Coeff.	z-value	Prob	Coeff.	z-value	Prob
Proximity of the beach (0 low, 1 high)	0.3633	10.70	0.000	0.3481	8.85	0.000
Risk of overcrowding (1 if no guarantee of access)	−0.5433	−16.53	0.000	−0.4944	−12.98	0.000
Good quality of natural environment (excluding dummy 'maximum quality')	−0.0762	−1.40	0.161	−0.0819	−1.30	0.195
Discrete quality of natural environment (excluding dummy 'maximum quality')	−0.3237	−4.96	0.000	−0.3085	−4.08	0.000
Minimal quality of natural environment (excluding dummy 'maximum quality')	−0.6226	−10.59	0.000	−0.5633	−8.26	0.000
Low availability of recreational services (excluding dummy minimum availability)	0.0423	0.76	0.449	−0.0183	−0.28	0.779
Good availability of recreational services (excluding dummy minimal availability)	0.3426	5.11	0.000	0.2612	3.36	0.001
Ample availability of recreational services (excluding dummy minimal availability)	0.3806	6.52	0.000	0.4085	5.98	0.000
Protected natural area in the surroundings (1 if present)	0.4202	12.92	0.000	0.4361	11.52	0.000
Daily cost of half board accommodation	−0.0044	−3.57	0.000	−0.0087	−5.94	0.000
Alternative specific constant	−0.0052	−0.13	0.893	0.0100	0.23	0.821

Diagnostic statistics and tests	Value	Value
Log likelihood function	−2839.95	−2099.66
Pseudo R-squared	0.1195	0.1151
Number of observations	9306	6846

that tourists do not seem to be particularly perturbed by slight modifications of the original environment, given that the coefficient is quite low and only slightly significant. What respondents have shown to be averse to are the substantial modifications of an untouched environment (i.e. from very high to low quality levels). Similar remarks can be made for the availability of recreational services, although with smaller values in absolute terms. There is a dichotomy between low and substantial endowment of services, so that only good and ample availability seem likely to affect the choice probability of a given destination. Finally, the vicinity of a natural protected area shows a quite relevant effect. This result has obvious important policy implications, both for a proper distribution of new accommodation services, and for the purpose of assisting a destination in difficulties. This high value could be partly determined by an option value effect, that is tourists appreciate the possibility to choose to visit a protected area, rather than the direct use they actually make of it. As a note of caution, however, we suspect that at least part of the estimated effect could depend on effects that contingent valuation analysts call 'symbolic bias' and 'part–whole bias', i.e. a tendency by respondents to express their support to environmental protection in general, rather than a precise evaluation of the benefit arising from a specific environmental good.[17]

The estimates based on the subsample of tourists not staying in luxury accommodation are reported on the right-hand side of the table. In fact, no striking differences emerge with respect to the sample as a whole. As expected, the only strong difference is in the sensitivity to the price of the half board accommodation, which is doubled. As it is clear from above, it is likely that this coefficient provides a more reliable measure of the marginal utility of income. On the other hand, this difference could also be interpreted as an indication of the quite low importance attributed by high spending tourists to variations in accommodation costs.

One property of the previous 'main effects' estimation is that of ensuring a constant marginal utility of income. In order to check if our results are robust to this condition, we could also relate the cost attribute to respondents' income. A common solution is to divide the cost attribute by the individual's income so that the coefficient of cost depends on income. We have found that parameter estimates are robust to this alternative specification.[18]

Simulations of the Probability of Choice for a Few Hypothetical Sites

The relative size of the various coefficients also provides an indication of which attributes and level variations determine the major effects on choice probabilities and market shares. A particularly interesting exercise is to predict choice probabilities for new or existing combinations of characteristics and study how different combinations of the attributes may affect the probability of choosing one or another site, as defined by some particular combination of the attributes. This simple exercise may be very useful for policy considerations regarding the shaping of main accommodation locations, with the caveat that the sample of tourists already arriving in Sardinia may suffer from self-selection problems, so that it would not be correct to extend the following analysis to the more general forecast of the behaviour of current national and international tourism flows.

As was outlined in section 9.2, it must be stressed that, in order to perform this exercise, the exploitation of the IIA hypothesis is of basic importance, given that it enables the researcher, on the basis of the estimated parameters only, to perform simulations regarding alternatives not actually chosen by the individuals. Of course, with IIA, what is unaffected by the addition of new choice alternatives in the choice set is the relative probability between two alternatives.

In practice, choice probabilities are determined by the expression (9.2) in section 9.2. It is straightforward to obtain estimated choice probabilities for different scenarios simply by inserting the levels of interest into the formula. For example, let us carry out a model simulation by hypothesising that tourists could choose among six holiday locations, which we have indicated with imaginary labels. There is no systematic structuring for all the hypothetical sites, but 'Paradise Resort' represents a situation where tourism is scarcely present, whereas '100 000 Beach' is the name of a mature location. The choice probabilities must of course be commented on under a *ceteris paribus* condition, that is a situation where there are no systematic differences among the destinations, beyond the attributes considered in the study.

As an example of how choice probabilities may be varied when intervening on some attributes, the first graph (Figure 9.2) considers a situation where the risk of overcrowding (where present) is eliminated by using the estimates on the whole sample.

Figure 9.3, based on subsample estimates to show that the quality of the results is unchanged, is modified introducing the effect of a € 10 price variation as a tool to get rid of overcrowding.

Finally, Figure 9.4 considers the case where overcrowding (where present) is eliminated in compensation for the greater distance of lodging from the beach.

WTP Estimates for the Main Characteristics

Let us now turn to the computation of implicit prices for the different qualitative levels of the attributes and of overall welfare measures for some representative scenarios. Table 9.4 below was constructed using expression

Table 9.3   *Simulation of the distribution of choice probabilities in a case with six choice alternatives*

Attributes	Paradise Resort	West City	East City	By the Stars	Lonely Beach	100 000 Beach
Proximity of main tourist attraction	Low	High	High	High	Low	Low
Risk of overcrowding in main point of attraction	Low	High	High	High	Low	High
An uncontaminated natural environment	Maximum	Good	Fair	Minimum	Good	Minimum
Availability of additional services	Minimal	Good	Good	Ample	Low	Ample
A nature reserve in the vicinity of your holiday location	Yes	No	Yes	No	Yes	No
Choice probabilities						
Whole sample, no difference in accommodation price	21.2%	15.2%	18.1%	9.1%	30.0%	6.4%
Subsample without high quality hotels, no difference in accommodation price	23.7%	15.9%	19.6%	11.4%	21.5%	8.0%

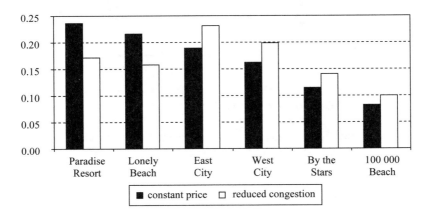

Figure 9.2   *Effects of the elimination of overcrowding (where present) on choice probabilities*

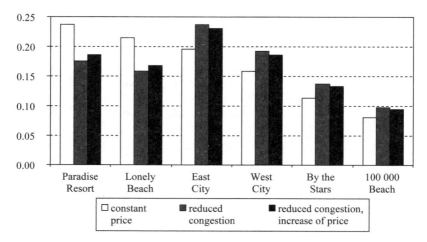

Figure 9.3   Elimination of overcrowding (where possible) without and with a price increase

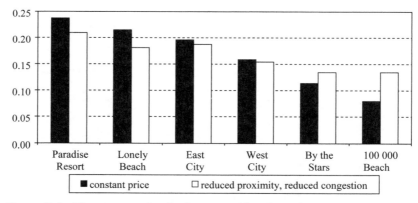

Figure 9.4   Elimination of risk of overcrowding by reducing proximity to the main attraction (if possible)

(9.4), whilst confidence intervals were estimated by means of the Krinsky–Robb (1986) procedure. What needs to be kept in mind is that we are dealing with discrete variations, but the hypothesis of constant marginal utility of income is mostly reliable when small level changes are considered.

As an indicator of marginal utility of income we use the 'conservative' estimates presented on the right-hand side of Table 9.4, which refer only to tourists not staying in 4–5 star hotels.[19] We have already pointed out that our sample (reflecting Sardinian tourism) consists of a large proportion of tourists who had lodged in expensive hotels. This practice has probably resulted in an 'anchoring' effect regarding the evaluation of the price of daily accommodation in the hypothetical scenario, regarding 3 star hotels, leading to a weak consideration of the cost attribute in the choice alternatives.

Table 9.4   Value of level changes for the various characteristics of the holiday locations

Level Changes	MNL estimation on subsample luxury hotels	
	Marginal WTP/WTA in Euros	95% Krinsky-Robb confidence intervals
Proximity of the main attraction	40.01	27.27 62.40
No risk of overcrowding	56.83	40.97 87.08
Variations in natural environmental quality		
From maximal to minimal	-64.75	-103.43 -4.60
From maximal to discrete	-35.46	-62.54 -17.81
From maximal to good	-9.33	-26.06 4.74
From discrete to minimal	-29.29	-59.25 -6.09
From good to discrete	-26.05	-54.82 -3.94
From good to minimal	-55.33	-93.57 -31.69
Variations in availability of recreational services		
From minimal to ample	46.95	28.93 76.23
From minimal to good	30.02	11.83 55.13
From minimal to low	Not significant	
From good to ample	16.93	-6.39 44.12
Existence of a protected natural area in the surroundings	50.13	35.73 75.97

The table was mainly built reporting willingness to pay (WTP) values for 'improvements' in individual utility functions, but it must be remembered that, with a constant marginal utility of income, the estimates obtained with the choice modelling approach yield the same result when the willingness to accept (WTA) case is considered (e.g. the environmental quality characteristic). Though based on the conservative estimates, we can see that the monetary values are quite large. However, for policy indications, 95 percent confidence intervals (whose width roughly depends on the MNL estimation of the standard errors of parameters) can offer a useful lower bound by means of which to assess the feasibility of some policy interventions. For example, 'packaging' solutions which guarantee 'no risk' of overcrowding seem to be easily ready to satisfy an unmet demand. Besides, proximity of the lodging to the sea clearly matters, but given the size of the aversion to the overcrowding effect, this could outweigh the value losses associated with accommodation which lacks proximity to the main tourist attraction. Finally, as expected from its international reputation, the environmental quality of Sardinia's sea is highly evaluated.

9.5   DISCUSSION AND CONCLUSION

This study has aimed to assess the potential of the discrete choice modelling approach in the analysis of international tourism preferences for a destination characterized by important natural resource endowments. Namely, the focus was on the demand-side economic effects of some broad characteristics of tourism supply which, according a growing stream of theoretical research, is likely to make the development of tourist destinations more sustainable from an environmental as well as an economic point of view.

The analysis was carried out on a sample of tourists interviewed when leaving Sardinia after their holiday. Therefore, in the first place, a note of caution is needed about the external validity of our results, as is generally the case for the outcomes of choice experiments. As was pointed out in section 9.2, we were faced with a rather rich niche of tourists that went beyond our original expectations. Moreover, the name 'choice experiments' must remind us that we are still dealing with a 'laboratory tool', where not all particularities of sites and accommodations can be modelled and captured.

Nevertheless, interesting indications about the relationship between the analysed attributes and destination choice have emerged. Results were all in accordance with economic theory, but what is even more important is the relative size of the various characteristics in determining consumer utility. We found that what tourists appreciate most is lack of overcrowding, in the form of being sure to have a fair access to the main attraction that motivated their holiday destination choice. Environmental quality is important, but real sensitivity seems to take place only where substantial losses with respect to original conditions are prospected. On the contrary, only high levels of recreational facilities as an accessory seem to be a relevant determinant of destination choice.

Useful policy indications emerge from such clear-cut effects. We know that an almost necessary condition for ensuring the physical carrying capacity of a site is that the concentration of accommodation and buildings near the main attractions (i.e. near the beaches and the coast) should be limited. Our results show, as expected, that giving up the proximity of the sea is not a 'free lunch'. In fact, the estimates indicate a quite relevant effect.[20] However, this is not a predominant one. Tourists seem well ready to give up having their room by the beach if they can get certain access to the natural resource, or if environmental quality is only slightly affected by tourism activities. Therefore, compensating effects in the form of granting access to the main attractive areas or ensuring the conservation of high standards of environmental quality seem to be feasible.

In general, we feel that the interest for this kind of approach should be fostered, both from the practitioner's and the academician's point of view. On the one hand, policy-makers and specialized agencies need to stay better informed about the determinants of tourists' behaviour, given the growing level of competition nourished by new tourist destinations, and the necessity to limit the market failures usually associated with a *laissez faire* management of natural resources. On the other hand, theoretical contributions can probably offer new useful insights if they would partially change the way environmental quality effects are framed in demand functions, in particular by shaping them more as a trade-off in comparison to other component characteristics, than as a simple upwards shift of consumers' willingness to pay.

ACKNOWLEDGEMENTS

This research has benefited of funding by the PRIN (National Interest Programme Research) project 'Sustainable local development and tourism'. We are grateful to the CRENoS members, especially to Stefano Usai, Raffaele Paci, Giovanni Sistu and Elisabetta Strazzera, for their participation in the definition of the survey questions and helpful comments and suggestions. We also thank the comments by the participants in the conferences held in Chia-Sardinia and Rio de Janeiro. The usual disclaimer applies. Finally, we wish to thank Riccardo Pinna, Fabio Mingoia and Fabio Manca for their important work in data collection.

NOTES

1. See, for example, Hazari and Sgrò (1995).
2. Recent reference texts are Louvière et al. (2000); Train (2003); Bateman et al. (2002).
3. For example, see the surveys by Hanley et al. (2001), Mazzanti (2003), and by Ryan and Gerard (2003), referring respectively to environmental economics, evaluation of cultural goods, and health economics literature.
4. See for example Train (2003).
5. This model is also referred to as the 'conditional logit' (e.g. Greene, 2003). Here we follow the terminology adopted by McFadden (1984) and Louvière et al. (2000).
6. The IID hypothesis implies that $\operatorname{cov}\left(\varepsilon_j^h,\varepsilon_i^h\right)=0$ and $Var\left(\varepsilon_j\right)=\sigma^2=\pi^2/6\mu^2$, $\forall j$, so that on the whole the variance–covariance matrix of the MNL is constant and simply equal to $\Sigma=\sigma^2 I$.
7. The parameter η is the mode of the distribution, μ is a positive scale parameter, $\pi=3.14159$ and $\gamma=0.577$ (the Euler constant).
8. Orthogonal designs are the most used solution for the design of choice experiments. See Louvière et al. (2000) for details, and the next section for the description of the design used in this chapter.

9.   More precisely, the effect on overall tourist expenditure would be zero only when the property of weak separability between regional destinations holds for international tourist demand. When the focus is on the forecast of the variation of choice probabilities, an analysis based on stated choices of potential tourists is to be recommended, in order to avoid the potential for incidental truncation with surveys of tourists at their destinations (e.g., see Morley, 1994; Huybers and Bennett, 2000; Huybers, 2003b).
10. The complete questionnaire which was prepared for the survey is available on request.
11. In fact, the pre-test of the questionnaire in the Easter 2005 period consisted of about 100 interviews, with a share of these devoted to test a version of the choice experiment where an attribute regarding the kind of holiday (sea versus natural-cultural holiday) was included. Tourists mainly opted (lexicographically) for a seaside vacation, so that we gave up examining different kinds of tourism attractions in the same choice experiment. At present, a survey with the natural/cultural-based holiday scenario is also being carried out.
12. The place where the interviews were carried out (directly by the gate area in the airport) made the administration of the questionnaire much more simple.
13. In order to check if this format of the choice experiment constitutes a strong limitation, we carried out a test on a subsample of respondents by introducing a follow-up question which allowed them to confirm the choice made or to say 'neither of these two alternatives'. We find that the inclusion or exclusion of these answers does not change the quality of the results.
14. The survey was part of a larger experiment that include another questionnaire with a scenario based on natural and cultural resources. The results of the complete survey will be presented in a future work.
15. The highest recorded income was € 500 000. Hence this result is not affected by the existence of outliers.
16. In Sardinia this quota is estimated particularly high.
17. See for example Bateman and Willis (1999).
18. Results are available on request. Given that a share of the respondents refused to answer the related question, this approach of course involves a reduction of the estimation sample. We are also aware that problems of measurement error, mainly due to rounding effects, cannot be ruled out. Finally, as Train (2003) remarks, if the cost coefficient depends on income, there is a violation of the assumptions needed for deriving welfare measures of the type expressed by equation (9.4). The violation may not be important for small level changes, but certainly relevant for large changes.
19. With the estimates from the whole sample, it is easy to verify that implicit prices would be more or less doubled.
20. Given the recent debates in Sardinia, where severe legislation has been established in order to limit the exploitation of costal areas, this attribute was in clear evidence in the choice set cards, in order to minimize the risk of underestimating the related aversion effects.

REFERENCES

Adamowicz, W., P. Boxall, M. Williams and J. Louviere (1998), 'Stated preference approaches for measuring passive use values: choice experiments and contingent valuation', *American Journal of Agricultural Economics*, **80**, 64–75.

Bateman, I.J. and K.G. Willis (1999), *Valuing Environmental Preferences: Theory and Practice of the Contingent Valuation Method in the US, EU, and Developing Countries*, Oxford: Oxford Economic Press.

Bateman, I.J., R.T Carson, B. Day, W.M. Hanemann, N. Hanley, T. Hett, A. Jones, G. Loomes, S. Mourato, E. Ozdemiroglu, D.W. Pearce, R. Sugden and J. Swanson (2002), *Economic Valuation with Stated Preference Techniques*, Cheltenham, UK and Northampton, MA, USA: Edward Elgar.

Cerina, F. (2006), 'Tourism specialization and sustainability: A long-run policy analysis', FEEM working paper 11.06.

Crouch, G.I. and J. Louvière (2000), 'A review of choice modelling research in tourism, hospitality and leisure', *Tourism Analysis*, **5**, 97–104.

Giannoni, X. and M.-A. Maupertius (2005), 'Environmental quality and long run tourism development: a cyclical perspective for small island tourist economies', FEEM working paper 145.05.

Greene, W. (2003), *Econometric Analysis*, fifth edition, New York: McGraw Hill.

Haab, T.C. and K.E. McConnell (2002), *Valuing Environmental and Natural Resources: The Econometrics of Non-Market Valuation*, Cheltenham, UK and Northampton, MA, USA: Edward Elgar.

Hanley, N., S. Mourato and R. Wright (2001), 'Choice modelling: a superior alternative for environmental valuation', *Journal of Economic Surveys*, **15**, 435–62.

Hazari, B. and P.M. Sgrò (1995), 'Tourism and growth in a dynamic model of trade', *The Journal of International Trade and Economic Development*, **4**, 243–52.

Huybers, T. (2003a), 'Domestic tourism destination choices: a choice modelling analysis', *International Journal of Tourism Research*, **5**, 445–59.

Huybers, T. (2003b), 'Modelling short-break holiday destination choices', *Tourism Economics*, **9**, 389–405.

Huybers, T. (2004), 'Destination choice modelling – to label or not to label?', TTRI discussion papers 2004/4, University of Nottingham.

Huybers, T. and J. Bennett (2000), 'Impact of the environment on holiday destination choices of prospective UK tourists: implications for Tropical North Queensland', *Tourism Economics*, **6**, 21–46.

Krinsky, I. and A.L. Robb (1986), 'On approximating the statistical properties of elasticities', *The Review of Economics and Statistics*, **68**, 715–19.

Lanza, A. and F. Pigliaru (1994), 'The tourist sector in the open economy', *Rivista Internazionale di Economiche e Commerciali*, **41**, 15–28.

Lozano, J., C. Gómez and J. Rey-Maqueira (2005), 'An analysis of the evolution of tourism destinations from the point of view of the economic growth theory', FEEM working paper 146.05.

Louvière, J., D.A. Hensher and J.D. Swait (2000), *Stated Choice Methods*, Cambridge: Cambridge University Press.

Mazzanti, M. (2003), 'Discrete choice models and valuation experiments', *Journal of Economic Studies*, **30**, 584–604.

McFadden, D. (1984), 'Econometric analysis of qualitative response models', in Z. Griliches and M.D. Intriligator (eds), *Handbook of Econometrics*, II, Amsterdam: Elsevier Science, pp. 1395–457.

Morimoto, S. (2005), 'A stated preference study to evaluate the potential for tourism in Luang Prabang, Laos', in A. Lanza, A. Markandya and F. Pigliaru (eds), *The Economics of Tourism and Sustainable Development*, Cheltenham, UK and Northampton, MA, USA: Edward Elgar.

Morley, C. (1994), 'Experimental destination choice analysis', *Annals of Tourism Research*, **21**, 780–91.

Morley, C. (1995), 'Tourism demand: characteristics, segmentation and aggregation', *Tourism Economics*, **1**, 315–28.

Nowak, J.J and M. Sahli (1999), 'L'analyse d'un boom touristique dans une petite économie ouverte', *Revue d'Economie Politique*, **109**(5), 729–49.

Nowak, J.-J., M. Sahli and P.M. Sgrò (2005), 'Tourism, increasing returns and Welfare', in A. Lanza, A. Markandya and F. Pigliaru (eds), *The Economics of*

Tourism and Sustainable Development, Cheltenham, UK and Northampton, MA, USA: Edward Elgar.

Rey-Maquieira, J., J. Lozano and G.M. Gomez (2005), 'Land, environmental externalities and tourism development', in A. Lanza, A. Markandya and F. Pigliaru (eds), *The Economics of Tourism and Sustainable Development*, Cheltenham, UK and Northampton, MA, USA: Edward Elgar.

Ryan, M. and K. Gerard (2003), 'Using discrete choice experiments to value health care programmes: current practice and future research reflections', *Applied Health Economics & Health Policy*, **2**, 55–64.

Sinclair, M.T. (1998), 'Tourism and economic development: a survey', *Journal of Development Studies*, **34**, 1–51.

Train, K.E. (2003), *Discrete Choice Methods with Simulation*, Cambridge: Cambridge University Press.

10. Linking Environmental Quality Changes and Tourism Demand with the Repeat Visits Method

**Sophie Avila-Foucat and
Juan L. Eugenio-Martin**

10.1 INTRODUCTION

Tourism demand has increased worldwide both as a consequence of a higher rate of participation in tourism and also due to an increase in the frequency of trips. The increase in frequency is accompanied by higher demand for diversified tourism products. Amongst them, nature-based tourism is becoming more popular, in particular with tourists who reside in urban areas. Nature-based tourism demand has evolved from day trips to weekend breaks and to international holidays. The success of the destination in attracting and sustaining such demand depends on the quality of the experience offered to the tourists. This depends, among other factors, on the environmental quality of the destination (Deng et al., 2002; Huybers and Bennett, 2003). In this sense, conservation of the environmental quality is critical to sustaining the attractiveness of the destination over time, not only to current tourists but also to future generations. To this end, a range of conservation programs have been implemented worldwide. Their implementation implies the need for regulating land use and/or the activities undertaken. The choice of regulations requires understanding of the impacts of all the activities undertaken in the area (Gartner, 1987; Alavalapati and Adamowicz, 2000) and how they affect the environmental quality and consequently tourism demand. Although the environmental impacts of tourism have been investigated (Price, 1981; Sun and Walsh, 1998; Hall, 2001), what remains unclear is how those impacts affect tourism demand.

The purpose of this chapter is to propose an innovative and interdisciplinary method for quantifying the link between changes in environmental quality and its effects on tourism demand. For this purpose, the chapter integrates ecological and socio-economic perspectives.

From an ecological perspective, environmental quality describes the quality of an ecosystem in terms of its ability or 'health' for supporting disturbances (known as resilience). Ecosystem health is based on energy flows between different groups of organisms (Costanza, 1992). In that sense, biomass flows are indicators of the ecosystem's response to environmental conditions. Sustainable use of natural resources implies maintaining economic production in the long run while minimizing impacts to the environment. This requires defining and understanding ecosystem health while taking account of ecosystem goods and services in the economy. This approach is considered in the chapter and is integrated with the socioeconomic perspective.

Tourists perceive environmental quality from a variety of perspectives. Amongst all the ecological attributes that define the environmental quality of a destination, it is necessary to identify those attributes of which tourists are significantly aware. These vary with the geography of the destinations, the kind of activities undertaken and the tourists themselves. For instance, a river can be used for two different recreation activities, fishing or swimming, so that the water quality required differs for each activity. For a specific destination and activity undertaken, the methodology proposed deals with the heterogeneity of the tourists using a utility framework. The model estimates the willingness of the tourist to repeat the visit to the destination. The model is also innovative in revealing which ecological attributes are significant for tourism demand, conditioned on certain socioeconomic characteristics of the individuals and their different preferences for the ecological attributes of the destination. This helps tourist destination managers to be aware of the ecological attributes that require protection.

The model is applied in a case study of Ventanilla, in the region of Oaxaca, Mexico, which is one of the few successful examples of community-based ecotourism management (CBEM). It is located alongside a coastal lagoon that is the destination of fertilizer run-off from upland activities. The effects on tourism demand of the ensuing environmental quality changes that occur should be measured to obtain policy implications for watershed management and the interests of the local community.

For this purpose, an innovative interdisciplinary methodology is developed. The research is innovative in two ways. On the one hand, this model is used to define what tourists mean by the environmental quality of a particular destination, and on the other hand, the model is also able to link changes in environmental quality to changes in tourism demand. Finally, the understanding of this link is inputted into an ecological economic model of the area. It allows running simulations between changes in biomass of ecological attributes of tourism interest and its effects to the profits of the community.

10.2   ENVIRONMENTAL QUALITY CHANGES, REPEAT VISITS, TOURISM DEMAND AND SUSTAINABILITY

There are several types of land use, such as housing, industry, agriculture or tourism and recreation. The economic activity chosen will have an economic impact for the region in terms of income and employment and also an environmental impact. Depending on whether the natural resource is renewable or non-renewable, the land use decision will affect the future to a greater or lesser extent, affecting its sustainability. In this sense, the choice of an economic activity has an opportunity cost (Norton-Griffiths and Southey, 1995) with respect to choosing other activities not only in the short run but in the long run as well. For this purpose it is critical to understand and measure the economic and environmental implications of each activity and their interrelationships. In some cases, conflicts between different activities are likely to arise (Schittone, 2001) and careful management is necessary (Skonhoft, 1998; Williams et al., 1998; Brown et al. 2001; Davis and Gartside, 2001). Such management requires understanding of the economic benefits of all the sectors involved (Wunder, 2000; Sekhar, 2003) and their consequences for the environment and sustainability.

Nature-based tourism is particularly sensitive to other activities in the area. These may cause positive or negative externalities. Positive externalities can arise from the construction of infrastructures for other activities, such as better transportation facilities, but can also cause negative impacts on the quality of the environment, such as pollution. In this sense, tourism destinations are particularly sensitive to the 'problem of the commons' (Briassoulis, 2002; Healy, 2006) and conflict with polluting activities may arise (Getzner 2002).

Thus, an integrated assessment of environmental quality and its effects in the economy is very important. This chapter focuses on coastal regions, where integrated coastal management is recognized as an important tool for understanding the links between different economic sectors and the environment. More precisely, it is defined as a continuous and dynamic process by which decisions are made for the sustainable use, development and protection of the coastal zone. Moreover, 80 percent of marine and coastal pollution is due to upland-based sources (GESAMP, 2001). To confront this issue it is essential to link coastal and watershed management. Watersheds are a natural ecological unit, which is self contained and connected by water flows and hydrological processes. Specifically, a watershed approach allows upland socioeconomic and ecological aspects to be linked to coastal ones. The case study presented in this chapter is located in a coastal region, and the effects of environmental quality on tourism demand would contribute an important part of the watershed management recommendations.

From an ecological point of view, environmental quality is referred to as the capacity of ecosystems in supporting disturbances. For instance, water quality and/or air quality are common indicators of environmental quality that can determine the level of pollution. But environmental quality is not only assessed with pollution measurements; it has been recognized that to assure sustainability, an understanding of ecosystem dynamics is crucial. Maintaining economic production in the long run while minimizing impacts on the environment (Arrow et al., 1995) requires an understanding of ecosystems ecology and an internalization of ecosystem goods and services in the economy. Ecosystem dynamics is the relationship between species populations and their habitat conditions. Thus, ecosystems dynamics are complex processes, and models have evolved from single species to multi-species models.

Over the last 30 years, ecosystem attributes have been studied based on research by Odum (1969) who distinguished a number of structural and functional attributes describing the energy moving between organisms and ecosystems stability and functions. Odum used such attributes to explore the differences between mature and immature ecosystem states, which provide insights into how structural and functional characteristics change as ecosystems mature and how they might respond to disturbances. Based on Odum's research, it has been recognized that understanding ecosystems, for maintenance of their services, biodiversity and structural integrity, implies the description of biomass flows between the different ecosystem elements. Biomass flows and other trophic indicators are used to assess environmental quality in terms of ecosystem health. Costanza (1992) has described a healthy ecosystem where there is absence of disease, given mainly by the presence of diversity, stability and vigor. Vigor is the flow of energy in the system and diversity is related to the complexity of trophic relations. Ecosystem flow studies have been carried out in order to link trophic relationships and energy fluxes to economic activities such as fisheries (Barbier and Strand, 1998; Vega-Cendejas and Arreguín-Sánchez, 2001). Biomass flows analysis is helpful to know if the system can support stress or impacts such as exploitation or pollution. Thus, biomass variations after a change in habitat conditions are used in this chapter as indicators of environmental quality.

Either the tourist activity itself or other activities in the surrounding area may cause environmental impacts that affect the quality of the experience. However, not all the environmental impacts have a real effect on the way that tourists perceive the environmental quality. In this sense, from the tourist's perspective, it is necessary to identify the ecological attributes that define the environmental quality. Such identification is useful for prioritizing the conservation of those ecological attributes that are relevant to sustainable tourism.

A definition of environmental quality from the tourist's perspective has hardly been considered in the literature. Most of the studies have considered surveys of visitors to obtain an impression of their preferences for the environment (Guyer and Pollard, 1997). The definition of environmental quality from the tourist's perspective varies with the individual, the destination and the activity undertaken. Some ecological attributes are more relevant to tourists, depending on the nature of the destination and the activity involved. Hence, the components of environmental quality are heterogeneous with respect to the destinations and the kind of activities undertaken. Furthermore, since each individual has different preferences in recreation (Jakus and Shaw, 1997; Hearne and Salinas, 2002), each has different perceptions and interests with respect to the quality of the environment for tourist purposes.

In order to deal with individual heterogeneity, a utility framework has been used prominently in the environmental economics literature. This approach incorporates the different socioeconomic characteristics that define the individuals, so that this information contributes to modeling the quantifiable individual heterogeneity. There is an unobservable part of the heterogeneity that, under certain assumptions, can also be modeled within the same methodology (Train, 1998). The way of assessing the relevance of the ecological attributes is by modeling recreational demand. This has been considered in the environmental valuation literature, employing different techniques such as contingent valuation, the travel cost method, hedonic prices or choice modeling (Hearne and Salinas, 2002).

Hedonic price methods have been applied in the tourism literature to identify the relationship between the prices paid by tourists and the bundle of services received from hotels or package holidays (Mangion et al., 2005). This may be extended to value the environmental attributes of a tourist destination if the tourists have to pay for the excursion and they have alternative excursions to choose from (Hunt et al., 2005). This is a feasible alternative method but is constrained by the fact that the tourists may not have paid for visiting the nature-based tourism destination. An alternative is the use of such non-market valuation techniques as contingent valuation or the travel cost method.

Contingent valuation studies are non-market valuation techniques that try to assess the environment by the formulation of questionnaires from a target population. Their main advantage is their flexibility and ability to deal with different use values. Most of the studies are based on the process of stated preferences from the interviewees, such as their willingness to pay for the existence of particular environmental attributes. There is a vast literature on this topic with different variations. Amongst them, it has been applied to tourism studies (Dharmaratne et al., 2000; Lee and Han 2002; Solomon et al.,

2004). However, there is some concern about the validity and reliability of the results (Venkatachalam, 2004), due to various biases and errors. This becomes more problematic when it is applied to developing countries (Schultz et al., 1998), where the willingness to pay concept may have a significantly different relative value than in developed countries and the design of the survey has to be adapted to the different conditions (Whittington, 2002, 2004).

Alternatively, the travel cost method has been widely used in recreation studies. The travel cost that an individual incurs in order to visit a destination is associated with his or her willingness to pay for visiting the place and, together with other variables, helps in constructing a demand function. The costs are usually the daily costs of traveling. This makes sense for recreation activities that take place in a day trip but it is unclear how to extend the methodology for tourists who stay longer than one day and whose travel costs are higher than those incurred by residents (Bell and Leeworthy, 1990). Case studies have been applied to different places, such as the USA (Douglas and Taylor, 1998), Spain (Font, 2000), Costa Rica (Menkhaus and Lober, 1996) and India (Maharana et al., 2000). These applications have tried to assess the non-market value of the environment of tourist destinations, but none has tried to link changes in the environmental quality with tourism demand. An exception is the work by Huybers and Bennett (2003), who model the destination choice of tourists as depending on the attributes of the destinations and simulate changes in tourism demand due to changes in these attributes. This approach is a relevant contribution to the field, but the methodology has the risk of having biased results because of the arbitrary decision of the researcher in choosing a limited number of worldwide regional destinations for the modeling.

This chapter proposes a new methodology to link environmental quality changes and tourism demand. It is based on the repetition of visits phenomenon, and as in the recreation demand models, the methodology relies on a utility framework that is able to consider individual heterogeneity. The model proposed is innovative and it belongs to the 'contingent behavior' family of models.

10.3   CASE STUDY

Ventanilla is located in Oaxaca State, on the South Pacific coast of Mexico. The village is situated in the Tonameca watershed between the two main resorts: Puerto Escondido and Huatulco. Ventanilla is a small village in a coastal lagoon with a mangrove forest. The main attraction consists of a lagoon boat trip for wildlife watching. The main ecological attributes of tourist interest are wild crocodiles, birds and the mangrove forest. Ventanilla has a conservation program for flora and fauna; thus, some other animals in captivity can be observed by visitors. Mangrove plants, sea turtle eggs and juvenile crocodiles are temporarily in captivity to avoid predation. Adult crocodiles, deer and raccoons can also be seen, having been captured by the Federal Mexican Agency for Environmental Protection (PROFEPA) and given to the community for conservation. Ventanilla has been registered, since 2001, as a Unit of Management and Wildlife Conservation (UMA). The UMA is a strategy of the Minister of Environment and Natural Resources for identifying and supporting communities with sustainable wildlife use.

Ventanilla has had a community-based ecotourism management (CBEM) since 1995, when the ecotourism cooperative was created, following a sea turtle exploitation ban. Sea turtle exploitation was the main source of revenue for many coastal communities. Ecotourism is now the main source of revenue in Ventanilla and involves 90 percent of families. CBEM is becoming an alternative way of living for rural communities of developing countries and is receiving increasing attention in the literature (Avila-Foucat, 2002; Wearing and McDonald, 2002; Jones, 2005).

Ventanilla is located alongside a coastal lagoon that receives impacts from upland activities, so that the environmental quality depends on the watershed management (Woolley et al., 2002). Agriculture is the main activity of rural communities in Tonameca watershed, where we can distinguish crops such as coffee (*café de sombra*), corn, beans, papaya and mangos. Fertilizer run-off from agriculture represents a potential impact to water quality in the river and finally in the lagoon. Water quality change in terms of nutrient concentration may affect negatively the biomass of groups such as fish. When fertilizer run-off is in small quantities, it increases the nutrient concentration in water causing sometimes positive effects on the biomass of some groups. However, when fertilizer run-off is above a certain threshold, the oxygen available in water might not be sufficient to support the biomass increase, reaching an eventual anoxia (or eutrophication). Under those circumstances, the fish population would decrease and consequently its predators. For instance, crocodiles or piscivorous bird populations can be adversely affected when the prey is less abundant. Hence, conflicts between agriculture and wildlife tourism may arise as reported in other places (Lewandrowski and Ingram, 1999; Reynolds and Braithwaite, 2001).

10.4   THE METHOD OF REPEAT VISITS

If tourists have enjoyed their visit to a destination, it is likely that they will think of returning and/or recommending the visit to a friend or a relative. The enjoyment depends on the appreciation of the quality of the experience. As commented above, in nature-based tourism demand, part of the quality of the experience depends on the environmental quality. Hence, changes in the environmental quality, as perceived by the tourists, will affect their willingness to repeat the visit and ultimately the tourism demand. The repetition of visits has been considered in the tourism literature for different purposes and with different methodologies but has not been applied for assessing the environmental quality of a tourist destination.

An early approach to modeling repeat visits was carried out by Gitelson and Crompton (1984), who showed that some tourists are risk averse since they prefer to return to a known place rather than taking the risk of spending their holidays visiting a new destination. Since then, repeat visits have been examined with respect to the effects on spending (Godbey and Graefe, 1991), the relevance of the socialization (Fakeye and Crompton, 1992), for lodging (Richard and Sundaram, 1994), for assessing satisfaction (Alegre and Cladera, 2006) or testing differences in behaviour by repeaters and first visitors (Kozak, 2001; Lau and McKercher, 2004; McKercher and Wong, 2004; Oppermann, 1997; Petrick, 2004). Different methodologies have been used, for example discriminant analysis (Tiefenbacher et al., 2000), multiple regression (Lee, 2001; Mazursky, 1989) or structural equation modeling (Lehto et al., 2004).

Research of particular interest for this chapter was carried out by Juaneda (1996) who employs a utility framework to estimate the probability of repeat visit and Darnell and Johnson (2001) who build a theoretical model with simulations of the individual frequency. This is based on the probabilities of revisiting a destination and how it may change over time as the number of repeat visits increases. Building on the work of these two papers, this chapter combines the modeling of the repeat visits with the assessment of environmental quality changes and tourism demand. It is applied to Ventanilla, in Oaxaca.

A model of the probability of repeating visits is proposed in order to assess the tourists' willingness to accept changes in environmental quality. A survey of tourists was conducted and interviewees were asked if they expect to repeat their visit or not. Those who stated that they will repeat the visit were asked whether they would repeat their visit if a particular attribute deteriorated by a certain percentage. If the individual still thinks of returning, similar follow-up questions were asked with higher percentage deterioration until he or she changed his or her mind. This process allows identifying each individual with a maximum percentage deterioration they are willing to accept in order to keep thinking of returning. In the same way, those who are not thinking of repeating their visit were asked about what percentage quality improvement they would be willing to accept in order to change their minds and repeat the visit. Similarly, they eventually stated the minimum percentage improvement they were willing to accept in order to change their mind and return to the destination. The sequence of questions in order to obtain these values is explained in Figures 10.1, 10.2 and 10.3.

The methodology provides the subjective value of each ecological attribute for each tourist. Those who are willing to return were asked to state the maximum percentage deterioration they are willing to accept in order to return. Thus, the higher the value given, the higher the perception of that individual of the environmental quality. For instance, consider two individuals who are willing to return. One will only come back if the number of crocodiles does not decrease by more than 10 percent. However, the other individual will still come back even if the population of crocodiles becomes half of its current size (50 percent deterioration). Hence, it is plausible to think that the second individual is attributing a higher value to the current number of crocodiles than the first individual. Each tourist reports his or her percentage. The use of a kernel density function of these values for the whole population of current tourists depicts how the value of each ecological attribute is distributed in the population. These percentage values are employed as an individual's indirect measure of the current level of environmental quality for each attribute. This is denoted by A_{il} and takes a different value for each individual i and ecological attribute l.

The decision to visit the site again is modeled as a binary choice, denoted by T_i, such that, $T_i = 1$ if the household or individual decides to visit the site again and $T_i = 0$ otherwise. As Darnell and Johnson (2001) concluded, the

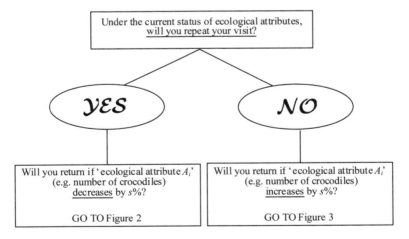

Figure 10.1   Discriminating question

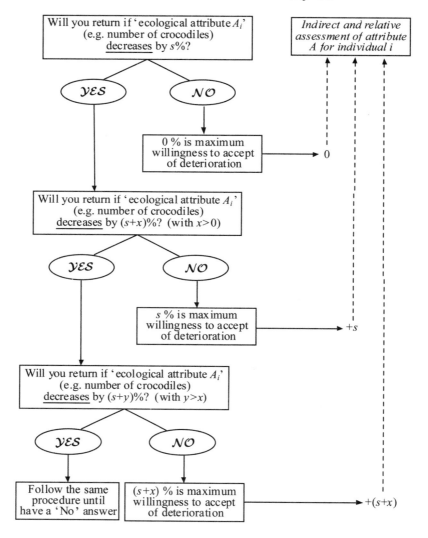

Figure 10.2   Method of assessment for those individuals who are willing to return

probability of visiting an attraction should be linked to the individual's characteristics. In this sense, it is assumed that $\Pr(T_i = 1)$ is linked to a set of exogenous variables. More precisely, for some appropriate function $g(\cdot)$,

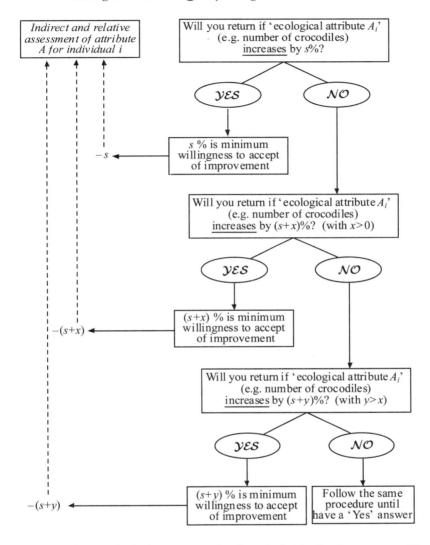

Figure 10.3   Method of assessment for those individuals who are not willing to return

$$\Pr(T_i = 1) = g\left(\alpha + \sum_{j=1}^{k} \beta_j SE_{ij} + \sum_{l=1}^{h} \beta_l A_{il}\right),\qquad(10.1)$$

where $0 \leq g(\cdot) \leq 1$, α denotes a constant, SE_{ij} denotes $j\text{-}th$ socio-economic variable of individual i, A_{il} denotes the value of attribute l as seen by individual i. β_i and β_l denote parameters associated with the previous variables. The model considers the existence of a latent variable T_i^*. Since this latent variable is unobserved by the researcher, we can consider it is composed of two parts: one observed by the researcher, which includes all the socio-economic variables, and another that is unobserved by the researcher and that corresponds to different behaviors among tourists. Thus, the model can be represented as:

$$T_i^* = \alpha + \sum_{j=1}^{k} \beta_j SE_{ji} + \sum_{l=1}^{h} \beta_l A_{il} + \varepsilon_i, \tag{10.2}$$

where ε_i denotes the unobserved part or error term. For our purposes, the latent variable will work as an index function, such that we will set $T_i^* = 1$ if $T_i^* > 0$ and $T_i^* = 0$ if $T_i^* \leq 0$.

Let

$$S_i = \alpha + \sum_{j=1}^{k} \beta_j SE_{ji} + \sum_{l=1}^{h} \beta_l A_{il},$$

such that $T_i^* = S_i + \varepsilon_i$. Then,

$$\Pr(T_i = 1) = \Pr(S_i + \varepsilon_i > 0) = \Pr(\varepsilon_i > -S_i)$$
$$= 1 - \Pr(\varepsilon_i \leq -S_i) = 1 - F_\varepsilon(-S_i)$$

where F_ε denotes the cumulative density function of the unobserved part. Due to a problem of identification of location and scale of T_i^*, it is necessary to choose a distribution and a value for the variance of ε_i. In our case, we assume ε_i is independently and identically distributed, following a normal distribution with zero mean and variance of one. Maximum likelihood estimation is applied to the probit model in order to estimate parameters of interest. We may obtain the change in the probability of revisiting the site under a marginal change in an attribute as:

$$\frac{\partial \Pr(T_i = 1)}{\partial A_{il}} = \phi\left(\alpha + \sum_{j=1}^{k} \beta_j SE_{ij} + \sum_{l=1}^{h} \beta_l A_{il}\right)\beta_l, \tag{10.3}$$

with

$$\phi(z) = \frac{1}{\sqrt{2\pi}} \exp\left(-\frac{1}{2}z^2\right).$$

being probability density function of a standard normal distribution. This will show how sensitive the probability of return is to a marginal change in environmental quality. From this approach, we can associate environmental quality changes with the variations in incoming tourists.

The model specification considers four main aspects: socio-economic variables, preferences for environmental attributes, length of stay and reasons for traveling. Among the socio-economic variables, we consider age, price and income. Price is divided into fixed price which is composed of travel cost to the coast of Oaxaca and travel cost to Ventanilla, and variable price which is composed of average daily expenditure on food, entertainment and accommodation. Total price with respect to income is considered in order to find out if the visit to Ventanilla is considered as a normal or inferior good.

Preferences for environmental attributes are examined in relation to four attributes: crocodiles, birds, mangroves and the fact that Ventanilla is a community based on ecotourism. The sensitivity of repeating the visit to changes in the number of crocodiles, birds and the size of the mangrove are explored as shown in Figures 10.1, 10.2 and 10.3, such that willingness to accept such changes are obtained from the survey and incorporated into the model.

Once the ecological attribute for visitors is identified, it is possible to estimate the production function considering variations in the biomass of this attribute. Biomass variations due to environmental changes, such as water quality, represent a measure of ecosystem health. That is, if the biomass of the main ecological attribute collapses, this means that the ecosystem is seriously affected and tourism arrivals would decrease since the main attraction is scarce. Supposing that the main attribute is crocodiles, changes in its biomass will be due to the fish biomass. For instance, let the ecotourism production function, Q_{vt}, be given by a function g($\cdot$), such that:

$$Q_{v_t} = g\left(B_{c_t}, L_{v_t}\right), \tag{10.4}$$

where B_{ct} denotes crocodiles biomass and L_{vt} denotes labour.

Crocodile biomass depends on the availability of food, therefore it is assumed in this model that an increase on crocodile biomass results from an increase in fish. Thus, it is possible to define crocodile biomass as a function of fish biomass given by a function v, such that:

$$B_{c_t} = v\left(B_{x_t}\right). \tag{10.5}$$

Fish biomass depends on phytoplankton biomass depending on nitrogen concentration as a measure of water quality and other variables such as predation:

$$B_{x_t} = f_x\Big[B_{p_t}(N_t), E_t\Big],$$ (10.6)

where B_{xt} is phytoplankton biomass in t/km^2, N_t is nitrogen concentration as a measure of fertilizer run off and E_t other ecological variables.

Substituting the expression (10.6) into expression (10.5) and this into the ecotourism production function (10.4) we have that:

$$Q_{v_t} = g\Big\langle L_{v_t}, v\big\{f_x\big[B_{p_t}(N_t), E_t\big]\big\}\Big\rangle$$ (10.7)

Ecotourism accordingly depends on labour, and biomass of crocodiles that is a function of fish biomass. Moreover, fish biomass is a function of nitrogen concentration in water due to urea run-off and other ecological variables.

Finally, tourism arrivals variations affect Ventanilla profits and can be estimated using tourism arrivals Q_{vt} (from expression (10.7)) multiplied by the price of the boat trip P_{vt} minus costs C_{vt}, as follows:

$$\Pi_{v_t} = P_{v_t}Q_{v_t} - C_{v_t}.$$ (10.8)

10.5   DISCUSSION OF RESULTS OBTAINED

Focus groups with tourists were carried out as a pilot survey. The questions were asked during and after visitors experienced wildlife watching. The purpose was to determine the degree of homogeneity of the visitor's perception of current environmental quality, for instance, if the number of current birds or crocodiles is perceived equally by each individual. This is a necessary condition in order to investigate whether, for instance, a decrease of 20 percent in the number of crocodiles will be perceived in a similar way. Pilot results were used to elaborate the final survey. A total of 552 structured questionnaires were completed in April and September 2003, providing information about the tourists' socioeconomic profile and the demand variations due to environmental changes. Open and dichotomous questions were asked in order to investigate a range of aspects of the visitors' perceptions.

The visitors mainly come from Mexico (86 percent). Specifically, 48 percent come from Mexico City and 13 percent from Oaxaca City. Visitors are mainly lodged in Huatulco (48 percent), followed by Puerto Escondido (12 percent). Ventanilla's accommodation infrastructure is non-existent but 35 percent of its visitors are lodged in nearby villages such as Mazunte. Visitors arrive mainly by tours organized from Huatulco (41 percent), by hotels or agencies, for day trips to the region. Seventy-one percent of the visitors have low earnings, since for 38 percent, income is less than US$500 per month and for 33 percent, between $500 and $1000 per month.

Preferences for crocodiles, birds, mangroves and community are ranked between 4 and 1, with 4 referring to the most preferred and 1 to the least preferred. On average, visitors' most preferred attribute is crocodiles (2.8) followed by mangroves and birds (both about 2.4) and finally preferences in enjoying an ecotourism community (1.8).

Index of Environmental Quality

This is carried out as explained in Figures 10.1, 10.2 and 10.3. A summary of results is shown using a Kernel density function for crocodiles in Figure 10.4 and for mangroves in Figure 10.5. The left-hand side of the density function corresponds to those tourists who are not willing to return and the right-hand side to those who will. Figure 10.4 shows that the willingness to accept changes in the population of crocodiles is bimodal and asymmetric. It shows the existence of two different groups of tourists with different interests in watching wild crocodiles. Those individuals who are willing to return will accept up to around 15 percent deterioration, whereas those individuals who are not willing to return might change their minds if the number of crocodiles increases by 40 percent (–40 in the figure).

Figure 10.5 shows a different picture. Willingness to accept changes in the mangrove area are more symmetrically distributed between those who will return and those who will not. Indeed, the distribution is also bimodal, but more similar to a normal distribution, with a higher proportion of the density concentrated around the mean and slightly skewed to the right. The comparison of the two distributions shows that those visitors who are keen on returning can accept more deterioration in mangroves than in the population of crocodiles, whereas those visitors who do not think of returning will need to see more crocodiles than mangroves in order to repeat their visit. The bimodal distribution suggests the existence of different market segments.

Model Estimation and the Definition of Environmental Quality from Tourists' Perspectives

The results from estimating the model are given in Table 10.1. Among more than 40 variables considered originally, the variables shown in this table were found to be the most relevant determinants for the repeat visit decision. The determinants are divided into four categories: socio-economic determinants, with age, income, travel cost from their places of origin, daily expenses, the proportion of total travel cost in their income; preferences, distinguishing preferences for crocodiles, birds, the community, mangroves, hotel-based

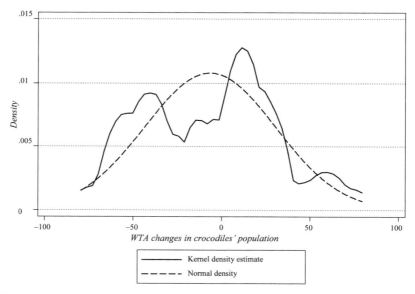

Figure 10.4　Kernel density function of the willingness to accept changes in the crocodiles' population

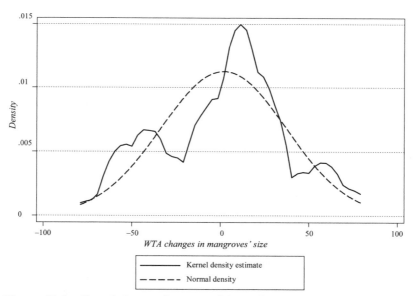

Figure 10.5　Kernel density function of the willingness to accept changes in the mangrove size

Table 10.1   Results of the repeat visits method

Variable	Mean	Parameter estimates	Marginal effects
Socio-economic characteristics			
Age	29.53	0.035	0.48
		(2.876)	
Income (in pesos)	13,769	-0.000016	-0.00022
		(-1.600)	
Travel cost (in pesos)	880	-0.00012	-0.0016
		(-1.881)	
Daily expenses (in pesos)	870	0.00024	0.0033
		(1.608)	
Total costs/Income	0.16	0.0023	0.032
		(2.050)	
Previous knowledge about the	0.18	0.890	10.2
existence of turtles in Ventanilla		(2.775)	
Ecological courses taken	0.40	0.493	6.3
		(2.241)	
Preferences			
Preferences on crocodiles	2.77	0.265	3.6
		(3.335)	
Preferences on birds	2.42	−0.139	−1.9
		(−1.727)	
Preferences on community	1.81	−0.181	−2.4
		(−2.685)	
Preferences on mangrove	2.52	−0.039	−0.05
		(−0.054)	
Purpose of visit: hotel	1.76	−0.219	−2.9
		(−2.163)	
Purpose of visit: nature	4.16	0.297	4.1
		(2.931)	
Willingness to accept changes in environmental quality of:			
Mangrove	2.95	0.008	0.12
		(1.854)	
Crocodiles	−4.98	0.013	0.18
		(2.821)	
Birds	−3.08	−0.001	−0.007
		(−0.125)	
Location			
Staying in Huatulco	0.44	0.519	6.9
		(1.905)	
Staying in Pto. Escondido	0.11	0.474	4.9
		(1.392)	
Log likelihood function		−100.182	
Number of observations		321	
Pseudo R^2		0.351	
Actual 1s and 0s correctly predicted		85.67%	

Notes: Marginal effects are calculated as the percentage change in the probability of repeat visits resulting from a marginal change in the variable. For dummy variables this is calculated as the difference between the probabilities conditioning the dummy to be equal to 1 and 0 for each case.

tourism or nature-based tourism; the indirect measure of environmental quality of the mangrove, crocodiles and birds and finally, the location and the length of the stay. The estimation was obtained by the maximum likelihood method and the number of well predicted cases was 85.67 percent.

The key finding is that crocodiles and mangroves are the only aspects that become relevant when assessing the willingness to repeat a visit. Furthermore, the presence of birds and the existence of a community-based ecotourism system are not seen as relevant by the current tourists. In this sense, changes in the current population of birds will not have an impact on the willingness to repeat their visit. Indeed, those visitors whose most valuable attribute is the presence of crocodiles, over other aspects such as birds or vegetation, are more likely to revisit the site, whereas those who prefer birds or vegetation are not necessarily so enthusiastic about repeating the visit. On average, in order to repeat the visit, visitors are willing to accept 3 percent deterioration in the mangrove forest, but they request an increase of 5 percent in the number of crocodiles and an increase of 3 percent in the number of birds.

The results of the model show that the number of crocodiles is the only sensitive (statistically significant) environmental attribute with respect to a change in its current size; whereas changes in the current number of birds and mangrove size are not so relevant for the decision to repeat the visit. This indicates that the presence of the crocodiles in the site is the main attraction for the visitors and that special emphasis needs to be put on their conservation.

Link Between Environmental Quality Change and Tourism Demand for Repeat Visits

The results (see Table 10.2) show that a 10 percent change in the number of crocodiles will vary the probability of repeating the visit by 1.8 percent. Similarly, a 10 percent change in mangrove biomass would affect the probability of repeating a visit by 1.2 percent, whereas changes in the number of birds have no significant effect.

The three main parts of tourism demand are distributed such that 11 percent of visitors are repeaters, 47 percent arrive by recommendation and 42 percent are visiting Ventanilla for the first time, without any kind of previous experience or recommendation. From the survey, we obtained the number of visitors in each of the three categories. Assuming that the proportion of visitors repeating their visit and arriving by recommendation is constant over time, the proportion that revisits the site is 58 percent. This percentage represents the part of the demand for which changes in environmental quality will have a further impact. Hence, out of a total number of visitors of 34 712, 20 042 visitors would repeat their visit or will come by recommendation the

Table 10.2   Tourism demand components and effects

Number of visitors in 2003	34, 712
% of visitors repeating visit	10.58% (3673)
% of visitors visiting by recommendation	47.16 % (16 370)
Repetition rate (repeat and recommended visitors)	57.74%
Potential repeat visitors for 2004	20 042
Ratio of recommended visitors by repeaters	4.45
Effect of probability change on repeaters by 10% change in the number of crocodiles	1.8%
Effect of probability change on potential visitors of 1% change in the number of crocodiles	0.18 + 0.18 * 4.45=0.98%
Effect on tourism demand of 1% change in the number of crocodiles	340

next year. From the sample, for every repeat visitor who comes, 4.45 (i.e. 47.16 percent/10.58 percent) recommended visitors come. Keeping this ratio constant in the short run, then the marginal change in the number of crocodiles has an impact on the demand for the next year of 0.98 percent (i.e. $0.18 + 0.18 * 4.45$). Hence, for instance, a decrease of 10 percent in the number of crocodiles, ceteris paribus, might decrease demand for the next year by 3400 tourists.

Market Segments

In terms of the purpose of the visit, two kinds of tourists can be distinguished: those who are interested in hotel entertainments and those who are keen on having contact with nature (Hvenegaard and Dearden, 1998; Perales, 2002). Nature is extremely or very important for 80 percent of visitors and hotel entertainment is not important for 48 percent. Moreover, 30 percent of visitors had already visited another coastal lagoon previously and 41 percent had attended an ecological course. Interviewees were asked to rank from 1 to 5 their purposes of visit. Amongst all of them, the purpose of enjoying being in a hotel with entertainments was negatively related to repeating the visit, whereas for those who were willing to have contact with nature, the relationship was positive. Both variables were ranked from 1 to 5, and a discrete change from one rank to another has a marginal change in the probabilities of repeating the visit of –3 percent and 4.1 percent respectively. Hence, we can distinguish two kinds of visitors with different willingness to repeat the visit, representing different market segments.

Simulations

The number of tourists is linked to the ecological model through a production function as was explained above in equation (1). The production function depends on the biomass of crocodiles, which is proportionally related to the number of crocodiles that can be observed by visitors. Crocodile biomass for 2000 was estimated using information derived from a local population study (Espinosa, 2000) and for the following years, the biomass was estimated using software for food web analysis called ECOPATH for ECOSIM. Details of this analysis are available upon request to the authors. The number of arrivals was extracted from the Ventanilla cooperative handbook for arrivals registration. Similarly, labor data were extracted from the Ventanilla cooperative costs handbook and include the number of both members and workers (Table 10.3).

Table 10.3   Tourism demand components and effects

Year	Number of visitors	Number of workers and cooperative members	Crocodile biomass (t/km^2)	Costs ($)	Profits ($)
2000	26 138	10	0.90	4 372	66 913
2001	32 457	15	0.85	12 737	75 782
2002	34 712	20	0.58	13 370	97 077

If crocodile biomass varies after five or ten years due to a change in fish biomass, the number of arrivals would also be affected. Simulations of these changes are shown in Table 10.4. An increase in fish biomass due to changes in nitrogen concentration and phytoplankton biomass initially have little effect on crocodile biomass, but after ten years a 50 percent increase in nitrogen and phytoplankton leads to an increase in crocodile biomass (0.95 t/km2) . Output in 2007 and 2012 was estimated using the ECOPATH model and the simulated crocodile biomass.

Cooperative profits were estimated as explained earlier, using equation (10.2). The number of workers is the main reason for an increase in costs. Price is the price of the trip in the boat which is $3.18 per person. Table 10.4 shows an increase in profits over time, implying that the number of arrivals has been increasing more than proportionately to costs. Profits for 2007 and 2012 increase proportionally to tourist arrivals and the crocodile biomass. After five years, arrivals and profits increase when the crocodile population increases by 0.58 t/km2, and by 0.85 t/km^2 after ten years, although

Table 10.4   Simulations of expected profits in five and ten years' time after changes in crocodile population biomass

% Change in crocodile biomass	After 5 years		After 10 years	
	Crocodile biomass (t/km^2)	Profits	Crocodile biomass (t/km^2)	Profits
−70	0.46	1 010 062	0.46	1 010 062
−50	0.46	1 010 062	0.57	1 066 314
−20	0.57	1 066 314	0.70	1 132 795
+20	0.56	1 081 656	0.85	1 235 072
+50	0.58	1 071 428	0.92	1 245 299
+70	0.60	1 061 201	0.90	1 209 502

population growth depends on the lagoon area. In contrast, profits are affected after five years when decreasing the crocodile population by 0.57 t/km2 and after ten years when decreasing the population by the same proportion. Cooperative profits in 2002 were $97 076, implying a gain per capita of around $8076 per year, which is $23 per day, similar to the gain by agriculture.

10.6   CONCLUSION

Nature-based tourism destinations are becoming a more popular alternative for holidaymakers. The long-run success of such destinations relies on the sustainability of their environmental quality from the tourists' perspective. Pressures from different activities or from the tourism industry itself may affect adversely this quality. Identification and understanding of the ecological attributes that are relevant to the tourists and anticipating how tourism demand will be affected by changes in the quality of those attributes is very important for sustainable tourism management. This will help to focus and prioritize protection where it is needed.

The innovative methodology proposed in this chapter shows that the willingness to repeat a visit can be used to identify the ecological attributes that are perceived by tourists as relevant in terms of environmental quality. It is also shown that the methodology is able to link changes in the environmental quality to changes in tourism demand. The model employs a utility approach that incorporates the socioeconomic characteristics and the preferences of the tourists. This allows us to model part of the heterogeneity of the tourists. Under this framework, different scenarios with alternative levels of deterioration are proposed for each of the environmental attributes, to evaluate how tourists' willingness to repeat the visit changes. This decision is used to identify and quantify their environmental preferences and test their relevance. Such identification is very important for showing, from amongst all the environmental attributes of a destination, those that require special protection for sustainable tourism purposes. Moreover, it allows us to measure the link between changes in the environmental quality and the tourism demand.

The repetition of visits phenomenon is very appealing for valuing changes in the attributes of a destination because the tourists interviewed have already experienced the destination and have good knowledge of all the environmental attributes of the place. A limitation that should be addressed in the specification of the model comes from the different attitudes of tourists towards experiencing new destinations. In this sense, two extreme cases can be identified. Some tourists are keen on looking for new places to visit, whereas others may be risk averse and prefer to revisit places where they are sure they will have pleasurable experiences (Pizam et al., 2004). Further research is required on this issue in order to identify its relevance and alternative ways to measure it.

The location chosen for applying the methodology is Ventanilla, a coastal lagoon in the region of Oaxaca, Mexico. In Ventanilla, amongst other environmental attributes, crocodiles have been shown to be the main tourist attraction, as tourism demand is mainly sensitive to changes in their population. Thus, for sustainable tourism purposes, the conservation of that species and its habitat needs to be encouraged.

Two market segments have been identified: nature-based tourism and traditional hotel-based tourism demand. Currently, Ventanilla only offers a lagoon trip for wildlife watching. It has been shown that each tourist segment has different preferences and that product differentiation could be implemented in order to maximize tourist satisfaction. Indeed, it would be convenient to diversify the offer, in order to attract more people with interests in nature, because the people in this market segment are more likely to return. Moreover, since the sensitivity of demand is low, diversification of the offer can be combined with price discrimination between different tourist market segments.

Ventanilla is one of the few community-based ecotourism management destinations in the region. If others are to be developed, investment in community conservation programs of species that are attractive to tourists is required. Habitat conservation depends on the impacts coming from upland activities. Thus, a watershed management program should be considered. For this purpose, the chapter develops an ecological model that can capture the key tourism and ecosystem dynamics of the area. The model permits simulations of the effects of environmental changes over the longer term. The simulations can incorporate the interrelated effects caused by environmental changes on the ecosystem, the tourism sector and the economy. In the specific modeling undertaken in the case study, watershed water quality is linked to the tourism sector in order to take account of the mutual externalities and to incorporate the effects on tourism demand, and consequently on the economy, of the community. The case study shows that profits increase in proportion to the number of crocodiles in the area, but also shows that the degree of pollution in the watershed would have to be very high before the population of crocodiles, and consequently the profits of the community, are affected significantly. This result is very useful for policy-makers because it provides evidence of the integrated effects of an environmental change and its consequences for the sustainability of the community at social, environmental and economic levels. It provides knowledge that can assist policy-makers in prioritizing conservation goals, helps to identify the main sources of environmental changes and contributes towards measuring their consequences over the short and long run. This interdisciplinary methodology is a very useful tool for tourism, watershed and integrated coastal management and long-run policy-making.

ACKNOWLEDGEMENTS

We are very grateful for comments and suggestions by M. Thea Sinclair and Charles Perrings, for the help provided by Ventanilla Community and to Conacyt, Mexico, for providing a grant which allowed the research work to be undertaken.

REFERENCES

Alavalapati, J.R.R. and W.L. Adamowicz (2000), 'Tourism impact modeling for resource extraction regions', *Annals of Tourism Research*, **27**(1), 188–202.
Alegre, J. and M. Cladera (2006), 'Repeat visitation in mature sun and sand holiday destinations', *Journal of Travel Research*, **44**(1), 288–97.
Arrow, K., B. Bolin, R. Costanza, P. Dasgupta, C. Folke, C.S. Holling, B.O. Jänsson, S. Levin, K.G. Maler, C. Perrings and D. Pimentel (1995), 'Economic growth, carrying capacity, and the environment', *Science*, **268**, 520–21.
Avila-Foucat, V.S. (2002), 'Community-based ecotourism management moving towards sustainability, in Ventanilla, Oaxaca, Mexico', *Ocean & Coastal Management*, **45**, 511–29.
Barbier, E.B. and I. Strand (1998), 'Valuing mangrove–fishery linkages', *Environmental and Resource Economic*, **12**, 151–66.
Bell, F.W. and V.R. Leeworthy (1990), 'Recreational demand by tourists for saltwater beach days', *Journal of Environmental Economics and Management*, **18**, 189–205.

Briassoulis, H. (2002), 'Sustainable tourism and the question of the commons', *Annals of Tourism Research*, **29**(4), 1065–85.

Brown, K., W.N. Adger, E. Tompkins, P. Bacon, D. Shim and K. Young (2001), 'Trade-off analysis for marine protected area management', *Ecological Economics*, **37**(3), 417–34.

Costanza, R. (1992), 'Towards an operational definition of ecosystem health', in R. Costanza, B.G. Norton and B.D. Haskell (eds), *Ecosystem Health: New Goals for Environmental Management*, Washington, DC: Island Press, pp. 239–56.

Davis, D. and D.F. Gartside (2001), 'Challenges for economic policy in sustainable management of marine natural resources', *Ecological Economics*, **36**(2), 223–36.

Darnell, A.C. and P.S. Johnson (2001), 'Repeat visits to attractions: a preliminary economic analysis', *Tourism Management*, **22**(2), 119–26.

Deng, J.Y., B. King and T. Bauer (2002), 'Evaluating natural attractions for tourism', *Annals of Tourism Research*, **29**(2), 422–38.

Dharmaratne, G.S., F.Y. Sang and L.J. Walling (2000), 'Tourism potentials for financing protected areas', *Annals of Tourism Research*, **27**(3), 590–610.

Douglas, A.J. and J.G. Taylor (1998), 'Riverine based eco-tourism: Trinity River non-market benefits estimates', *International Journal of Sustainable Development and World Ecology*, **5**(2), 136–48.

Espinosa, G. (2000), 'Densidad poblacional y estructura de tallas de la población del cocodrilo de río Crocodylus acutus en el Estero la Ventanilla, Oaxaca', *Benemérita Universidad Autónoma de Puebla*, **63**.

Fakeye, P.C. and J.L. Crompton (1992), 'Importance of socialization to repeat visitation', *Annals of Tourism Research* **19**(2), 364–67.

Font, A.R. (2000), 'Mass tourism and the demand for protected natural areas: a travel cost approach', *Journal of Environmental Economics and Management*, **39**(1), 97–116.

Gartner, W.C. (1987), 'Environmental impacts of recreational home developments', *Annals of Tourism Research*, **14**(1), 38–57.

GESAMP (2001), *Protecting the Oceans from Land-based Activities, Land-based Sources and Activities Affecting the Quality and Uses of Marines, Coastal and Associated Freshwater Environment*, UNEP.

Getzner, M. (2002), 'Investigating public decisions about protecting wetlands', *Journal of Environmental Management*, **64**(3), 237–46.

Gitelson, R.J. and J.L. Crompton (1984), 'Insights into the repeat vacation phenomenon', *Annals of Tourism Research*, **11**(2), 199–217.

Godbey, G. and A. Graefe (1991), 'Repeat tourism, play, and monetary spending', *Annals of Tourism Research*, **18**(2), 213–25.

Guyer, C. and J. Pollard (1997), 'Cruise visitor impressions of the environment of the Shannon–Erne waterways system', *Journal of Environmental Management*, **51**(2), 199–215.

Hall, C.M. (2001), 'Trends in ocean and coastal tourism: the end of the last frontier?', *Ocean & Coastal Management*, **44**(9–10), 601–18.

Healy, R.G. (2006), 'The commons problem and Canada's Niagara Falls', *Annals of Tourism Research*, **33**(2), 525–44.

Hearne, R.R. and Z.M. Salinas (2002), 'The use of choice experiments in the analysis of tourist preferences for ecotourism development in Costa Rica', *Journal of Environmental Management*, **65**(2), 153–63.

Hunt, L.M., P. Boxall, J. Englin and W. Haider (2005), 'Remote tourism and forest management: a spatial hedonic analysis', *Ecological Economics*, **53**(1), 101–13.

Huybers, T. and J. Bennett (2003), 'Environmental management and the competitiveness of nature-based tourism destinations', *Environmental and Resources Economics*, **24**, 213–33.

Hvenegaard, G.T. and P. Dearden (1998), 'Ecotourism versus tourism in a Thai national park', *Annals of Tourism Research*, **25**(3), 700–720.

Jakus, P. and D. Shaw (1997), 'Congestion at recreation areas: empirical evidence on perceptions, mitigating behaviour and management preferences', *Journal of Environmental Management*, **50**, 389–401.

Jones, S. (2005), 'Community-based ecotourism. The significance of social capital', *Annals of Tourism Research*, **32**(2), 303–24.

Juaneda, C.N. (1996), 'Estimating the probability of return visits using a survey of tourist expenditure in the Balearic Islands', *Tourism Economics*, **2**(4), 339–52.

Kozak, M. (2001), 'Repeaters' behavior at two distinct destinations', *Annals of Tourism Research*, **28**(3), 784–807.

Lau, A.L.S. and B. McKercher (2004), 'Exploration versus acquisition: a comparison of first-time and repeat visitors', *Journal of Travel Research*, **42**, 279–85.

Lee, C.C. (2001), 'Predicting tourist attachment to destinations', *Annals of Tourism Research*, **28**(1), 229–32.

Lee, C.K. and S.Y. Han (2002), 'Estimating the use and preservation values of national parks' tourism resources using a contingent valuation method', *Tourism Management*, **23**(5), 531–40.

Lehto, X.Y., J.T. O'Leary and A.M. Morrison (2004), 'The effect of prior experience on vacation behaviour', *Annals of Tourism Research*, **31**(4), 801–18.

Lewandrowski, J. and K. Ingram (1999), 'Policy considerations for increasing compatibilities between agriculture and wildlife', *Natural Resources Journal*, **39**(2), 229–69.

Maharana, I., S.C. Rai and E. Sharma (2000), 'Valuing ecotourism in a sacred lake of the Sikkim Himalaya, India', *Environmental Conservation*, **27**(3), 269–77.

Mangion, M.L., R. Durbarry and M.T. Sinclair (2005), 'Tourism competitiveness: price and quality', *Tourism Economics*, **11**(1), 45–68.

Mazursky, D. (1989), 'Past experience and future tourism decisions', *Annals of Tourism Research*, **16**, 333–44.

McKercher, B. and D.Y.Y. Wong (2004), 'Understanding tourism behaviour: Examining the combined effects of prior visitation history and destination status', *Journal of Travel Research*, **43**, 171–9.

Menkhaus, S. and D.J. Lober (1996), 'International ecotourism and the valuation of tropical rainforests in Costa Rica', *Journal of Environmental Management*, **47**(1), 1–10.

Norton-Griffiths, M. and C. Southey (1995), 'The opportunity costs of biodiversity conservation in Kenya', *Ecological Economics*, **12**(2), 125–39.

Odum, E.P. (1969), 'The strategy of ecosystem development', *Science*, **164**, 262–70.

Oppermann, M. (1997), 'First-time and repeat visitors to New Zealand', *Tourism Management*, **18**(3), 177–81.

Perales, Y. (2002), 'Rural tourism in Spain', *Annals of Tourism Research*, **29**(4), 1101–10.

Petrick, J.F. (2004), 'First timers' and repeaters' perceived value', *Journal of Travel Research*, **43**, 29–38.

Pizam, A., G. Jeong, A. Reichel, H. van Boemmel, J.M. Lusson, L. Steynberg, O. State-Costache, S. Volo, C. Kroesbacher, J. Kucerova and N. Montmany (2004), 'The relationship between risk-taking, sensation-seeking, and the tourist behaviour of young adults: a cross-cultural study', *Journal of Travel Research*, **42**, 251–60.

Price, C. (1981), 'The impact of tourism on the environment', *Journal of Environmental Management*, **12**(3), 279–80.

Reynolds, P.C. and D. Braithwaite (2001), 'Towards a conceptual framework for wildlife tourism', *Tourism Management*, **22**(1), 31–42.

Richard, M.D. and D.S. Sundaram (1994), 'A model of lodging repeat choice intentions', *Annals of Tourism Research*, **21**(4), 745–55.

Schittone, J. (2001), 'Tourism vs. commercial fishers: development and changing use of Key West and Stock Island, Florida', *Ocean & Coastal Management*, **44**, 15–37.

Schultz, S., J. Pinazzo and M. Cifuentes (1998), 'Opportunities and limitations of contingent valuation surveys to determine national park entrance fees: evidence from Costa Rica', *Environment and Development Economics*, **3**, 131–49.

Sekhar, N.U. (2003), 'Local people's attitudes towards conservation and wildlife tourism around Sariska Tiger Reserve, India', *Journal of Environmental Management*, **69**(4), 339–47.

Skonhoft, A. (1998), 'Resource utilization, property rights and welfare – wildlife and the local people', *Ecological Economics*, **26**, 67–80.

Solomon, B.D., C.M. Corey-Luse and K.E. Halvorsen (2004), 'The Florida manatee and eco-tourism: toward a safe minimum standard', *Ecological Economics*, **50**(1–2), 101–15.

Sun, D. and D. Walsh (1998), 'Review of studies on environmental impacts of recreation and tourism in Australia', *Journal of Environmental Management*, **53**(4), 323–38.

Tiefenbacher, J.P., F.A. Day and J.A. Walton (2000), 'Attributes of repeat visitors to small tourist-oriented communities', *The Social Science Journal*, **37**(2), 299–308.

Train, K. (1998), 'Recreation demand models with taste variation over people', *Land Economics*, **74**(2), 230–39.

Vega-Cendejas, M.E. and F. Arreguín-Sánchez (2001), 'Energy fluxes in a mangrove ecosystem from coastal lagoon in Yucatan Peninsula, Mexico', *Ecological Modeling*, **137**, 119–33.

Venkatachalam, L. (2004), 'The contingent valuation method: a review', *Environmental Impact Assessment Review*, **24**(1), 89–124.

Wearing, S. and M. McDonald (2002), 'The development of community-based tourism: the relationship between tour operators and development agents as intermediaries in rural and isolated area communities', *Journal of Sustainable Tourism*, **10**, 191–206.

Whittington, D. (2002), 'Improving the performance of contingent valuation studies in developing countries', *Environmental & Resource Economics*, **22**(1–2), 323–67.

Whittington, D. (2004), 'Ethical issues with contingent valuation surveys in developing countries: a note on informed consent and other concerns', *Environmental & Resource Economics*, **28**(4), 507–15.

Williams, P.W., R.W. Penrose and S. Hawkes (1998), 'Shared decision-making in tourism land use planning', *Annals of Tourism Research*, **25**(4), 860–89.

Woolley, J.T., M.V. McGinnis and J. Kellner (2002), 'The California watershed movement: science and the politics of place', *Natural Resources Journal*, **42**(1), 133–83.

Wunder, S. (2000), 'Ecotourism and economic incentives – an empirical approach', *Ecological Economics*, **32**(3), 465–79.

11. Social Carrying Capacity of Mass Tourist Sites: Theoretical and Practical Issues about its Measurement

Silva Marzetti Dall'Aste Brandolini and Renzo Mosetti

11.1 INTRODUCTION

Tourism[1] is one of the fastest expanding sectors of the world economy. In the EU its contribution to the total GDP is about 4.7 percent. Visitors influence the social, cultural and economic activities of a site, resident life style and public policy-making. They are very sensitive to social, cultural and environmental quality; therefore tourist sites have to be managed according to sustainable criteria otherwise they will lose their ability to generate welfare.

Every process of tourism growth has to be sustained by the tourism carrying capacity (TCC) of the site. Policy-makers must pursue sustainable tourism through 'a rational distribution of tourism activity . . . without exceeding the saturation limits of each area . . . according to its vulnerability and characteristics' (Decleris, 2003, p. 86). In general, the concept of carrying capacity applied to the human species 'is foremost socially determined, rather than biologically fixed due to the important influence of human consumption patterns, technologies, infrastructure, and impacts on the environment or food availability' (Seidl and Tisdell, 1999, p. 403). Applied to tourism, this concept requires tourist economic growth to be responsible towards local society and its cultural values, and compatible with the preservation and improvement of the local natural environment and with the conservation of the local traditional economic activities. Therefore, since a tourist system is an integrated system constituted by different sub-systems, such as the ecological (biological and physical), social, cultural, institutional and economic (infrastructural and management) sub-systems (World Tourism Organisation, 1998, 2004), the TCC is the result of the carrying capacities of all these sub-systems. The levels of these different carrying capacities may be in conflict; for example, mass tourism may be desirable from the economic point of view because it increases the local aggregate income, but from the social and ecological point of view it can be damaging if criminality increases and the natural environment is (in part or totally) destroyed. This means that, in practice, policy-makers have to mediate between these different carrying capacities, also stimulating discussion about society values in order to change their plans and actions if necessary.

In this chapter we focus on the social aspect of the carrying capacity related to overcrowding. In literature, the social carrying capacity (SCC) is in general analysed both from the point of view of residents and from that of visitors. We consider mass tourism sites, because high-density recreational activities today are the predominant kind of tourism in Europe, and congestion is a major management problem at mass tourist sites. Tourism is generally a seasonal economic activity and, on the most crowded days of the year, traffic, criminality, waiting time, and noise by day and by night are major causes of residents' discomfort, and the quality of the visitors' recreational experience may deteriorate. Therefore, we present a joint analysis of these two aspects of the SCC in order to establish the site SCC, as an indicator of residents' and visitors' perception of crowding. Two methods are used: i) the cost–benefit analysis (CBA) based on the maximisation of individual cardinal preferences; and ii) the majority voting rule (MR) when sufficient data for applying the CBA are not available.

Section 11.2 briefly describes the CBA in order to measure the TCC as an indicator of sustainable tourism. In section 11.3 the focus is on the site SCC, when the residents' SCC is lower than the visitors' SCC. Assuming that it is possible to measure the utility loss due to crowding, a solution of this conflict is described by a CBA model in which the policy-maker mediates between residents' and visitors' claims. Section 11.4 focuses on the situation in which the policy-maker does not have all the data for the solution of the maximisation problem, and applies the MR to the results of a survey by questionnaire. Finally, in order to show how this voting criterion works, it is applied to the data of a coastal tourist site in Marina di Ravenna (Italy). Section 11.5 presents conclusions.

11.2   TOURISM CARRYING CAPACITY

Different indicators are used for the TCC measurement, such as tourist density (the number of visitors within a specific area per day), length of stay, visitors' life style and their impacts on the natural environment, facilities, infrastructures and residents' life style. Nevertheless, there continues to be a demand for representing the TCC with a single indicator. This approach is simpler and easier to apply than that of multiple indicators, and can be carried out with lower expenses and less time (Shelby et al., 1989). In economic literature the number of visitors is generally used (Fisher and Krutilla, 1972; Cicchetti and Smith, 1973; Canestrelli and Costa, 1991). We make reference to the number of visitors present on a site per day. Given the specific characteristics of a tourist site, the TCC is defined as the maximum number of visitors (MNV) that can be contained in that tourist area per day.

In order to estimate a sustainable and efficient MNV, the CBA is applied. Economic efficiency states that tourist resources are rationally used if the difference between their benefits and costs is maximised; while sustainability requires social and environmental goods that the market does not evaluate to be estimated in monetary terms and considered in this computation. Therefore, by making reference to a CBA model the TCC, or the MNV that can be contained in a tourist area, is identified with the optimum number of visitors which maximises the collective net benefit (Fisher and Krutilla, 1972). Let us consider the following very simple static model:

$$\max_{Q} [\Pi(Q) \equiv NB(Q) - C_S(Q) - C_E(Q)], \qquad (11.1)$$

where: $\Pi(Q)$ is the total net benefit from tourism activity, Q the number of visitors per day in a specific site, $NB(Q)$ the private net benefit from tourist production, $C_S(Q)$ the social costs, and $C_E(Q)$ the value of environmental losses. It is, in general, assumed that the net marginal private benefit from tourism decreases as the number of visitors increases, while the social marginal cost and the environmental marginal cost increase as the number of visitors increases. The optimum number of visitors Q' has to satisfy the condition of equality between the net marginal benefit and the sum of the social and environmental marginal costs.

11.3   SOCIAL CARRYING CAPACITY

We cannot deal here with all the different aspects of the TCC. As regards the optimal use from the ecological point of view, we assume that it is not a limiting factor, and that $C_E(Q) = 0$. This may be the case of very extensive natural resources used for recreational activities (such as numerous beaches), and of resources whose ecological aspect has lost much of its importance because they have already been sacrificed heavily to tourist growth (such as dunes).

Our attention is devoted to the SCC computation in situations in which mass tourism determines overcrowding effects. When overcrowding reduces the individual satisfaction, it is considered 'a negative evaluation' of tourist density (Ditton et al., 1983, p. 275). In particular, in situations of overcrowding, people may feel irritated because physical congestion, noise, criminality and waiting time increase. Therefore, residents' quality of life and visitors' recreational experience may deteriorate as the number of visitors increases. These individual losses of enjoyment, when they are not compensated, have the nature of external diseconomies[2] which 'behave like public bads' (Starrett, 1971, p. 191).

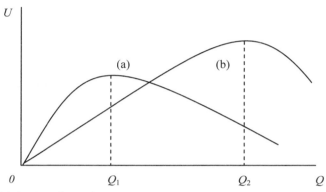

Figure 11.1   Residents'/visitors' utility function

The psychological nature of the perception of overcrowding is represented through a utility curve. In general, when an overcrowding sensation begins to be felt, the individual total utility U starts to reduce, the marginal utility becomes negative, and this means that the total number of visitors on the site exceeds the maximum number preferred or tolerated. In addition, different individuals (whether residents or visitors) may be sensitive to different levels of crowding. Figure 11.1 shows, as an example, two different situations: curve (a) represents the total utility U of an individual (or a group of individuals) whose satisfaction from the presence of visitors is quite low, and who is quite sensitive to crowding because the overcrowding sensation begins to occur to the right of the fairly low daily number of visitors Q_1; while curve (b) represents an individual (or a group of individuals) whose satisfaction is high and who becomes sensitive to crowding with large numbers of visitors (overcrowding begins at Q_2) (Clawson and Knetsch, 1978; Marzetti, 2003).

The Site SCC

The SCC of a tourist area must be considered from two different points of view. From the point of view of residents, the SCC represents the social interaction between residents and visitors, and is the optimum number of visitors which maximises the host population's utility. From the point of view of visitors, the SCC describes the interaction between the visitors themselves, and is the optimum number of visitors which maximises visitors' utility.

According to the CBA, the SCC of a tourist site (site SCC) can be defined as the optimum number of visitors per day to which the maximum social welfare or satisfaction corresponds.[3] The site SCC is here obtained by comparing the visitors' SCC, which we indicate with Q^*, with the residents' SCC, indicated with Q^{**}. Visitors' SCC and residents' SCC may in fact be conflicting since the MNV preferred by the visitors themselves may be different from the MNV tolerated by residents. Therefore the site SCC is seen as the result of a compromise between these two specific carrying capacities.

In general, three situations are possible:

a) $Q^* = Q^{**}$, which is the ideal site SCC because it is the social equilibrium.

b) $Q^* < Q^{**}$, which indicates that visitors reach the maximum utility before residents. This can be the result of an inadequate quality of tourist services. The policy-maker's action could be promoting the organisation of crowd-attracting activities.

c) $Q^* > Q^{**}$, where residents reach the maximum utility before visitors. Our attention is on this last case. It represents a situation of congestion, quite frequent in mass tourism sites, which we model in the following way.

A Site SCC Model: The Maximisation Criterion

The site SCC represents a compromise between the need to preserve residents' life style and the need to preserve or to increase the economic benefits of the site recreational use. Therefore, when $Q^* > Q^{**}$, a resource re-allocation is needed. In general, in situations of overcrowding, it is reasonable to think that residents and visitors are so numerous that in practice they cannot directly negotiate by creating a market for utility loss due to overcrowding. In this case public action is justified in order to achieve the social optimum. The task of policy-makers is pursuing social welfare. Local policy-makers are elected by residents not by visitors, and they identify the social welfare with residents' welfare. Therefore, in this chapter we consider that in the local political context visitors' interests are represented by those residents who produce tourist services (the tourist offer).[4] We distinguish three kinds of residents: (i) those who are directly and wholly tourism-dependent (the local tourist sector), and who represent visitors' needs, (ii) those who are in part indirectly tourism-dependent (such as those who benefit from the fact that a well developed tourist sector increases the local economic welfare); and (iii) those who are totally independent from tourism (such as those who work in the public administration, housewives and pensioners).

For simplicity, we also assume that residents who belong to category (i) do not feel irritated by the presence of tourists; while those who belong to categories (ii) and (iii) suffer a loss of enjoyment or utility in overcrowded situations due to tourism. Therefore, we specify two aggregated utility functions about residents: (i) the utility function of residents wholly dependent on tourism; and (ii) the utility function of partially or totally independent residents. Thus we suppose that the optimum number of visitors tolerated by wholly tourism-dependent residents is obtained by maximising their aggregated utility curve. This optimum number represents not only their own SCC but also the visitors' SCC, and for simplicity we refer to it as the visitors' SCC. The residents' SCC is, instead, assumed to be the optimum number of visitors which maximises the utility function of partially and wholly tourism-independent residents. As an aggregation procedure, let us assume that all individuals are alike and have the sample mean characteristics, such as the sample mean income (Cicchetti and Smith, 1973).

Visitors' SCC

Let us assume that the local tourist sector is a perfect competition market which offers a basket of tourist goods (such as recreational activities and accommodation) per visitor at the price p. The representative wholly tourism-dependent resident maximises her/his utility U_1. Utility depends on income y_1, and for simplicity we write $U_1(y_1) = y_1$. We consider $y_1 = pQ - C(Q)$, where $C(Q)$ is the production cost function, and Q the tourist production measured in number of visitors per day. The optimal problem of the representative wholly tourism-dependent resident is:

$$\max_Q \ [U_1(y_1) \equiv pQ - C(Q)]. \qquad (11.2)$$

The first order condition is:

$$p = C'(Q), \qquad (11.3)$$

where $C'(Q)$ is the first order derivative of $C(Q)$, which we assume to increase with Q. The solution is the tourist offer, or visitors' SCC:

$$Q^* = h\,(p). \qquad (11.4)$$

Residents' SCC

As regards the (ii) and (iii) categories of residents we use the following model, which considers a loss of utility due to overcrowding. Their total utility function is $U_2(y_2) = y_2 - C_s(Q)$, where: income y_2 is equal to the sum of the non-tourism income y_0 and the partially tourism-dependent income $a(pQ - C(Q))$; a is the coefficient of tourism benefit, $0 \leq a < 1$; and $C_s(Q)$ is the social loss of utility due to overcrowding. When $a = 0$, it means that residents are wholly tourism-independent.

The optimal problem of the representative resident who is partially or wholly independent of tourism is:

$$\max_{Q} \ [U_2(y_2) \equiv y_0 + a(pQ - C(Q)) - C_s(Q)]. \tag{11.5}$$

The first order condition is:

$$p = C'(Q) + C_s'(Q)/a, \tag{11.6}$$

where $C_s'(Q)$ is assumed to increase with Q. The utility function, described in Figure 11.1, is consistent with the residents' utility function here defined. By assuming $C''(Q) > 0$, $C_s''(Q) > 0$ and $a > 0$, it follows that the utility function U is strictly convex since U'' is negative.

The solution is residents' SCC, which we write:

$$Q^{**} = f(p). \tag{11.7}$$

According to equation (11.6), given the price p, Q depends on the ratio between the marginal utility loss due to overcrowding and the coefficient of tourism benefit a. If there is no loss due to overcrowding, $C_s'(Q)/a = 0$, and Q^* is equal to Q^{**}; while, when there is a loss due to overcrowding, $C_s'(Q)/a > 0$ and $Q^{**} < Q^*$.

The Ideal Site SCC

When $C_s'(Q)/a > 0$, the optimum number of visitors tolerated by partially or wholly tourism-independent residents is lower than that claimed by wholly tourism-dependent residents (or visitors). A policy-maker's task is to consider the different interests of the different categories of residents in order to find the number of visitors which maximises the social welfare, here intended as the sum of all residents' utilities. Let us assume that policy-makers' intervention has no costs. This maximisation problem is:

$$\max_{Q} \langle U_1(y_1) + U_2(y_2) \equiv [pQ - C(Q)] +$$
$$+ \{y_0 + a[pQ - C(Q)] - C_s(Q)\}\rangle. \qquad (11.8)$$

The first order condition is:

$$p = C'(Q) + C_s'(Q)/(1+a), \qquad (11.9)$$

and we write

$$Q^\circ = g(p). \qquad (11.10)$$

At the price p, Q° represents the site SCC. It is between Q* and Q**
because $C_s'(Q)/(1+a) < C_s'(Q)/a$, as shown in Figure 11.2, by assuming the
marginal cost to be linear in Q. According to equation (11.9), the price p is
the social price of the tourist basket because it is comprehensive of the social
cost due to crowding.

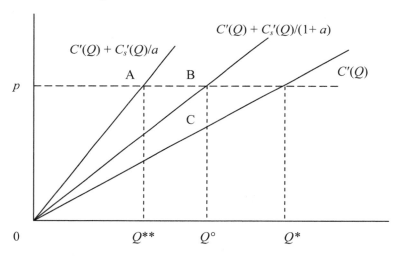

Figure 11.2   Site SCC

In order to pursue a sustainable management of the tourist resort, let us
finally assume that the policy-maker decides to internalise the social loss due
to congestion by taxing the tourist sector, and by compensating residents
wholly or partially independent from tourism. According to our model, we
write $\tau = C_s'(Q)/(1+a)$, where τ is the Pigouvian tax that the tourist sector
pays, and which represents the unit compensation of wholly or partially
tourism-independent residents. Once τ has been computed, it has the nature of
a unit price of the 'social bad', which is constant regardless of Q and uniform

for all individuals. If we include taxation in the maximisation problem (11.2), it becomes:

$$\max_{Q} \; [\,'U_1(y_1) \equiv pQ - C(Q) - \tau Q], \qquad (11.11)$$

the solution of which is:

$$p = C'(Q) + \tau. \qquad (11.12)$$

The same solution is obtained in the maximisation problem (11.5) by including τ as unit compensation of the social loss:

$$\max_{Q} \; \{\,'U_2(y_2) \equiv y_0 + a[pQ - C(Q)] - C_s(Q) + \tau Q\}. \qquad (11.13)$$

Through τ, the tourist sector is compelled to consider the social price $p = C'(Q) + \tau$ instead of $p = C'(Q)$, and therefore to reduce the tourist offer from Q^* to Q°; while the other residents, being compensated, accept the level of crowding Q° higher than Q^{**}. In Figure 11.2 the tax amount τ is equal to BC.

The model here presented describes a case of externality similar to that represented by Meade's social atmosphere (Meade, 1952). Here the tourist sector creates an unfavourable atmosphere, or condition, for the activities of wholly or partially tourism-independent residents, which are assumed to be passive actors in the sense that they cannot escape substantially the effect of overcrowding through private defensive actions (Starrett and Zeckhauser, 1971). In the mathematical model presented here, the utility loss due to congestion is treated as an unpaid factor. The internal solution has been obtained by assuming diminishing marginal social utility and increasing marginal loss due to overcrowding, and the creation of a favourable atmosphere is promoted through τ. Other situations can be imagined. In particular, we can admit that residents are active in the sense that they defend themselves from the negative effect of overcrowding in some way (by moving off the site, or by installing double-glazing, for example) (Starrett, 1972; Courant and Porter, 1981; Shibata and Winrich, 1983; Helfand and Rubin, 1994). These situations may imply non-convexity of the possibility set,[5] and are beyond the scope of this chapter.

11.4 SOCIAL CARRYING CAPACITY: THE VOTING CRITERION

Sustainability requires real actions to be made. Therefore, we cannot avoid highlighting some difficulties in the practical computation of the site SCC when the maximisation of utility is the social choice criterion. From the operational point of view, measuring the SCC through the CBA requires individual cardinal preferences to be known. In particular, the losses of welfare due to overcrowding have to be valuated in money terms with some specific method, because they are not established by the market.

Measuring the Utility Loss Due to Crowding

There are different methods of estimating cardinal preferences. Individual benefit/loss from the tourist use of a site, or consumer surplus, can be estimated by using an indirect or direct approach. According to the indirect approach, data can be obtained by applying the travel cost method (TCM). Nevertheless, this method is not suitable for sites in densely populated regions, where visitors incur relatively low travel costs. Nor is it suitable for residents who do not have travel costs (McConnell, 1977; Marzetti, 2006). In these cases, the Contingent Valuation Method (CVM) is the most used technique conceived by economists for directly estimating in monetary terms those gains and losses of satisfaction which are not established by the market. The CVM is based on the economic theory of demand, which considers individual cardinal preferences.[6] It can be conceived in different versions, and its philosophy is: when the value of something is unknown, go to those who might value it and ask how much they evaluate it (Price, 2000). Through a survey by questionnaire the CVM creates a hypothetical market which permits respondents to elicit, according to their preferences, the value of the non-marketable consequences of a change in the number of visitors to a site. The value so elicited is contingent to the scenario created through the questionnaire. In particular, if the CVM is applied in the willingness to pay version (WTP), the individual WTP for a project which reduces the level of crowding represents the individual value of the avoided loss of utility due to overcrowding (i.e. $C_s(Q)$).[7]

Since the questionnaire provides information about variables which determine the WTP, this method enables a model of resident's/visitor's satisfaction to be built:

$$WTP = r\,(Q_{,}\ C,\ A,\ L,\ R,\ O,\ S,\ I), \qquad (11.14)$$

where: WTP = willingness to pay; Q = daily number of visitors; C = crowding consequences (advantages and disadvantages); A = a vector of site attributes, such as infrastructure capacity and facilities; L = factors representing individual quality of life; R = recreational activities; O = reactions to overcrowding; S = socio-economic attributes; I = survey influences, such as interviewer characteristics. Taking other variables as constant, it is expected that the relation between U and Q is represented by an individual utility curve such as one of those indicated in Figure 11.1. Guidelines for the specification of model (11.2) cannot be provided by the economic theory. Through regression analysis, different attempts are generally made in order to estimate equation (11.14), and an extensive literature exists on this topic (see Bateman and Willis, 1999, for example).

Nevertheless, experience shows that a CVM survey is not always successful. In particular, a respondent may declare that s/he is unable to reply to the valuation questions, or may behave like a 'free-rider'. If the number of no responses and protest answers is high, it is not possible to estimate a valid WTP function (in particular $C_s'(Q)$), the aggregated utility curve[8] and the site SCC through a CBA model. Therefore $Q°$ has to be estimated by applying some other criterion of social choice.

Voting criterion

The closest substitute for the maximisation criterion is a voting procedure. The MR is generally used for social choices.[9] The majority may be of different size, ranging from a simple majority to unanimity. By denoting with M the majority size, and n the numbers of voters, the limits of M are given by $n \geq M > \frac{1}{2} n$ (Black, 1948, p. 246). The larger the majority is, the more closely the social choice is to the Pareto optimum. Therefore, unanimity (i.e. $M = n$) is widely considered the best rule for making a Pareto-efficient choice, because proposals which make someone worse off do not pass (see, in particular, Mueller, 1979, chapter 3); while when $n > M > \frac{1}{2} n$ this voting rule may lead to a Pareto-inefficient choice, because an alternative that makes someone worse off may pass. The simple majority (i.e. $M = \frac{1}{2} n + 1$) is the smallest majority that can be required in order to make a social choice; it is the median optimum.

In politics the MR is applied to results obtained by universal suffrage. Nevertheless, a referendum is expensive, and policy-makers entitled to act in the public interest can carry out a less expensive survey by questionnaire, where respondents are directly asked the maximum number of visitors (MNV) tolerated on the site considered (Marzetti and Mosetti, 2004). We call this method the 'MNV survey' in order to distinguish it from the CVM survey. More specifically, through this method no questions are asked about the monetary value of respondents' satisfaction (dissatisfaction) due to crowding. Interviews must be carried out on the most crowded days of the year, and respondents are asked if they would prefer a daily number of visitors greater or lower than that present on the site, or if they prefer the number of visitors present at the survey time. If interviewees are well informed, if they are aware that their choice will influence the policy-maker, 'if a poll is based on a representative sample of the population, and if the questions are put in the same way as if the entire citizenry were voting, the results can of course be interpreted in exactly the same way' (Bowen, 1943, p.128).[10]

The site SCC computed through the MR is, therefore, intended as the MNV preferred by the majority of residents and of visitors themselves. Making reference to the model presented in section 11.3, when some data are not available for the solution of the maximisation model, the method of the MNV survey can be applied in order to compute the residents' SCC and the visitors' SCC. Experience shows that respondents generally have no problem in establishing the MNV preferred on the site considered (De Ruyck et al., 1997; Saveriades, 2000). As regards residents' SCC, partially or wholly tourism-independent residents are interviewed; while as regards visitors' SCC, the policy-maker can decide to interview wholly tourism-dependent residents or directly visitors themselves.

If we maintain the assumption that all individuals are alike, and we assume that they are able to rank all the alternatives in an order of preference, and that each respondent (resident/visitor) declares as MNV preferred the number corresponding to her/his maximum net satisfaction, it is reasonable to think that the number of visitors obtained by maximising residents'/visitors' utility is equal to the MNV obtained with the MR, even if respondents are unable to establish the monetary value of their satisfaction. Let us assume that the economic variables p and a, and the $C'(Q)$ economic function are known, but $C_s'(Q)$ is unknown because a CVM survey failed. In this case, as regards visitors' SCC, the policy-maker can estimate the optimum Q^*; while, as regards residents SCC, Q^{**} cannot be computed. Let us imagine that the policy-maker obtains Q^{**} through a MNV survey. In this situation, in Figure 11.2, where $Q^* > Q^{**}$, only the point A of the function $C'(Q) + C_s'(Q)/a$ is known. In the case of linearly increasing marginal costs, as assumed in model (11.8), it is easy to show that, given p, a, and $C'(Q)$, the site SCC $Q°$ and the optimum amount of τ can be computed.

Other situations can be conceived. When not only $C_s'(Q)$, but also $C'(Q)$ are unknown, the policy-maker could resort to an MNV survey for estimating the visitors' SCC too; while when $C_s'(Q)$ and a are unknown, τ cannot be computed with the procedure presented above, even if Q^* and Q^{**} are established through a MNV survey. Given this lack of data, only by intuition or by chance could the policy-maker establish the correct value of τ on a single occasion. Otherwise, τ may be obtained through successive 'trials and errors' over a certain period of time. If we admit that the policy-maker can learn about the correct value of τ, this situation can be represented through an adaptive or learning model in a dynamic context (Pesaran, 1987, p. 19), which is beyond the scope of this chapter. Here we only stress that adaptation is a 'rule of thumb' which permits the policy-maker to obtain new data by observing (the two categories of) residents' behaviour, when a certain level of τ is established. Residents' reaction to τ generates new information, and consequently the policy-maker can modify the level of τ. Through this learning process, τ may be corrected until it is equal to the level which makes the residents' SCC equals to the visitors' SCC.

A Case Study: The Well Developed Tourist Site of Marina di Ravenna

The mass tourist site here considered is Marina di Ravenna (Italy) on the Northern West Adriatic sea. It is visited for the recreational activities done on its sandy beach, which is about 4 km long and on average 200 mt wide (see Figure 11.3). From the recreational point of view, the beach is well developed because there are 42 sunbathing buildings, while only a small part of it is completely free. A wide strip of pinewood is behind the beach, but the dunes have been almost completely destroyed.

Beach services were successfully innovated by some sunbathing establishment managers in this resort. The sunbathing area has been reorganised, and traditional services (such as bar, showers, and the renting of cabins, seating and sun umbrellas) have been expanded with restaurant services, new sport activities, parties, cultural and music events (called 'happy hours') by day and night. This economic innovation has turned out to be a profitable business because it attracts numerous visitors, mainly young (20–40 years old) day-visitors. Consequently, in the spring/summer season crowding phenomena have been occurring mainly during weekends.

As regards this site, data for highlighting the main practical problems about the estimate of the site SCC are available. They are the results of two experimental surveys about crowding effects, from the point of view of residents and visitors respectively. One is a CVM/MNV survey about residents (Medoro, 2004–5), the other a MNV survey about visitors (Vitali, 2002–3).[11] As regards visitors, the TCM was not applied to this case study, because this site is in a densely populated region, and numerous visitors do not spend much money to arrive in Marina di Ravenna. This is a case where 'the distribution of facilities and population is such that travel costs are relatively unimportant determinant of demand'; therefore the TCM would not work (McConnell, 1977, p. 188, note 5).

The MNV preferred by residents

In autumn 2004 a CVM/MNV survey by questionnaire of 95 interviews (random sample) was carried out by Medoro (2004–5) in Marina di Ravenna, in order to find out residents' opinions about tourist crowding in this resort. Partially or wholly tourism-independent residents were found to be 89, and

Figure 11.3   The Marina di Ravenna beach

wholly tourism-dependent residents were six. In the questionnaire, specific questions were included in order to estimate the gain or loss (in monetary terms) of satisfaction due to tourist crowding, and to find out the WTP for a project to change the level of crowding. In addition, a question about the MNV preferred was asked. In particular, as an introductory question, a multiple response question about the kind of advantages and disadvantages from tourism was asked. As regards the whole sample, among the advantages 29 percent of respondents included general economic welfare, and 27 percent said they like being with a lot of people; while among the disadvantages, 60 percent of respondents included the increase in traffic, 43 percent criminality, 42 percent noise and 23 percent price increases.

In order to estimate the residents' SCC, we consider only the subsample of 89 partially or wholly tourism-independent residents. About 47 percent of them work, and the others are pensioners, housewives, students aged 18 plus, and unemployed people. About 58 percent receive benefits from tourism, and 50 percent of these respondents work; while 42 percent do not receive benefits from tourism, and 43 percent of these respondents work. In particular, respondents who work, who benefit from tourism, and who declare that tourism is a source of general welfare, are 17 percent of partially or wholly tourism-independent residents. This means that *a* is positive for a certain number of Marina di Ravenna residents, but this survey does not provide data for establishing its numerical value.

As regards the WTP for a project which changes the level of crowding, about 6 percent of people are willing to pay, but only one person stated a specific amount while the others declared they are unable to establish how much. About 70 percent stated they are unwilling to pay, as they suffer discomfort due to overcrowding; while 22 percent did not reply to the question. A certain number of respondents justified their unwillingness to pay by saying that the public authority has to pay, others claimed they already pay a lot of taxes, or have a low income. Therefore, this CVM survey does not provide data for estimating $C'(Q)$, mainly due to respondents' unwillingness to pay, but also due to a certain number of non-responses to the evaluation question and inability to establish the WTP monetary value.

This survey instead provides data on the MNV preferred. About 90 percent of this sub-sample of residents replied to the MNV question. They were presented with five alternatives, which were established making reference to the number of visitors in summer 2004, which we call 'present number': double the present number, four times the present number, the present number, half that number and less than half. The majority of respondents (about 55 percent) stated that they prefer the present number, while about 19 percent would prefer double the visitors and about 14 percent fewer visitors. Only 1 respondent would prefer four times the present number. In this case, there is no unanimity of preference, and the number of respondents representing the majority is very near to the median optimum. Since on the most crowded days in Marina di Ravenna there are about 20 000 visitors per day (Marzetti and Mosetti, 2004),[12] this is the residents' SCC for that majority of respondents.

MNV Preferred by Visitors

As regards visitors' SCC, we have data on the MNV preferred about wholly tourism-dependent residents, and also visitors themselves; while data about the true marginal cost of tourist production $C'(Q)$ are more difficult to obtain. Therefore, in order to estimate the visitors' SCC, we use the survey data.

Let us first consider the results about the six wholly tourism-dependent residents (random sample) interviewed by Medoro (2004–5). Fifty percent of them are willing to pay, but are unable to establish how much, and the other 50 percent are unwilling to pay. As regards the MNV preferred, 33 percent stated the present number, and 50 percent double; the rest did not specify the number preferred, and declared that it is not a question of number of visitors but of quality of visit. Even if the number of wholly tourism-dependent residents interviewed is very small, this result about the MNV preferred is substantially confirmed by an MNV survey, where visitors were interviewed directly.

In 2002 an experimental MNV survey of 62 face-to-face interviews (random sample) was carried out by Vitali (2002–3). Visitors, all Italian, were interviewed on a representative area of the beach, because they visit Marina di Ravenna mainly for beach recreational activities. Interviews were done on two very crowded weekends of spring/summer. The De Ruyck et al. (1997, p. 824) questionnaire was adapted for the Marina di Ravenna situation, with some modifications and integrations made. In particular, the question about the number of visitors tolerated by visitors themselves is: How many more/less than the number present do you feel the site can accommodate without you feeling uncomfortable: less than half; half; present number; double; four times?

At the survey time, just over 45 percent would feel comfortable with double the present number, and just under 10 percent with four times that number; while 20 percent of respondents would feel comfortable with the present number, and about 25 percent with half the present number. Since in this site 55 percent of visitors declared that they would feel comfortable with at least double the number of people, for the majority of respondents the visitors' SCC is about 40 000 visitors per day. The fact that this majority is not very different from that of wholly tourism-dependent residents confirms the validity of the hypothesis, made in section 11.3, that in the local political context visitors can be represented by wholly tourism-dependent residents.

The Marina di Ravenna Site SCC

Given the results of the two surveys by questionnaire about the MNV preferred by residents and by visitors, in Marina di Ravenna the residents' SCC (the present number) is lower than the visitors' SCC (double the present number). Figure 11.1 summarises this situation: Q_1 is the residents' SCC; while Q_2 is the visitors' SCC. The site SCC Q_0 can be thought of as an intermediate level between Q_1 and Q_2. The policy-maker could pursue Q_0 through taxing the tourist sector to reduce their MNV preferred, and by spending tax revenues for increasing residents' satisfaction (through noise reduction and new facilities, for example) and their MNV preferred. This tax can be established, given the lack of data about a and $C_s'(Q)$, through the procedure of trials and errors mentioned above. Both SCCs are supported by a majority which is nearer to the median optimum than unanimity. This means that a site SCC between 20 000 and 40 000 visitors per day may be

Pareto non-efficient, because the new situation created by the policy-maker may leave some residents and visitors (those who prefer a number of visitors higher/lower than Q_0) worse off.

11.5 CONCLUSIONS

In this chapter the site SCC is intended as the result of a compromise between residents' and visitors' interests. Two different criteria of social choice for measuring the site SCC have been discussed, when the residents' SCC is the limiting factor: the CBA and the MR. According to the CBA, the site SCC is defined as the number of visitors which maximises the social welfare of residents. Under the assumption of full convexity, we have shown that the site SCC is obtained through the internalisation of the social loss due to overcrowding by considering the social price instead of the market price. In particular, the site SCC is computed by assuming that in the local political context visitors are represented by those residents who are wholly tourism-dependent.

The validity of this hypothesis is shown by the data of the case study presented. Nevertheless, this case study also confirms that individuals may be incapable of eliciting a monetary value for their satisfaction, thus cardinal preferences cannot be estimated for applying the CBA. In this case, since in social deliberation the MR is generally applied, we present how this voting criterion works when applied to the computation of the site SCC.

We highlight that, if the sampling design is conceived in a way that the sample well represents the relevant population, if interviewees are well informed about the scenario considered and told that their preference will influence the policy-maker's action, and if the questions are put in the same way as if they were voting in a referendum, the survey results can be interpreted in the same way as a universal suffrage. In addition, we claim that, by assuming that all individuals are alike, that they are able to rank all the alternatives in an order of preference and they declare as MNV preferred the number corresponding to their maximum satisfaction, it is reasonable to think that the optimum number of visitors obtained through the CBA is equal to the MNV obtained with the MR, even if respondents are unable to establish the monetary value of their satisfaction.

The creation of a favourable social atmosphere is promoted by internalising the social loss due to overcrowding through a Pigouvian tax. According to the information available to the policy-maker, we present different procedures for establishing the tax amount which makes the visitors' SCC and the residents' SCC equal. In a condition of complete information the policy-maker must resort to the maximisation procedure;

while when information is incomplete, the procedure depends on the kind of data which are lacking. In particular, when only the marginal loss due to overcrowding cannot be estimated, the policy-maker can estimate the visitors' SCC through the CBA, and if the optimum residents' SCC is obtained by applying the MR and the marginal costs are linearly increasing, the site SCC and the optimum level of tax can equally be computed.

Finally, our case study shows not only that respondents have no problem in establishing the individual MNV tolerated for applying the MR criterion of choice, but that in practice unanimity about the MNV preferred by residents and by visitors is difficult to obtain. Whether a SCC is Pareto-efficient or not depends on the majority which has established the MNV preferred; therefore, if the majority is different from unanimity, the site SCC may not be Pareto-efficient.

ACKNOWLEDGEMENTS

We thank the Municipality of Ravenna and Giovanni Gabbianelli (University of Bologna) for Figure 11.3.

NOTES

1. The tourism sector is intended in the broad sense, in that it is made up of both tourists or overnight visitors (people who visit the site and stay at least one night) and same-day visitors (people who visit the site, but do not sleep there) (World Tourism Organisation, 1998).
2. In modern terms, an externality is the result of the direct interaction between different agents or groups of agents. This interdependence violates market efficiency, because it is 'external to the price system, hence unaccounted for by market valuations. Analytically, it implies the non-independence of various preference ... functions. Its effect is to cause divergence between private and social cost-benefit calculation' (Bator, 1958, p. 358). More specifically a Pareto-relevant externality has to satisfy the following sufficient conditions: i) the activity of agent or group is in equilibrium; ii) the marginal effect of the activity of agent or group on another individual or group is non-zero, i.e. $C_s'(Q) \neq 0$ (Buchanan and Stubblebine, 1962). Baumol (1964) highlights that sometimes not only the total utility of others is influenced, but also their marginal utility. In this case, 'externalities directly reduce the likelihood that the second-order conditions will be satisfied, thereby significantly complicating the pertinent problems of public policy', caused by the presence of different local maxima when externalities are of sufficient magnitude (ibid., pp. 358–64). This last case is not considered here.
3. We highlight that, because crowding is a complex phenomenon, numerous studies on visitors' perception of crowding show that it does not only depend on the number of visitors present on a site per day, but also on other variables such as visitor's expectation and experience, impacts, desirable conditions (ideals), standards for acceptable level of impact and other aspects of visit quality (Shelby et al., 1983 and 1989; Ditton et al., 1983). This is also true for residents, whose perception of crowding also depends on impacts, desirable conditions and standards for an acceptable level of impact. Nevertheless, for the SCC it is advantageous to use a single variable such as the number of visitors because, as Shelby et al. (1989, p. 275) highlight, 'when people evaluate an area as being crowded, they have at least

implicitly compared the impact that they experienced with their perception of a standard (a personal or social norm or some combination thereof). If they conclude that the area is crowded it would appear that the impact exceeded the standard ..., even though no more precise data about the standard or the absolute level of the impact are available.'

4. Canestrelli and Costa (1991, p. 298) highlight that the WTP of tourists 'can be easily translated' into the incomes of the 'tourist-dependent population'.

5. A non-convexity situation is characterised by the existence of multiple local optima, which make the choice of the optimal policy-making more complex.

6. We highlight that numerous studies also exist which measure utility or satisfaction by considering ordinal preferences. See, for example: Shelby (1980); Ditton et al. (1983); Whishman and Hollenhorst (1998); Inglis et al. (1999); Stewart and Cole (1999). Satisfaction may be measured by a single question such as, for example: How did the number of people you encountered today affect the overall enjoyment of your visit? Responses may range from 1 (greatly reduced) to 7 (greatly increased) (Ditton et al., 1983, p. 277). Nevertheless, the mean level of satisfaction measured in this way cannot be used for computing the SCC in a CBA model, because it does not represent a monetary value but only a degree of satisfaction.

7. The WTP question format changes according to the specific situation considered. For example, in Cicchetti and Smith (1973) respondents are asked how much they are willing to pay for a certain change in crowding; while in McConnell (1977) respondents are asked whether or not they would come to a specific site if a suggested price is incremented by a certain amount.

8. Some respondents may give a false response or no response to the evaluation questions if they fear that they will be asked to pay for the good under evaluation, even when assured that no payment will be asked. In addition, if survey studies describe scenarios that respondents find unclear or unrealistic, or are based on relatively small samples, the estimates obtained could differ widely from the true value; therefore great attention has to be paid to these two aspects. Furthermore, even if a main survey of at least 500–600 interviews is carried out in order to estimate values with a confidence level of at least 95 percent, some coefficients – important from the economic point of view – may be statistically non-significant. Nevertheless, even where most coefficients are statistically significant, the overall explanatory power of the relationship considered may be quite low (Bowen, 1943; Cicchetti and Smith, 1973; Mueller, 1979).

9. Rawls (1971, revised 1999, p. 313) claims that the best available way of ensuring 'just and effective' choices is some form of majority rule.

10. As regards the general management of social goods, Bowen (1943, p.33) discusses – when preferences are unknown – the 'possible use of voting as a means of measuring or inferring marginal rates of substitution and hence of determining ideal output', and highlights the conditions under which the ideal or optimum output of a social good obtained by a maximisation utility model is equal to the output preferred by a majority of voters.

11. As regards both surveys, the questionnaires were created by Marzetti Dall'Aste Brandolini, S.

12. Marzetti Dall'Aste Brandolini and Mosetti (2004) make reference to 2002. Nevertheless, between 2002 and 2004 the number of visitors did not change substantially, and the number of residents has remained almost the same.

REFERENCES

Bateman, I.J. and K.G. Willis (1999), *Valuing Environmental Preferences: Theory and Practice of the Contingent Valuation Method in the US, EU and Developing Countries*, Oxford: Oxford University Press.

Bator, F.M. (1958), 'The anatomy of market failure', *The Quarterly Journal of Economics*, **72**, 351–79.

Baumol, W.J. (1964), 'External economies and second-order optimality conditions', *The American Economic Review*, **54**, 358–72.
Black, D. (1948), 'The decisions of a committee using a special majority', *Enonometrica*, **16**, 245–70.
Bowen, H.R. (1943), 'The Interpretation of voting in the allocation of economic resources', *The Quarterly Journal of Economics*, **58**, 27–48.
Buchanan, J.M. and W.G. Stubblebine (1962), 'Externality', *Economica*, **27**, 371–84.
Clawson, M. and J.L. Knetsch (1978), *Economics of Outdoor Recreation*, London: John Hopkins University Press.
Canestrelli, E. and P. Costa (1991), 'Tourist carrying capacity. A fuzzy approach', *Annals of Tourism Research*, **18**, 295–311.
Courant, P.N. and R.C. Porter (1981), 'Averting expenditure and the cost of pollution', *Journal of Environmental Economics and Management*, **8**, 321–9.
Cicchetti, C.J. and V.K. Smith (1973), 'Congestion, quality deterioration and optimal use', *Social Science Research*, **2**, 15–31.
Decleris, M. (2003), *The Law of Sustainable Development, General Principles*, Luxemburg: European Union Commission.
De Ruyck, M.C., A.G. Soares and A. McLachlan (1997), 'Social carrying capacity as a management tool for sandy beaches', *Journal of Coastal Research*, **13**, 822–30.
Ditton, R.B., A.J. Fedler and A.R. Graefe (1983), 'Factors contributing to perceptions of recreational crowding', *Leisure Sciences*, **5**, 273–87.
Fisher, A.C. and J.V. Krutilla (1972), 'Determination of optimal capacity of resources-based recreation facilities', *Natural Resources Journal*, **12**, 417–44.
Helfand, G.E. and J. Rubin (1994), 'Spreading versus concentrating damages: environmental policy in the presence of non-convexities', *Journal of Environmental Economics and Management*, **27**, 84–91.
Inglis, G.J., V.I. Johnson and F. Ponte (1999), 'Crowding norms in marine settings: A case study of snorkeling on the great barrier reef', *Environmental Management*, **24**, 369–81.
Marzetti Dall'Aste Brandolini, S. (2003), *Microeconomia. Un'applicazione al settore turistico*, Bologna: CLUEB.
Marzetti Dall'Aste Brandolini, S. (2006), 'Investing in biodiversity for recreational activities: the natural coastal area of Lido di Dante (Italy)', *Chemistry and Ecology*, **22**, 443–62.
Marzetti Dall'Aste Brandolini, S. and R. Mosetti (2004), 'Sustainable tourism development and social carrying capacity: a case-study on the North-Western Adriatic Sea', in F.D. Pineda and C.A. Brebbia (eds), *Sustainable Tourism*, Southampton: WIT Press, pp. 211–20.
McConnell, K.E. (1977), 'Congestion and willingness to pay: a study of beach use', *Land Economics*, **53**(2), 185–95.
Meade, J.E. (1952),'External economies and diseconomies in a competitive situation', *The Economic Journal*, **62**, 54–67.
Medoro, M. (2004–5), *Sviluppo Sostenibile e Capacità di Carico Turistica: Un Caso di Studio*, Laurea thesis, co-ordinator Prof. S. Marzetti, Bologna: University of Bologna.
Mueller, D.C. (1979), *Public Choice*, Cambridge: Cambridge University Press.
Pesaran, M.H. (1987), *The Limits of Rational Expectations*, Oxford: Basil Blackwell
Price, C. (2000), 'Valuing of unpriced products: contingent valuation, cost–benefit analysis and participatory democracy', *Land Use Policy*, **17**, 187–96.
Rawls, J. (1971, revised 1999), *A Theory of Justice. Revised edition*, Oxford: Oxford University Press.

Saveriades, A. (2000), 'Establishing the social carrying capacity for the tourist resorts of the East Coast of the Republic of Cyprus', *Tourism Management*, **21**, 147–56.

Seidl, I. and C.A. Tisdell (1999), 'Carrying capacity reconsidered: from Malthus' population theory to cultural carrying capacity', *Ecological Economics*, **31**, 395–408.

Shelby, B. (1980), 'Crowding models for backcountry recreation', *Land Economics*, **56**, 43–55.

Shelby, B., T.A. Heberlein, J.J. Vaske and G. Alfano (1983), 'Expectations, preferences, and feeling crowded in recreation activities', *Leisure Sciences*, **6**, 2–14.

Shelby, B., J.J. Vaske and T.A. Heberlein (1989), 'Comparative analysis of crowding in multiple locations: results from fifteen years of research', *Leisure Sciences*, **11**, 269–91.

Shibata, H. and J.S. Winrich (1983), 'Control of pollution when the offended defend themselves', *Economica*, **50**, 425–37.

Starrett, D.A. (1972), 'Fundamental non-convexities in the theory of externalities', *Journal of Economic Theory*, **4**, 180–99.

Starrett D.A. and R. Zeckhauser (1971), 'Treating external diseconomies – markets or taxes?', *Public Policy Program Discussion Paper No.3*, Cambridge, MA: Harvard University.

Stewart, W.P. and D.N. Cole (1999), 'In search of situational effects in outdoor recreation: Different methods, different results', *Leisure Sciences*, **21**, 269–86.

Vitali, E. (2002–3), 'Turismo sostenibile: le conseguenze economiche dell'affollamento a Marina di Ravenna', Laurea thesis, co-ordinator Prof. S. Marzetti Dall'Aste Brandolini, Bologna: University of Bologna.

Whishman, S.A. and S.J. Hollenhorst (1998), 'A path model of whitewater boating satisfaction on the Cheat River of West Virginia', *Environmental Management*, **22**, 109–17.

World Tourism Organisation (1998), *Guide for Local Authorities on Developing Sustainable Tourism*, A Tourism and Environment Publication, Madrid: World Tourism Organization.

World Tourism Organisation (2004), *Indicators of Sustainable Development for Tourism Destinations. A Guidebook*, Madrid: World Tourism Organisation.

Conclusion

Rinaldo Brau, Alessandro Lanza and Stefano Usai

Sustainability, not only from an environmental perspective but also from a social and economic viewpoint, is, to a great extent, considered a critical element to exploit the whole potential of the tourist sector – a sector which can be, in turn, key to enhancing the economic development of many economies, including less developed countries and peripheral regions in highly industrialised countries.

This book highlights the economic potential of tourism, as well as some crucial drawbacks usually disregarded, such as the negative impact on employment in traditional sectors and the volatility of tourism earnings. The contributions, selected from the papers presented at the 'Second International Conference on Tourism and Sustainable Economic Development: Macro and Micro Economic Issues', organised by the Centre for North–South Economic Research (CRENoS) and the Fondazione Eni Enrico Mattei (FEEM), focus on the understanding of those narrow conditions under which economic growth of open economies specialized in tourism can be sustainable. In this respect, most of the chapters also draw some interesting conclusions regarding strategies that would aid the optimal exploitation of the potential of nature-based tourism for economic development

The empirical contributions illustrate the use of a number of empirical instruments intended to put theory into practice. In particular, as far as the measurement of economic and social sustainability of tourism is concerned, special emphasis is given to the assessment of the volatility of tourism receipts, the impact of environmental preservation on tourists' preference, and the identification of social sustainability in tourism development policies.

The book will be of interest to economists, geographers, social scientists and policy makers, but also to all who have a direct or indirect interest in tourism economics.

Index